Way

THE SEARCH FOR ORDER
1877–1920

Books by Robert H. Wiebe include

Businessmen and Reform

The Segmented Society

THE SEARCH
FOR ORDER

1877–1920

By

ROBERT H. WIEBE

The Making of America

GENERAL EDITOR: DAVID HERBERT DONALD

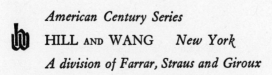

American Century Series

HILL AND **WANG**   *New York*

A division of Farrar, Straus and Giroux

Standard Book Number (paperback edition): 8090–0104–7
Standard Book Number (clothbound edition): 8090–8510–0
Library of Congress catalog card number: 66–27609

FIRST EDITION JANUARY 1967

Manufactured in the United States of America
Twenty-second printing, 1984

For My Mother and Father

Foreword

DURING the four decades between the close of the Reconstruction period and the end of the First World War the United States underwent a major transformation. Some historians have seen this change chiefly as a matter of settling the remaining territories, closing the frontier, and admitting new states. Others have stressed the shift of both numerical preponderance and political power from the farm to the city. Still others have found the basic change in the decline of the independent small businessman in the face of the giant monopolies. For many historians these forty years are most notable for the emergence of large-scale reform movements, from Populism through Progressivism. Writers more concerned with foreign policy have emphasized the drift from self-containment and isolation as the United States became a true world power.

The Search for Order endeavors to show that beneath all these surface ripples of rapid change there lay a deep-flowing current, which gave unity and meaning to the period as a whole. It is Professor Robert H. Wiebe's thesis that these years witnessed a fundamental shift in American values, from those of the small town in the 1880's to those of a new, bureaucratic-minded middle class by 1920. Arguing that the United States at the end of the Reconstruction period was "a society without a core," afflicted by "a general splintering process," Mr. Wiebe shows how the nation was incapable of facing the challenges of urbanization, industrialization, and immigration. Some embattled defenders of the faith tried to close their eyes to change, clinging the more tightly to the old-fashioned values of the small town simply because they were now outmoded. Others, like Henry George with his single-tax plan, hunted for a magical formula to reduce the complex dilemmas of an industrial society to the simple moral equations of small-town America. Still others sought to impose some kind of social stability through force.

Ultimately it was none of these but a "new middle class"—largely urban professional men and women—who developed the new values of "continuity and regularity, functionality and rationality, administration and management" in order to cope with twentieth-century problems. Inevitably this new value system, consciously in conflict with that of nineteenth-century America, led the new middle class to see "the need for a government of continuous involvement" and to emphasize executive administration. The Progressive movement was the triumph of this new middle class with its bureaucratic mentality.

Such, in brief, is the transformation Mr. Wiebe traces, in economic life, in social structure, in political behavior, and in patterns of ideas. To all these subjects he brings formidable learning and acute insight. Much of what he has written will be new even to close students of the period. For instance, his discussion of the actual workings of large businesses in "the distended society" and his analysis of the rise of the professions in the United States are strikingly original. Much is also highly controversial, particularly his new interpretation of Progressivism. Rejecting both the old view that these reformers were simply crusaders for clean government and the new theory that they were a displaced elite seeking to reclaim their slipping social status, Mr. Wiebe presents the Progressives as members of a dynamic and optimistic new middle class deliberately attempting to substitute an entirely new set of values for traditional but outmoded American beliefs.

Both thoughtful and brilliant, *The Search for Order* is at the same time a careful synthesis of present-day historical scholarship and a major new interpretation. For many years to come this will be not merely the standard book in its field, but the take-off book—the book that every serious student of American history will have to read and ponder, the book that will shape the pattern of future research and writing on the whole broad era from 1877 to 1920. It is, therefore, with special pleasure and excitement that the publishers and I welcome Professor Wiebe's book to The Making of America series.

DAVID HERBERT DONALD

The Johns Hopkins University

Contents

Preface

AMERICA during the nineteenth century was a society of island communities. Weak communication severely restricted the interaction among these islands and dispersed the power to form opinion and enact public policy. Education, both formal and informal, inhibited specialization and discouraged the accumulation of knowledge. The heart of American democracy was local autonomy. A century after France had developed a reasonably efficient, centralized public administration, Americans could not even conceive of a managerial government. Almost all of a community's affairs were still arranged informally.

My purpose is to describe the breakdown of this society and the emergence of a new system. The health of the nineteenth-century community depended upon two closely related conditions: its ability to manage the lives of its members, and the belief among its members that the community had such powers. Already by the 1870's the autonomy of the community was badly eroded. The illusion of authority, however, endured. Innumerable townsmen continued to assume that they could harness the forces of the world to the destiny of their community. That confidence, the system's final foundation, largely disappeared during the eighties and nineties in the course of a dramatic struggle to defend the independence of the community.

Although no replacement stood at hand, the outlines of an alternative system rather quickly took shape early in the twentieth century. By contrast to the personal, informal ways of the community, the new scheme was derived from the regulative, hierarchical needs of urban-industrial life. Through rules with impersonal sanctions, it sought continuity and predictability in a world of endless change. It assigned far greater power to government—in particular to a variety of flexible administrative devices —and it encouraged the centralization of authority. Men were now separated more by skill and occupation than by community; they identified themselves more by their tasks in an urban-industrial society than by their reputations in a town or a city neighborhood. The new system, moreover, had applications as important in foreign as in domestic affairs. This, in sum, was America's initial experiment in bureaucratic order, an experiment that was still in process as the nation passed through the First World War.

My outstanding debts, other than those suggested by the bibliography, begin with the one I owe my wife Lonnie, who not only encouraged and criticized in sensitive proportions but maintained a family's good temper throughout. Richard W. Leopold and Carl Resek stole time to offer very valuable advice on the entire manuscript. I am especially grateful to David Donald, whose extensive and incisive commentary improved the final product immeasurably. James E. Sheridan helped me in more ways than I am able to calculate. I also benefited from conversations with Herbert Bass, Claude Barfield, George Daniels, John Keiser, Grady McWhiney, Robert Marcus, Zane Miller, Robert Reid, and Joel Tarr. Northwestern University granted me a timely leave of absence, and once again the Social Science Research Council generously supported my efforts.

                                                                    R.H.W.

THE SEARCH FOR ORDER
1877–1920

1

Prelude

THE OUTLINES OF DEPRESSION in the 1870's were simple and severe. An economy buoyed by extravagant railroad construction sank abruptly when further expansion could no longer attract long-term investments. Bankers such as the celebrated Jay Cooke had precipitated the panic of 1873 by their use of any available short-term credits to keep afloat railroad promotions that foreign investors were scorning, and when no European money materialized to rescue them, those who had lived dangerously died as desperately. The manner in which the House of Cooke collapsed foreshadowed conditions lasting until the end of the decade. Falling prices and uncertain profits continued to discourage long-term investments even after the American economy might otherwise have enticed Europeans back again. The nation's youthful heavy industry experienced six very lean years.

Yet in other respects it was a strange depression. The longest in the nation's history, in human terms it proved one of the mildest. The same falling prices that deterred investors facilitated commerce, as migrants filled the land along the new railroad lines and enterprising businessmen, adequately supplied with those short-term credits which had lured Cooke into disaster, rushed to exploit the new possibilities in trade. While overbuilding the railroads had brought depression, it had created a commercial reservoir which for years afterward sustained much of the economy, including the railroads themselves. The volume of freight, growing as fast as rates declined, maintained the income of the roads. Because industrialists cut prices much more often than they did production, employment in most sectors of the economy remained reasonably high, and because prices dropped so markedly, real income rose over 60 percent between 1869 and 1879.

A depression of this nature, distressing but not devastating, shed a uniquely revealing light on the workings of American society. In a nation geared to promotion and expansion, stagnant years had traditionally carried a special frustration. They were quite literally soul-searching times, for throughout the nineteenth century a great many looked upon economic downturns as a moral judgment, precise punishment for the country's sins. They were, moreover, times of release when those strained human relations which prosperity often cloaked would burst into the open. Now lines cleared, and the contours sharpened.

Small-town life was America's norm in the mid-seventies. Depending upon the lines of transportation, groups of these towns fell into satellite patterns about a larger center, to which they looked for markets and supplies, credit and news. But however much they actually relied upon an outside world, they still managed to retain the sense of living largely to themselves. With farms generally fanning around them, these communities moved by the rhythms of agriculture: the pace of the sun's day, the working and watching of the crop months, the cycle of the seasons. Relatively few families lived so far from town that they did not gravitate to some degree into its circle, and there people at least thought they knew all about each other after crossing and recrossing paths over the years. Usually homogeneous, usually Protestant, they enjoyed an inner stability that the coming and going of members seldom shook. Even when new towns were established in fresh farm country, the gathering families brought the same familiar habits and ways so that a continuity was scarcely disturbed.

From a distance the towns exemplified a levelled democracy, sustaining neither an aristocracy of name nor an aristocracy of occupation. Almost anyone with incentive, it seemed, could acquire the skills of a profession. Lawyers and doctors, ministers and teachers, either trained themselves or, like the town's craftsmen, apprenticed themselves briefly with masters. But beneath that flat surface, each community was divided by innumerable, fine gradations. Distinctions that would have eluded an outsider —the precise location of a house, the amount of hired help, the quality of a buggy or a dress—held great import in an otherwise undifferentiated society. In fact, what Thorstein Veblen made famous as "conspicuous consumption" carried a far more exact meaning in the town where everyone looked on and cared than in the cities where only squandered millions would attract attention. At the top stood the few who not only had greater wealth than their neighbors but controlled access to it as well. These men— merchants, bankers, successful farmers—were "Mister" or "Major," not "Bill" or "Sam." In the same fashion, variations in religion, accent, and skin coloring distinguished individuals, groups, and even entire communities from one another. Except in rare circumstances, custodians of a genteel but explicit Protestantism with Anglo-Saxon names enjoyed a powerful advantage over all competitors.

Many lives diverged from the norm. Nevertheless, coal and mill towns with a different work discipline, or somewhat larger commercial centers with a quicker tempo and a greater heterogeneity, usually shared enough of these qualities, including many of the ties with agriculture, to keep them in the same social camp. Even in the cities, life often retained much of the town's flavor. Within the city limits yet detached from its core, neighborhoods provided fairly cloistered way stations between urban and rural living. In these years garden plots and a smattering of livestock came as standard accouterment to the city scene. Apart from the rest, urban elites of wealth and family—the nation's closest approximation of an aristocracy—also qualified as small self-contained communities. Enjoying little interchange with the rich and well-born in other cities, they fashioned private lives that would protect their exclusiveness and intermarry their young. In all, it was a nation of loosely connected islands, similar in kind, whose restless natives often moved only to settle down again as part of another island.

Men searched for the explanation of America's economic punishment from that provincial, community-centered base. If there was an American philosophy in the seventies, it was a corrupted version of Scottish common-sense doctrines, taking as given every man's ability to know that God had ordained modesty in women, rectitude in men, and thrift, sobriety, and hard work in both. People of very different backgrounds accommodated themselves to this Protestant code which had become so thoroughly identified with respectability, and the keepers of the national conscience applied its rules with slight margin for the deviant. An age in which the Supreme Court justified oppression of the Mormons because no right-thinking man could consider theirs a religion would not be remembered for its cosmopolitan tolerance. Americans were judging the world as they would their neighborhood. Their truths derived from what they knew: the economics of a family budget, the returns that came to the industrious and the lazy, the obnoxious behavior of the drunken braggart, the advantages of a wife who stayed home and kept a good house. In an island community people had little reason to believe that these daily precepts were not universally valid, and few doubted that the nation's ills were caused by men who had dared to deny them.

Consequently, cries for reform sounded much like the counsel of reaction. Deep inside, everyone knew the path of virtue; and those who had strayed would simply have to return. In depression, small-town America took its stand against "the credit system, the fashion system, and every other system tending to prodigality and bankruptcy." The government in particular would have to relearn the fundamentals of thrift. From the Midwestern farmers and shopkeepers to the editors of Eastern literary magazines came demands for "retrenchment and reform": drastically reduced appropriations, austerity on all public occasions, and lower salaries. Reform must continue, declared the Illinois Grange, "until every department of our government gives token that the reign of licentious extravagance is over, and something of the purity, honesty, and frugality with which our fathers inaugurated it, has taken its place." Newspapers across the land denounced a reasonable, if mishandled effort to raise Congressmen's stipends as a "salary grab."

Never had so many citizens held their government in such low regard. A part of that reputation had been acquired as a result of the extraordinary experiments in reconstructing the former Confederate States, experiments that had been predicated on the existence of a new national sovereignty. Without the tradition, the means of communication, the legal framework, or the administrative apparatus—in effect, without anything beyond an army and the tenuous cooperation of some local citizens to implement a detailed public policy—reconstruction had guaranteed confusion, disappointment, and recrimination. Yet even after a large majority had agreed upon its failure, extrication was extremely complex. Men with reputations and vital interests at stake had continued to clutch their disintegrating program, and some remnants of reconstruction remained until 1877. Out of this process had come a haunting sense of the war's failure, a vague feeling of political betrayal.

In fact, war and reconstruction had helped to disrupt an entire system of government. The sudden departure of eleven states and their erratic return, the years of preoccupation with strange problems, had invited endless distortions in the making of policy. Those internalized restraints which the traditional ways of governing had bred no longer operated. Corrupt bargains, crude force, and extralegal expedients had become the new standard, as the methods of Congressional reconstruction and the techniques of white redemption in the South so amply illustrated. The irregular distribution of public favors to satisfy a passion for railroad construction and the inability of city governments to provide even minimum services each added its measure to the chaos. Little wonder that Americans everywhere were crying out in scorn and despair. Unable to comprehend that they had heaped impossible tasks upon officials with woefully deficient

means, they explained all crimes in the time-honored manner—
unique failures in leadership and public morality.

Somehow, some way, it seemed, ruthless men had usurped the
government and were now wielding it for their private benefit.
"Those who administer the laws," the rising politician John Peter
Altgeld told his audience in Savannah, Missouri, "have been
taken from classes of citizens who live off the farmer [and other
honest laborers] and who profit by [their] distress. . . ." One
increasingly popular proposal was a Federal civil service to drive
the marauders away and force them, as the independently
wealthy Richard Henry Dana, Jr., put it, to "begin the unaccustomed business of earning a living by legitimate work." Politics
as a vocation was never truly "legitimate work"; most successful
politicians continued to designate themselves lawyers or businessmen or generals, as if they were temporarily on leave from their
real occupations. And as the very title of the Senate Committee
on Civil Service and Retrenchment indicated, pure government
always meant parsimonious government.

Currency posed a knottier problem of morals, with greenbacks,
the paper currency issued in quantity as a war measure, creating
the major complication. Silver, too scarce, had been quietly
demonetized in 1873. In the boom times before the panic, greenbacks had offered some relief from an insufficient gold currency,
some encouragement to expansionists little and big who feared
deflation and tight credit. More important, gold was already
acquiring a vague association with fat, parasitic bondholders.
Nevertheless, the impulse to recapture fundamentals proved too
strong, and throughout the countryside waverers selected currency with a feel and a ring that crinkly paper could never
match. In 1875 Congress passed the Specie Resumption Act.
Although it was a compromise in that it did not actually retire
the greenbacks, the law still represented a moral commitment to
currency that citizens could recognize as safe, sound, and honorable.

More than the chance of politics pitted Rutherford B. Hayes
against Samuel J. Tilden in the Presidential campaign in

1876. Both hard-money men who promised an austere, limited government, they were models of probity, untouched by scandal and impervious to all wild schemes. Dull perhaps, and certainly unimaginative; but this was no year to choose between a captive general and an aging faddist. Time now for the bedrock values.

In communities across the land, railroad promotions collapsed as the first casualties of the panic. But if new construction practically ceased, payments on the old bonded debt did not. In the cold morning after, hundreds of counties and dozens of states swore they would never gamble again. A reasonable vow in the mid-seventies, it would prove too severe in many localities that still lay outside the nation's railroad network. The panic had frozen a mere infant system. Just four years earlier, the Union Pacific and Central Pacific had linked tracks to complete the first transcontinental line. Even in the Northeast, which already boasted an impressive railway mileage, what at first glance looked like continuous road was often fragmented by a score of competing companies, several widths of track, and gaps where citizens had excluded the sooty monsters from the center of town. Again only four years before the panic, Cornelius Vanderbilt had consolidated the first trunk line from the Atlantic to Chicago; and not until 1901 did one management operate the Union Pacific–Central Pacific route.

A pall of thwarted opportunity, of frustrated dreams, hung over large parts of the nation. Innumerable townsmen had been looking to the railroads as their avenues to greatness. Now nothing could entice a company to build past their community. Or if the track had already been laid, it had too often brought trouble instead of glory. Towns that had tied their future to a local line almost never owned it. Nor did they have any part in deciding the rates charged, the services offered, the distant connections made or not made. That power lay elsewhere, in "alien" hands. Moreover, crops were increasingly processed well beyond the farmer's ken, and the goods he needed came more often from strange, remote places. What would later be known as "trusts"

were "rings" in the seventies—the Harvester Ring, the Plow
Ring, and many more—whose very existence may have depended
upon agitated imaginations but whose control seemed ominously
complete from an agrarian perspective.

When Commodore Vanderbilt died in 1877, he left a fortune of
$90 million. While the people struggled day by day, the argument
ran, a few men far away were hoarding the nation's wealth and
power. "The time was when none were poor and none rich," the
Texan John Reagan told his constituents that year as he left for
Washington to battle the monopolists. "There were no beggars
till Vanderbilts and Stewarts and Goulds and Scotts and Hun-
tingtons and Fisks shaped the action of Congress and moulded
the purposes of government. Then the few became fabulously
rich, the many wretchedly poor . . . and the poorer we are the
poorer they would make us."

Reagan's destination was not the usual one. Most of the angry
townsmen turned instead to the local and state governments,
which had traditionally supported their enterprise. Here, in a
familiar setting, the townsmen would defend themselves.
Through countless, now-forgotten local ordinances and a cluster
of state measures known as the Granger laws, they tried to hold
those elusive, threatening forces. A legislature or a commission
would fix railroad rates, establish just practices at the mill and
warehouse, set the rules of business behavior. From an agrarian
viewpoint these laws were simply the preconditions for fair play.
By determining such matters once and for all, they would free the
American people's natural initiative. It was another return to
fundamental morality.

Even at the height of their popularity, the Granger laws held
only a qualified appeal. Some of those who cursed one road were
simultaneously wooing another. Just beyond the temporary obstacles grand opportunities always seemed to beckon. Most states,
moreover, never passed such measures, despite undercurrents of a
similar spirit. The prime strength of the Granger movement lay
in that portion of the Midwest which bordered the Mississippi
River. Farther west, where everything remained to be done; in

the South, just now reviving and eager to build; in the East, which had already experienced the first shocks of a railroad economy, the emotions of depression generally found other outlets.

Nor did the Granger legislatures wish to outlaw all large enterprise. Too many ambitious men pictured themselves as tomorrow's kings to proscribe royalty. The townsmen had had relatively little time to ponder the evils of big business. That pathfinder in monopoly, John D. Rockefeller, had just acquired the basis for control in petroleum, and few Americans would know much about his practices until the end of the decade. Even great fortunes were still rare enough to be regarded as oddities. A token of the future, the Commodore's son William more than doubled his inheritance before dying only eight years after his father. In all, the Granger movement hinted at problems that one day would assume giant proportions, but it neither formulated them clearly nor held its followers tightly to the cause.

The nation of small towns and big enterprise was the America of popular fancy. Songs and stories romanticized it, orators honored it, and faith in the sovereign public was predicated on it. Yet millions inhabited another world. *"My people do not live in America,"* declared a Slavic immigrant, *"they live underneath America."* The same held true for many more who had recently arrived from Europe, for the gangs of Chinese who had laid the Central Pacific tracks, for Negroes a step from slavery, for the growing bands of migratory workers, and for other marginals in industry and agriculture. When William Dean Howells, who came out of Martin's Ferry, Ohio, to serve as the arbiter of literary fashions, excluded violence and casual brutality from his definition of realism because they were "unnatural" and "sensationalist," he denied everyday life in the slums and shanty towns. When the famous minister Washington Gladden rebuked gamblers by invoking the orderly, prudent values of his Ohio town, he ignored that precarious existence where only chance made sense. Addressing the American Social Science Association in

1875, the economist David A. Wells, who worked a few blocks from the densest tenement district in the world, remarked in passing, "But few are so poor nowadays as not to be able to afford some sort of a carpet for their parlor." So many dwelled in the city and never saw it.

In the summer of 1877, a portion of that hidden America rose momentarily into view. By announcing yet another wage cut that July, the management of the Baltimore and Ohio touched off a wildcat strike that soon spread north and west along the railroad lines to Philadelphia, Pittsburgh, Chicago, San Francisco, and scores of stops between. In the towns, people expressed a rather orderly hostility to the roads. But in the cities crowds gathered and milled, clashed with trigger-happy vigilantes and militia, then drifted downtown to riot and loot. Frightened state officials convinced a reluctant President to send Federal troops. The mobs dwindled, then disappeared. Called America's first national strike, it was actually the first national holiday of the slums. The rioters, rather than self-conscious wage earners, were simply the inhabitants of center city who had taken advantage of a singular opportunity to come out and roam.

As shaken as substantial Americans were by the explosion, they put it out of mind with surprising ease. The Great Railroad Strike of 1877 was quickly classified an exception and, once categorized, it became no more than a bad memory, an incident rather than an index to fear or failure. By the end of the decade, the nation was preoccupied once again with building, growing, expanding.

2

The Distended Society

AFTER A PAUSE during the depression, three more trans-
continentals—the Southern Pacific, the Northern Pacific, and the
Atchison, Topeka, and Santa Fe—were completed at two-year
intervals early in the eighties. A fourth, the Great Northern,
reached the West Coast just before the panic of the nineties.
Though none could re-create the drama of the first, together the
four lines gave the sudden impression of an integrated country.
The rush into the Black Hills in 1877 marked the last bonanza
frontier in western mining. The tragic dispersal of the Indians
moved fitfully toward an end, with Congress debating their
future as it might have discussed taxes. Territory so recently a
part of the Great American Desert was now brought into the
Union: Colorado in 1876; after interminable delays, the Dakotas,
Washington, and Montana in 1889, and Idaho and Wyoming in
1890; then that sober land of tantalizingly immoral images, Utah,
in 1896. In fact from afar the West appeared much more settled
than it actually was, and Easterners were already fashioning a
mythical land of tall men, brave women, and valorous deeds.

So great numbers of Americans came to believe that a new
United States, stretched from ocean to ocean, filled out, and
bound together, had miraculously appeared. That, it seemed, was
the true legacy of the war, and by the early eighties publicists
were savoring the word "nation" in this sense of a continent
conquered and tamed. It was a term that above all connoted

growth and development and enterprise. The talk had such a breathless quality: so much so fast, with so much still coming. An age never lent itself more readily to sweeping, uniform description: nationalization, industrialization, mechanization, urbanization.

Yet to almost all of the people who created them, these themes meant only dislocation and bewilderment. America in the late nineteenth century was a society without a core. It lacked those national centers of authority and information which might have given order to such swift changes. American institutions were still oriented toward a community life where family and church, education and press, professions and government, all largely found their meaning by the way they fit one with another inside a town or a detached portion of a city. As men ranged farther and farther from their communities, they tried desperately to understand the larger world in terms of their small, familiar environment. They tried, in other words, to impose the known upon the unknown, to master an impersonal world through the customs of a personal society. They failed, usually without recognizing why; and that failure to comprehend a society they were helping to make contained the essence of the nation's story.

The rush to the cities, swelling established centers like New York and Chicago and creating new ones like Denver and Kansas City out of overgrown towns, brought a constant influx of inexperienced newcomers who required jobs, homes, and a sense of belonging. Older residents were inundated. Not only did masses congest the center of the city, but in response to pressures for living space, transportation lines thrust outward, cutting into communities that had existed apart and pulling them into a greater urban area. Patterns of development followed little logic beyond the availability of dry land and the enterprise of speculators, builders, and trolley companies. Even then leaders often turned into followers as the fate of Harlem soon after 1900 demonstrated. The collapse of real estate values suddenly trans-

formed an area for the well-to-do into a fashionable slum for
New York's Negroes.

Each city desperately needed such fundamental services as fresh
water, sewers, paving, and transportation, yet the same conditions
that made the need so imperative diminished the capacity to meet
it. Pell-mell expansion destroyed the groups and neighborhoods
that sustained social action. The thousands recently arrived, the
thousands more moving about, concentrated narrowly on their
own security. Men struggling to learn new skills or to preserve
old ones in a rapidly changing economy could not afford to think
about city-wide issues. Without stability at home or on the job,
the civic spirit had no place to take root. When a city depended
upon industries with absentee owners, the problem was that
much more acute. Local leaders who might otherwise have
championed civic improvements protected that distant railroad
king or machinery manufacturer from the higher taxes and closer
regulation which they feared would drive him away. Beyond all
of these obstacles lay an archaic system of government. Originally
designed so that a handful of city fathers could express the community's purpose, the intimate club had now grown into an un-
wieldy council, mirroring a fragmented and confused city. Essential services became the playthings of private profit, and a busy
people paid the price of danger, dirt, and disease.

A later generation thought it saw a neat three-class system
emerging in the cities of the late nineteenth century, with men of
great wealth and power at the top, lesser businessmen, professionals, and white-collar workers in the middle, and the mass of
wage earners below. At close range, the scheme vanished. Established wealth and power fought one battle after another against
the great new fortunes and political kingdoms carved out of
urban-industrial America, and the more they struggled, the
more they scrambled the criteria of prestige. The concept of a
middle class crumbled at the touch. Small business appeared and
disappeared at a frightening rate. The so-called professions meant
little as long as anyone with a bag of pills and a bottle of syrup
could pass for a doctor, a few books and a corrupt judge made a

man a lawyer, and an unemployed literate qualified as a teacher. Nor did the growing number of clerks and salesmen and secretaries of the city share much more than a common sense of drift as they fell into jobs that attached them to nothing in particular beyond a salary, a set of clean clothes, and a hope that somehow they would rise in the world. The proletariat included a few with important skills, a number of demoted artisans, many families fresh from the farms, an increasingly complex array of immigrants, and an admixture of Negroes, some of Northern and some of Southern background. No pot melted these bits and pieces into a class. Fearful of each other's competition and ignorant of each other's ways, they lived in mutual suspicion, as separated into groups of their own kind as they could manage.

From the outside, however, the cities seemed monolithic in their strangeness, centers of alien ways and murky power. Sermons, popular verse, and tales of country lasses corrupted on a Saturday night all taught small-town Americans to think of the city as fundamentally different and thoroughly dangerous. The message contained its kernel of truth. Immigration poured largely into centers of 25,000 or more, and as the flow quickened the major source of immigrants shifted in the mid-eighties from Northern and Western to Southern and Eastern Europe. Each year the cultural gap between city and countryside widened. Moreover, the very process of urban living generated its own special values. The individualism and casual cooperation of the towns still had their place in a city. But new virtues—regularity, system, continuity—clashed increasingly with the old. The city dweller could never protect his home from fire or rid his street of garbage by the spontaneous voluntarism that had raised cabins along the frontier.

In addition, urban centers were collecting more and more power over regional finance, over the marketing of farm products and the distribution of finished goods, and over the dispensing of news and opinion. Although few city dwellers held any of that power, still fewer recognized that they had it, and fewer yet knew what to do with it, country people cared only that someone in a distant center was pulling the strings that moved their affairs. The shock of sudden subservience was particularly severe. If relations between a Boston and its hinterland were never smooth, they at least rested upon decades of experience. But the abrupt appearance of a city where none had existed before brought sharp qualitative changes, all the more disturbing because often neither holder nor beholden comprehended what was happening between them.

The same country spokesmen who fostered the illusion of a monolithic city also perpetuated the myth of the united farmers, the sturdy people of America who saw their world through a single lens. Yet the countryside was undergoing as marked a reorientation as the cities. Railroads, machinery, and scientific advances opened more farmland in the last third of the century than in the nation's previous history. Pioneers transformed huge barren tracts on the Plains into America's primary wheat and livestock regions, and in the Far West, farmers brought large, rich areas under cultivation for a variety of fruit, vegetable, and grain crops. Responding both to the new competition and to the expanding urban market, the Midwest combined smaller amounts of wheat with corn and hog farming, dairying, and various perishables for the region's cities; and Eastern farmers concentrated even more heavily on serving the nearby urban centers. In the Deep South cotton dominated as it never had prior to the war.

Crop specialization told only part of the story. The spread of machinery revolutionized agriculture in the Midwest and the Plains, where it spawned large-scale, entrepreneurial farms. In the South, by contrast, the value of farm implements had declined by 1900 to less than half that of 1860; the land was increasingly worked in small pieces by families who either had mortgaged their coming crop for living essentials or took a share of the proceeds in return for seed, tools, and perhaps a mule. Developments in agricultural science also left the South behind, while they were encouraging a hardheaded, business approach in the dairy and livestock areas to the north and west.

Distinctive patterns of credit, transportation, and markets deepened these regional differences. In general the newer areas suffered both from inadequate financing and from incomplete transportation. Skeletal banking facilities meant higher interest rates, the greater likelihood of failures, and financial stringency at almost every harvest. Absolutely dependent upon the railroads, the lands across the Plains also encountered the most rudimentary, monopolistic network of carriers. Wheat and cotton farmers suffered from the most perplexing, treacherous markets, where highly variable prices were determined in international competition, and interest rates reflected this fact as well. In the case of the South, neolithic farming techniques and hopeless migrations among the victims of sharecropping and the crop lien pushed rates to cruel heights. The East, on the other hand, had a relatively mature banking system and extensive, often competitive transportation, conditions that also prevailed in much of the Midwest by the eighties. Their domestic markets, moreover, were generally steady and expanding.

The changes that had the most immediate impact upon the farmer were those he saw directly about him, ones that affected his daily relations in the community. Especially in the wheat country, men who could add acreage and purchase the latest equipment enjoyed a rising advantage over their neighbors. Lesser farmers might pool resources to buy machinery or to hire itinerant harvesting teams, but they easily overextended themselves in the scramble to advance. Many fell back; others held their own as the big farms grew bigger. Farther west, California offered particularly bald examples of this maldistribution. Livestock created equally grand empires; Richard King of Texas was a millionaire even before the advent of systematic cattle raising in the mid-eighties. These divisions spread to some extent through all areas, as the distance increased between those who could benefit from a more complicated, expensive agriculture and those who in varying degrees could not.

The significance of capital drew successful farmers into the commercial life of the town just as it attracted well-to-do townsmen into farm ownership. A blended elite dominated the rural communities. These businessmen wore their Sunday suits every day, and no one mistook them for tillers, least of all the dirt farmers. Increasingly, townsmen were exercising an important supervisory power over the countryside. Like it or not, the Southern merchants with funds invested in local liens had to care who grew what on that land, and the decisions of these conservative creditors accounted for much of the postwar emphasis upon a familiar cash crop, cotton. At the same time, commercial farmers came more and more to rely upon wage earners, and consequently "hired hands" found a larger place in the low rungs of rural society. Harvest time brought the most pressing demand. Although some part-time laborers might be recruited locally, most of them moved in bands with the crop seasons. Scorned, feared, yet desperately needed, migrant workers comprised the indispensable outcasts of rural America.

A certain friction always existed between those who lived on the land and those who operated out of the local banks and stores and law offices. But the effects of that friction varied widely. Where families worked their own land and the town obviously served as no more than a way-station for their produce, the average farmer found it relatively easy to merge his antipathies with those of the local businessmen, especially when one agency such as a railroad provided a natural focus for their hostility. On the other hand, where tenantry predominated in the countryside, the relationship changed, sometimes radically. The man without control over his land who pushed along under an everlasting debt to local creditors usually did not see beyond the town: its boundaries marked his world. Then the local merchant became in effect the fertilizer trust, the local banker the merciless bloodsucker, and the local lawyer the tool of the rich. Particularly in depressed sections of the South, anger that in another setting would have flowed onward toward distant villains stopped close to home, holding town and country in a continuous state of tension.

By reputation, the men of the late nineteenth century who understood the currents about them, and the future as well, were the successful businessmen. Friends called them the prophets of progress, foes the evil wizards of manipulation. Yet as shrewdly as some of them pursued the main chance, they were also trapped by the present, scurrying where they appeared to stalk. An unprecedented number of vast fortunes told much less about some ethereal genius than about fortuitous positions in an explosive economy, particularly the advantages of having money if you wished to make money. Even the most able among them excelled not in the breadth of their visions but in their concentrated purpose. Fastidious, consumptive Jay Gould, who left $77 million at his death in 1892, perfected sleights-of-hand that drew into his own pocket the assets of the railroad and telegraph companies he dominated. "His touch is death," marvelled an equally unscrupulous magician, Daniel Drew. Andrew Carnegie, the lively little Scot who relished a scrap above all else, developed such a remarkable facility for dog fighting that in 1901 his holdings in iron and steel brought almost half a billion dollars. John D. Rockefeller, humorless exemplar of the prudent maxims, amassed an even greater fortune by demonstrating the profitability of a tight-fisted acumen. Tacticians rather than strategists, they bought and sold, bargained and traded, as the requirements of a daily struggle dictated. Even Rockefeller, the most impressive leader of the lot, added endlessly to his domain instead of integrating it. Self-conscious empire builders such as J. P. Morgan and Edward H. Harriman did not rise to prominence until the mid-nineties.

The railroads nicely illustrated this emphasis upon the immediate and the particular. Here the primary objective was control of as many critical junctions as possible. Vicious battles for access to such basic cities as Chicago or for monopolization of such newer centers as Omaha filled the late nineteenth century. Although rate cutting attracted the greatest attention, warfare by construction was actually more significant, as competing roads frantically threw down tracks in a profusion of tactical maneuvers. Almost no one emerged the victor. Losers tended to build onward, plunging further into debt on the dubious logic of better luck next time. Ostensible winners usually found that the enemy had devised some alternative route, or that new roads had to be purchased at exorbitant prices, or that an inadequate system of feeders left their main lines unprofitable. Yet despite a past strewn with disappointment, railroad executives continued to lay track they did not want to build, engage in rate wars they had wished to avoid, and count on a perpetual prosperity that would never come. What seemed to them a series of rational responses added up to an utterly irrational industrial policy that courted danger for large portions of a dependent economy.

Here as elsewhere the executives in the home office relied so heavily upon the initiative of their scattered subordinates that it was difficult to know who made the major decisions. As the range and complexity of a corporation's affairs increased, executives quite naturally extended the familiar methods of management. But far-flung networks did not respond to the personal, casual procedures of a small company, and the result was an unplanned diffusion of power. If those who thought of the new industrial giants as diabolically perfect organisms could have peeked inside, they would have found jerry-built organization, ad hoc assumptions of responsibility, obsolete office techniques, and above all an astonishing lack of communication among its parts. The immense power that came from dominance over transportation, as in the case of Standard Oil's stranglehold on pipelines, or through a monopoly of raw materials, as in the case of the later holding companies in copper and lead, did not translate into personal control. Presiding over ramshackle concerns, the officers could only command and hope.

Distribution demonstrated the same confusion. Marketing goods in a limited area required a few agents who operated directly under the guidance of a superior, often the president himself. As the product spread outward, the company would add more agents and yet more agents, simulating the old intimate system with reams of correspondence from somebody who knew neither his representatives nor their local situations. Rewarded by the quantity of sales, agents devised their own methods, set their own terms and prices, and told the home office only what they wanted it to learn. The picture of the sturdy Captain Frederick Pabst trying to command a scattered army of salesmen with scribbled aphorisms as his beer moved from Milwaukee into a national market was a harmless blend of the quaint and the ludicrous. Customers would not die from watered beer. But an autonomous life insurance agent might play at will with his customers' deepest hopes for family security, restrained only by his conscience and the faint chance of being fired.

Even in the factories beside them, executives let a great deal of control slip away by clinging to the familiar. The plant expansion that accompanied America's rise to world leadership in manufacturing came in hasty disorder. New buildings often retained the arrangement of men and material that discarded machinery had made traditional, hampering the very improvements in technology that had inspired their construction. No cosmic reason determined that the organization of a factory to suit mass production should await Henry Ford's assembly line of 1914. A great urban market lay at hand by the late eighties, advances in machine-tool technology guaranteed the necessary precision, and pioneers in rational factory procedure had already compiled considerable data. But corporation leaders who took pride in their practical, dollars-and-cents wisdom thought they were attending to greater affairs. Inside the factory the customary ways were the sensible ways.

Employers proved equally impervious to the impact of factory life upon their workers, to the alienation and uncertainty and degradation bred in these impersonal establishments. Often the transition from shop to factory had occurred so quickly that the executive who boasted his office was open to any man on the payroll deluded himself into believing the old paternalism still obtained. Or he resisted understanding, because the fatherly care of employees was still widely regarded as his Christian duty. Thus discontent became perversity or the influence of "outsiders," usually a form of personal disloyalty as well. Actual control in the shop had fallen to the foreman. Like the insurance agent in the field, he ruled his little kingdom as a tyrant, hiring, helping, firing, and frustrating as he pleased.

These dispersals of power were just one part of a general splintering process. Superimposing a national market upon a locally oriented business system brought small entrepreneurs across the land into the scramble for some piece of its riches. The hands of independent middlemen reached out at every short step to complicate what would otherwise have been simple transactions. Moreover, most industrial innovations still came out of small concerns and backyard workshops. Testing each of these prospects meant in most cases still another company. In the infant electrical industry, for instance, where ambition far outran knowledge, innumerable firms expressed everyone's bright ideas during the late seventies and eighties. Nor did one company's success necessarily destroy its many competitors. When improved methods of printing enabled cheap dailies to reach a new mass audience, the giants ran parallel with, instead of replacing, the more sedate papers and the countless publications that catered to small ethnic and interest groups.

What was true of business in general applied as well to banking. A few institutions in the major cities experienced a phenomenal growth during the eighties, in part from the demand for commercial banking facilities and in part through the correspondent system which encouraged lesser banks to deposit their surplus with these titans. Yet the apparent leaders, like their industrial counterparts, presided over vast mechanisms that had developed beyond their control. With intuitive methods for gauging the business cycle and rule-of-thumb measures for evaluating credit risks, they relied on stabs of shrewdness, not long-range wisdom, in conducting their affairs. Bankers at all levels strained to comprehend an increasingly complex, impersonal operation. The correspondent system seemed as much beast as blessing: big bankers lived with the possibility of massive withdrawals they could neither predict nor absorb, and smaller ones never understood what was happening to their deposits. Nevertheless, they and the many new firms that operated under lax state laws continued to enter a variety of unexplored fields, multiplying the hazards of the system as they pushed onward.

Little wonder, then, that businessmen could not recognize the economy was entering an important transition. Since mid-century the railroads had served as America's great generator of opportunity, opening new avenues of commerce, consuming quantities of steel and coal, and fostering a host of subsidiary industries. During the nineties the sources of growth shifted to a varied and increasingly complex urban market which would require a far broader range of refined materials and finished products. Under the most favorable circumstances such a major change would have unsettled the men caught up in it. Vested interests were always difficult to readjust. But in these years of exceptional stress, businessmen adamantly refused to acknowledge the process their everyday actions were creating. As prospects within the old system narrowed, they railed against the government, accused radicals of destroying confidence, and demanded an immediate expansion of foreign commerce—any explanation in favor of still another general reorientation. This resistance, in turn, further complicated the transition, especially during the depression that followed the panic of 1893. Businessmen could scarcely attract the foreign investor when they themselves found such scant hope and so few alternatives at home. Contrary to the depression of the seventies when both manufacturing and commerce maintained a brisk pace, hard times in the nineties brought sharp cutbacks with high unemployment and widespread misery. Great urban markets lay before them, markets that would spell prosperity a few years hence, but in the mid-nineties, businessmen saw only trouble. Their worried decisions, not the ineluctable laws of economics, deepened the severity of the depression.

Of course the changing scope and nature of economic activities did not actually paralyze all businessmen. Many fought hard to impose some order on their affairs, and their successes, by contrast to the confusion around them, often gave men still groping in a half-light reputations for genius. One such accomplishment was the nationwide adoption of a standard railroad track gauge,

4'8". Although the mature systems of the East and Midwest had already adopted that gauge by 1880, over 80 percent of the Southern lines still measured 5', in large part from strangely perverse decisions made after the war. Moreover, several Western roads, hoping to minimize the dangers of mountain traffic, laid miles of extremely narrow tracks early in the eighties. Then uniformity came with a rush. Countless townsmen in the South and West demanded a smooth connection with the mainstream of national transportation; and many executives were simultaneously discovering the advantages of cooperation with contiguous roads. Highlighted by a dramatic changeover through much of the South on May 31, 1886, the drive for a single width was essentially complete by the end of the decade. Supplementing this basic achievement, railroad leaders replaced a crazy quilt of local times in 1883 with the modern system of standard time zones and belatedly installed uniform air brakes and automatic couplers.

Incorporation was also helping to standardize business procedures. Although a majority of concerns had still not incorporated by the end of the century, a successful elite had, and that device greatly facilitated their financing, their interstate operations, and their interrelations. Incorporation also encouraged the vertical integrations that a few companies were exploring in an effort to simplify transactions. These might lead a steel company, for example, to buy coal and ore lands and barge lines and to diversify the range of its finishing plants, an insurance company to seek ways of making its salesmen dependent upon the home office and therefore obedient to its regulations, or a manufacturer to distribute its goods through exclusive agents and a uniform credit program. With very mixed results, home offices were trying to lessen the disruptions, the uncertainties, created by those innumerable autonomous links in the chain.

The endless attempts to minimize competition within an industry produced equally uneven results. The classic sequence from tooth-and-claw competition to gentlemen's agreements to pools*

* Precise but legally unenforceable divisions of business.

to trusts* to holding companies† properly suggested the development of larger consolidations and more sophisticated means of cooperation. But it also implied a smooth evolution that certainly did not take place. New techniques for cooperation, rather than supplanting the old, joined them to form a more intricate mosaic of business practices. Both gentlemen's agreements and that cousin of the pool, informal price maintenance, enjoyed greater popularity after the arrival of the holding company than before. Furthermore, the trust, a brief vogue following its adoption by Standard Oil in 1882, influenced no more than a fraction of the economy. Nor did the holding companies necessarily diminish competition. Standard Oil, for instance, controlled a larger percentage of the nation's refining capacity in the late seventies— that is, before it became either trust or holding company— than it ever would again. Jagged fluctuations in competition remained the norm through the nineteenth century and into the next. Finally, the more complex the consolidation, the greater the internal confusion it tended to bring. Paper monopolies that were struggling to establish communications within their companies, to bail water from their financial structures, and to weather dips in the business cycle did not function with robotlike efficiency.

Of the various movements toward economic order, the emergence of a new form of financial leadership easily ranked first both in breadth and in significance. Gathering momentum in the eighties, this process, commonly known as finance capitalism, accelerated at a startling rate during the nineties, when a combination of circumstances suddenly cleared the path for its arrival. The most important of these was the accumulation of ample resources at the disposal of a few American financiers. By the early nineties the economy had matured to the point where it held sufficient concentrated surplus capital to dominate its own investment market. Prior to that time, despite the growing

* Contracts that placed the voting stock of several companies in the hands of "trustees."

† Paper corporations absorbing the assets and legal identities of several companies.

importance of domestic sources, the expansion of heavy industry in particular had depended upon foreign money. English investors alone had placed over $2 billion in American railroad securities by 1890. After the boom of the eighties, however, the total funds of banks and trusts, life insurance companies, some corporate reserves, and a few private fortunes gave the United States a new kind of independence, a relative yet vital freedom.

The right to allocate these resources fell to a few men whose companies were so established that their chief executives could operate with practically no internal restraints. Nevertheless, most of them had no clear idea how to use the surplus. Like other Americans, they sensed the passing of familiar opportunities without recognizing alternative areas for investment. Consequently, they were most receptive to somebody's strong-willed guidance. That responsiveness perfectly suited the half-dozen men, an elite within the monied elite, who not only did have plans but also had recently acquired the eminence to command a hearing. Led by J. P. Morgan, whose imaginative policies in railroad cooperation had already won him fame during the eighties, a handful of financiers, almost all of them private investment bankers, took charge of the new surplus. While agents for European capital, they had lacked the leeway to act quickly and consistently; now Morgan in particular enjoyed such respect that a caravan of domestic followers gladly marched to his beat.

The second precondition for finance capitalism, the readiness of heavy industry for outside leadership, had also been developing for several years. The continuous need for credit as a matter of course made industrial executives vulnerable to a banker's direction. Foreign investors, however, had scarcely used that potential, with the result that overexpansion, befuddled management, and profitless competition grew unabated. Partly for this very reason, companies that had fought every intrusion during the seventies and eighties were now showing some interest in the benefits of an enforced peace, especially where a first generation of stubborn captains no longer dominated. Just at this juncture circumstances allowed, then almost demanded, a shift in the patterns of finance and leadership. By 1891 economic difficulties in Europe were pushing American securities back across the Atlantic, and because a few Americans now had the funds, they gathered them in at reasonably steady prices. Despite the delay, depression finally struck the United States as well, and before it lifted, about 40 percent of the nation's railroad mileage had entered receivership. Such an astonishing quantity of bankruptcies seemed to pose a monumental task of salvage.

The solution proved simple, though breathtaking in its sweep. By and large the receiverships did not reflect economic disaster. In an effort to entice investors during the prosperous years, many railroads had financed their expansion through bonds with payments enforceable at law, and now sudden hard times led them to pass a dividend. Still reasonably solid enterprises, they entered a technical bankruptcy. Technical bankruptcy served the investment bankers admirably. With Morgan showing the way, they reorganized the corporations by paring the bonded debt and weighting their finances with common stock. For the first time in a depression domestic capitalists had appreciable money to invest; railroads were traditionally considered a sound risk; Morgan's name gave the financing sufficient prestige; and as if by magic America's basic heavy industry emerged with chief executives who repudiated helter-skelter competition and looked toward Wall Street for strategic guidance. The economy's surplus had brought power—and very handsome fees—to a small pocket of investment bankers, whose reorientation of a fundamental industry pointed toward broad changes in the structure of business.

As impressive as these accomplishments were, in no sense did they lay the basis for an integrated economy. Indeed, their most pronounced effect was additional upheaval. Even a systematizer as able as Morgan thought and worked in single channels. It never occurred to him that his railroad empire was upsetting innumerable relationships and destroying a thousand dreams. Yet that is precisely what finance capitalism and the lesser attempts at consolidation did: while trying to resolve particular problems, they aggravated the general dislocations out of which they had grown.

America in the late nineteenth century was a nation of intense partisanship and massive political indifference. With the order of things so uncertain, party identification gave men a common label, a comfortable rhetoric, to share with their group; it might also provide some sort of national attachment at a time when any rewarding ties between the community and the world beyond were rare indeed. Moreover, politics served as a grand recreational device, a reason for picnics and rallies, social busy work and oratorical festivities, without the restraining hand of the pastor or employer. Politics was the great national avocation, and as many a coach and manager would discover, Americans took their pastimes with an almost vicious seriousness. Leaders were loved and hated, their private lives and public behavior relentlessly dissected. Factional names like Stalwart, Half Breed, and Mugwump carried the kind of emotion that determined who could and who could not become a man's intimate. Yet the rules of the game required that these passions stay within the bounds of a single party commitment. When certain Mugwumps actually left the Republican party, praising each other as they departed, Republicans and Democrats alike generally regarded them as freaks.

Partisanship of this variety grew out of lives narrowly circumscribed by a community or neighborhood. For those who considered the next town or the next city block alien territory, such refined, deeply felt loyalties served both as a defense against outsiders and as a means of identification within. Appropriately, the only operations of government that roused the same emotions were local ones. Here the struggles over ordinances and appropriations, over what clique or ethnic group held which offices, merely extended the involvements they were expressing through partisanship. But as the process moved beyond their community, interest dwindled rapidly. To the degree that they could still find parochial relevance in state and national affairs, they remained alert. Yet at best that meant haphazard attention and for many none at all.

This was the era when, as Henry Demarest Lloyd remarked, Standard Oil did everything to the Pennsylvania legislature except refine it, when lawmakers by the score came to expect cash and whiskey as their due, when anyone who watched knew and so few cared. Why should they have cared? The issues that would loom large to a later generation had little or no meaning from the perspective of the village or city neighborhood. If a legislator far away pocketed a few dollars, wasted a few hours, did it really matter that much? He was still the right or wrong man by local standards, representing the right or wrong party faction; or he simply did not count at all. No one expected great men in politics; saints entered the ministry, geniuses made fortunes in business. So the same men or their facsimiles returned year after year to repeat the same practices, underwritten by a general, understandable apathy.

Parochialism split the major parties into a myriad of little units that no one had the capacity—or even the inclination—to combine. Like the society that produced them, the parties lacked a central nervous system. Neither Republicans nor Democrats had the dependable income or the broad range of favors that might have held a nationwide organization together. National leaders never thought to devise integrated political programs, and their followers, immersed in local affairs, would only have been shocked if they had. Feeble national committees had neither the resources nor the prestige to conduct campaigns. Each candidate managed his own affairs, and unless he was a person of exceptional prominence, he could usually dissociate himself from the national platform without appearing either hypocritical or necessarily disloyal. Under the circumstances, the best that a man seeking political power could do was to pile a few units into a temporary structure in an effort to achieve limited objectives.

Presidential politics, a special yet representative art, highlighted many of these characteristics. Ideally, an aspirant would have the services of an expert in conventions, someone like Mark Hanna, the industrialist turned king-maker, who laid the foundations for William McKinley's nomination with pledges from the weak, often corrupt Southern Republicans. Ideally also, the candidate had already attracted a wealthy patron. Sponsoring a fine gentleman for the Presidency, which appealed to some rich men as a mixture of philanthropy and sport, almost never implied repayment. In this capacity Hanna doubled as one of McKinley's angels, the steel magnate Wharton Barker supported Benjamin Harrison, and the industrialist Amasa Stone subsidized James A. Garfield. The nominee's campaign strategy, contrary to his finances, did constitute one kind of party function, shared by the factional leaders who had nominated him, and those efforts definitely did carry political obligations. Only McKinley was spared most of that debt by virtue of Hanna's shrewd management.

Immediately after election, the winner faced the most delicate ritual of his term, the selection of a Cabinet. With the party crisscrossed by rivalries, each camp hypersensitive to slights, and Cabinet posts graded by importance, the challenge taxed the ablest political mind; a worrier like Garfield spent months of torturing labor on his slate. For regardless of the official deference he received, the President was still just a factional leader, a chieftain among peers, whose election gave him considerable power through his control over Federal offices but in no way raised him to leadership of the entire party. Cabinet appointments formed a political tableau telling the other chieftains what coalition his administration hoped to represent.

As he accepted the office, a Cabinet member obligated himself to further his chief's renomination. Unquestionably the executive branch served as the most important staging ground for the convention, and except for the lazy Chester A. Arthur, every President who sought renomination won it. But if the President demurred, he could not designate an heir, a fact that helped to deadlock the Republican convention in 1880 and that greatly increased the difficulties of Cleveland's allies during his second term. As every Senator and Governor also knew, the so-called patronage machines operated only in behalf of one man's nomination and election; otherwise they left the appointees almost completely free.

A few urban machines constituted the one important exception to this rule. Excessive mobility, disrupted neighborhoods, and waves of Europeans all contributed to a peculiarly apolitical climate in the major cities, and in this atmosphere the ward boss gained a particularly deep loyalty from old and new residents alike by acting as their intermediary in a bewildering world. The ward politician, on his part, required wider connections in order to manage many of his clients' problems—finding jobs, explaining away minor crimes, and the like. Therefore clusters of these men allied to increase their bargaining power in city affairs. But if logic led to an integrated, city-wide organization, the instinct of self-preservation did not. The more elaborate the structure, the more independence the ward bosses and area chieftains lost and the more violent their feuds became. Then in the eighties two interrelated factors hastened the first, full-blown city machines to maturity. Improvements in urban transportation, spreading a common malaise and wiping out pockets of political resistance, practically assured control of the city to an organization that could overcome enough local rivalries. Just as this reward dangled, the very scope of the expanding city had so increased the difficulty of providing services that only a central agency could handle them. In such a setting, men like Richard Croker of Tammany Hall and George B. Cox in Cincinnati brought their machines of age.

Serving as coordinator rather than dictator, the successful urban boss determined the general division of favors, managed such city-wide issues as public utilities, designated certain candidates whom the organization would support, and represented the machine beyond the city limits. Control came only through careful attention to the intricate workings of his federation. Unlike any other political arrangement of the time, this type of organization functioned continuously to meet a full range of problems in its sphere. At its best, it approximated a self-perpetuating mechanism. Access to jobs and funds won friends who in turn voted the officials back into office. Even prosperous business-men negotiated at a disadvantage: the machine enjoyed its own independent sources of power. Yet the very fluidity that brought the machine to power posed a constant threat to its life. Rarely did one operate for as long as a decade without some major failure. Even this notable achievement barely coped with the disorganization around it.

In a manner comparable to the consolidations in business, the success of the urban machines meant additional disruptions elsewhere in politics. By their very nature, the urban machines tended to turn inward, and national leaders could seldom find leverage in bargaining with a powerful city boss. Nor were there state or national organizations for general political purposes to which the urban machine might have attached itself. Its arrival, in other words, contributed that much more to a particularism that overwhelmed the workings of the national government.

The primary responsibilities of the national government late in the nineteenth century were gathering income and appropriating funds. During the eighties these problems assumed the form of what to do about a surfeit of money in the Treasury. One line of argument suggested giving it away, either by direct distribution to the states or through larger pork-barrel bills. The other recommended cutting income, which in effect meant lowering the tariff. Phrased in another way, the legislators debated how best to allow a multitude of groups outside of Congress decide the fate of that surplus. While distribution promised the simplest transfer of authority, either an appropriation or a tariff bill would accomplish the same end. Because no one in Congress had the power to regulate the contestants, to coordinate the many specific requests into a legislative program, the process in each case resembled a free-for-all with countless interests grabbing what they could until the money had disappeared or the gamut of tariff schedules had been run. In this fashion legislators tinkered with the tariff and threw together appropriation measures throughout the decade, climaxed by the high McKinley Tariff of 1890 and a "billion dollar" Republican Congress. Congress, in other words, provided a forum in which private groups served themselves as best they could.

"National policy" was an illusion in another sense as well. With neither the will nor the apparatus for continuous super-vision, administrators in Washington declared the law at the outset and perhaps checked a few of its results at some later date. The nature of party power determined that almost all Federal agents would come from the localities where they served, and the agent then tailored the laws in his keep to local specifications. Isolated forays might uncover occasional corruption, filling the headlines for a time, but these chance discoveries did not alter the basic process: once Congress had acted, power effectively dispersed to the recipients. Even where broad government management seemed imperative, people simply muddled along without it. Settlers in the Western territories, peculiarly the wards of Washington, were by default forced "to improvise mining laws, exercise the harsh prerogatives of vigilante justice, preempt lands illegally . . . and shape a confused, unrealistic Indian policy to serve their own ends." The rare administrator who sought continuity in policy had to find private means for implementing it. The Treasury Department, for example, tried several times from the seventies through the nineties to beg or buy cooperation from New York's leading bankers in its attempts to stabilize the currency. What a later generation would regard as humiliating and corrupt was the natural administrative procedure of the day.

The only men with resources sufficient to counter such pervasive political decentralization were a handful of magnates who alone had tangible national interests. A network of railroads, a steel company with markets across the land, a financial house with investments throughout the economy, had no logical home. The titans of Wall Street would have made the same decisions if they had operated from Denver; the same spate of holding companies would have appeared if Oregon instead of New Jersey had passed a lax incorporation law. Yet even in Washington,

American government did not offer interests of that nature any natural means of expression. The weak executive branch was almost useless as a source of broad influence. Perforce, these big businessmen relied upon Congress because despite its local orientation Congress at least addressed the subject of national policy.

Consequently, some magnates set about detaching legislators from their localities to serve as representatives for national business interests. As incentive they used a form of insurance policy, including long-term guarantees of campaign funds, lucrative tips and jobs, and often a promise of employment upon retirement from politics. This attractive package appealed especially to those who could justify service to a corporation as one expression of their constituents' current interests. A Congressman from Kansas, for example, could argue that as long as his district cried out for more transportation, friendship toward the major railroads automatically fulfilled the voters' mandate. Expanding gradually during the eighties and nineties, the collection of detached representatives constituted a striking innovation: the beginnings of a new political system, grafted upon the old, that operated from the top down rather than block by block from the bottom up. Still, it did not function with high efficiency. Many big businessmen never cultivated the practice, and not all of those who did pursued it consistently enough to derive full advantage. Perhaps most important of all, party leaders grimly resisted the new system as direct competition with their own partisan power. Once again, a narrow attempt to impose order tended to increase the disorder around it.

If the government's main operational task concerned money, its major public function was debate. Where the House of Representatives made most of the important decisions on allocation, the Senate acted as the center of oratory. The agenda varied only slightly. Tradition had invested certain topics—tariff, currency, land policy, and more recently railroads—with an eternal quality that set them apart as touchstones of public morality. These issues required constant examination. By the same token, there was seldom a widespread demand for immediate solutions. Relatively few took it amiss that the Senate talked more than a decade before settling upon a law to regulate the railroads or that it discussed the tariff directly after passing a bill on the subject, as if no decision had been made. Legislative and rhetorical functions were largely separated, and the Senate enjoyed greater prestige than the House precisely because it seemed to give measures that unhurried consideration which was a government's prime responsibility. Traditionally the statesman had served as the people's mentor, and a citizenry weaned on the perorations of Daniel Webster and Patrick Henry hoped for authentic heroes in their own time. Partisans waited eagerly for their champion's turn in debate, and Senators distributed their speeches as the finest products of each session.

Congressmen could follow such a leisurely pace because so few influential citizens demanded any more of them. It was this absence of counterpressures that allowed Presidents Hayes and Garfield and Senator Roscoe Conkling, the strutting chieftain from New York, to devote about a year of the government's working time between 1879 and 1881 to the question of whose man dedicated to whose faction and whose Presidential nomination would serve as Collector for the Port of New York. Congress filled its slack schedule with an astonishingly elaborate partisanship.

Under certain circumstances that leeway might have freed Congress to answer at least some problems boldly. It did not largely for two reasons. First, the dominance of partisan over governmental considerations militated against clear decisions. Where the ultimate task of a legislature was to legislate, the fundamental responsibility of a party was to maintain communication among its parts. With both Republicans and Democrats fragmented and faction-ridden, leaders shied from any solution that might damage those fragile networks. Second, an extremely close balance between the parties magnified the normal difficulties of compromise. Every factional dispute threatened a crisis. Interparty cooperation became the more imperative in an age of professional partisanship. As a result, the urge to postpone decisions grew almost irresistible, and the measures that did materialize were outstanding only for their vacuity.

Government of intricate partisan maneuver and token legislation elevated certain types to leadership. Congress required the skills of a politician who would dedicate practically all of his energies to its problems, who had absorbed the details of factional division, and above all who placed his party's welfare ahead of any other consideration. A self-evident formula, it was neither simple nor common, as the careers of two such technicians suggest. Arthur Pue Gorman, Democratic Senator from Maryland, and William Boyd Allison, Republican Senator from Iowa, both entered politics as an adjunct to business. Undramatically, perhaps unknowingly, both reversed that normal relationship, first subordinating their business interests and then immersing themselves solely in politics. Like other successful Senators, Gorman and Allison discovered that once removed from the state, they could no longer really influence its politics. Both soon dropped the pretense of any more active participation than filling Federal offices carefully and on occasion mediating almost as outsiders. Consequently, each man required a powerful silent partner—Isaac Rasin for Gorman, James Clarkson for Allison— who cared enough to work every six years in the Senator's behalf. Although Gorman initially achieved prominence as Cleveland's campaign manager in 1884, neither he nor Allison permanently attached himself to any faction. Both men were free to act as intermediaries and adjudicators. At the same time, whatever their dreams, they were too occupied in Congress to fight effectively for the Presidency, a prize that went in almost all cases to those who concentrated on it. Specialization exacted its price.

Contrary to his role in party affairs, the President played only a peripheral part in the domestic operations of government. Although he presented subjects for Congressional consideration, he did so generally and permissively. The one exception was Cleveland's message in 1887 calling for a lower tariff. Yet even that bold pronouncement was more declaratory than legislative in intent. "I shall keep right on doing executive work," he had replied to suggestions that he coerce Congress. "I did not come here to legislate." Instead, the President served as a model for the nation, exemplifying decent, honorable behavior. When Arthur took office in 1881 upon Garfield's assassination, the New York *Sun,* a sophisticated paper, listed the logical reasons of that era why the incumbent, despite his background in machine politics, might well "make a successful administration. He is a gentleman in his manners, neither obsequious nor arrogant. His bearing is manly, and such as to prepossess in his favor all whom he meets. Truth in speech and fidelity to his friends and his engagements form a part of his character. He has tact and common sense."

By and large the Presidents of the time—Hayes, Garfield, Arthur, Cleveland, Harrison, and McKinley—fulfilled their role quite well. Kind to their families and noteworthy for some small list of brave or generous acts, they comported themselves with an almost ostentatious propriety. Hayes served lemonade in the White House and Garfield tea; before the camera McKinley set aside his cigar so that the youth of America would not see their President smoking. Because scandal in the executive branch reflected directly upon them, as leaders and as judges of character, they tried hard to conduct scrupulously honest administrations. Moreover, they kept the government's conscience. The veto was the most significant Presidential power, the test of the truly moral man. Here Cleveland, whose youthful boarding-house indiscretions had linked his name to a bastard, more than compensated for his private lapse by striking down bill after bill with a bluff righteousness. And although Cleveland won the highest distinction, Hayes and Arthur also received an amount of public approval approximately equivalent to the number and importance of their vetoes.

The irrelevance of government to most citizens' lives placed a continuous if elusive strain upon its operations. Out of a need to square the political system with democratic ideals came a justification that combined the government's primary concerns—partisanship, lawmaking, and oratory—with the nation's one common denominator, voting. American politics, it read, was based upon certain fundamental principles which the major parties embodied and their spokesmen enunciated; the electorate judged between these sets of principles, and the government then translated the decision into laws. Nothing better attested to the strength of the myth than the tremendous human effort expended in its behalf. Congressmen explained the precepts behind their votes in quantities of print; leaders solemnly contorted the meaning of their bills to fit the party's commandments; and convention speakers praised the purity of the party's record to thunderous applause. Citizens accepted as much of all this as they could because in that way they remained participants in their government. States rights and a low tariff among Democrats, national unity and protection among Republicans, attracted people who with nothing tangible to gain would nonetheless stake their reputations on the absolute truth of these slogans. Politicians believed as best they could because they were conscious actors' in a democracy. How else could they legitimize decisions? What other encouragement did they have to rise above their factional squabbles?

With state capitols and city halls duplicating roughly the same characteristics, government outside the smaller communities was government in the gross. The flow of responsibility toward the periphery restricted most laws to a form of moral pronouncement, or advisory opinion. Central administration had neither the incentive nor the equipment to make them a substantial part of society's everyday affairs. Later, Americans would look back with contempt at these officials who did so little so poorly. Yet the only popular mandate that politicians in the nineteenth century received demanded an even further curtailment of their powers as the one cure for the government's failure.

The United States in the late nineteenth century offered a peculiarly inviting field for coarse leadership and crudely exercised power. Inhibitions that restrained a man in his own community scarcely applied when his decisions involved distant, invisible people. Witness, for example, the treatment accorded

dissident Western miners by such firms as the American Smelt-
ing and Refining Company and its immediate predecessors.
Absentee owners ignorant of life around the mines readily gave
subordinates a free hand to eliminate troublemakers. Acting
behind the shield of the corporation, underlings then shot and
beat, trampled the strikers' rights as citizens, and blacklisted them
throughout the region. Western laborers who came to sneer at
the democratic process, who looked upon justice as synonymous
with injunctions, martial law, and the bull pen, were absolutely
correct in believing they had no peaceful, orderly recourse. They
worked in a basically inhuman system made more brutal by its
insidious anarchy. As late as 1913, when bullets raked a strikers'
camp outside Ludlow, Colorado, who could say that the local
agents of the Colorado Coal and Iron Company were more than
bloody tools? Yet the owner, John D. Rockefeller, Jr., a kindly
man busy with his philanthropies, really knew little about it.
Shocked by the affair, he felt approximately the same responsibility that he might have for any unfortunate act of nature. The
situation did not differ significantly in the steel and textile mills,
the lumber camps and slaughtering houses. Henry Clay Frick,
who made his fortune in coke and steel, "should not be allowed
in the same room with children," an acquaintance once remarked. "I have always had one rule," a veteran employer
announced from his New York office. "If a workman sticks up
his head, hit it."

Inhumanity in no way depended upon physical distance. Traditionally urban slums had lain outside of the boundaries that
most respectable citizens recognized as the true city. As long as a
cordon sanitaire had sealed the world of hovels from theirs, they
did not have to concern themselves about the very poor. Officials,
reflecting this attitude, had made little effort to police these
outcast districts, only to contain them. With the rise of the
industrial city, however, slums deepened and spread at an alarming rate. Slum dwellers were no longer mere pariahs; they
comprised essential labor that had woven itself throughout the
city's fabric. Trouble in the tenements potentially touched every-

one, and knowing nothing about the slum except that it frightened them, respectable citizens demanded aggressive protection. Now officials were expected to break up gatherings, crack the heads of demonstrators, and generally show the masses that "society," as it was called, stood armed against any menace. Utterly ineffectual as law enforcement, these desultory acts of violence brought cheers from anxious men of property in and around the city, a kind of exultation over the brutality toward their fellow citizens.

A similar spirit permeated business competition, the mixtures of bribery and extortion in politics, the increasingly scurrilous yellow press of the large cities, in fact, the full range of impersonal activities in urban-industrial America. Of course the strains affected employees as well as employers, townsmen as well as railroad kings, and given the opportunity they proved equally intemperate. Rural leaders, for example, were at least as quick as urban to purge unorthodox professors from the college faculties under their control. Yet here as elsewhere the opportunity seldom offered itself to the farmer and wage earner. The capacity to influence quantities of people, however imperfect in a distended society, belonged almost exclusively to those who held strategic positions in an expanding urban-industrial complex. Because they had the power, their irresponsibility spread the great blights over the era.

Irresponsibility in a disorganized society generated a host of ethical evasions no more subtle than the evils they were meant to hide. Some idealized the past and the passing. A flood of fiction sighed over the lost virtues of another day: the valiant men of the Wild West, the touching warmth between master and slave, the quite peace of the New England village, the happy innocence of the barefoot boy with cheek of tan. The peculiar ethical value of an agricultural life, long taken for granted by so many Americans, now became one of their obsessions. (While city dwellers counted the blessings of the pastoral way, men from the farms like Hamlin Garland were simultaneously introducing a different rural literature—of loneliness and poverty and pain.)

Others preached a segmented morality that divided a man's life into compartments and judged each part by a separate standard. A gracious warmth in the living room, decent manners in the street, pious thoughts on Sunday, a formal honesty in dealing with acquaintances, and animal cunning before the rest of the world all passed at the bar of justice. Knowledgeable politicians like Harrison and McKinley could turn their backs on the unsavory tactics that had placed them in the White House and still feel they walked in the light as God's humble servants. Another variation exonerated the individual through forms of determinism. Everyone knew that in the United States the people ruled; therefore, a politician could never alter a government the people had established. Everyone knew that corporations and their products lay helpless before the inexorable laws of economics; therefore, a businessman's methods and goods fell beyond his own ability to control. This scheme made such catch phrases of Darwin's biology as "natural selection" and "survival of the fittest" particularly attractive, an added comfort to the powerful who still had lingering inner doubts.

More generally, Americans emphasized the obvious. What they saw about them were more tracks and more factories and more people, bigger farms and bigger corporations and bigger buildings; and in a time of confusion they responded with a quantitative ethic that became the hallmark of their crisis in values. It seemed that the age could only be comprehended in bulk. Men defined issues by how much, how many, how far. Greatness was determined by amount, with statistics invariably the triumphant proof that the United States stood first among nations. Appropriately, China and Russia, with so much land and so many people, enjoyed a vogue late in the century among soothsayers who talked knowingly about the rise of these "sleeping giants." Problems arose when corporations grew too big, immigrants arrived in too large numbers, strikes idled too many men. Increasingly people were judged in the public arena by dollars, raw not refined. A man rose or fell in common parlance according to the slide of his bank balance, and the cult of the millionaires arrived, focusing rapt attention upon how many there were and how much money each had.

Successful businessmen understandably led the nation in the quest for goodness in bigness. Not only did a quantitative ethic influence their decisions to expand and consolidate, but it usually dominated their sense of personal importance as well. The rich spent their money on the large and the concrete, importing whole castles and purchasing old masterpieces by the gross. In the midst of depression, rival branches of the Vanderbilt family matched taste in the construction of summer homes, the one a $5 million palace of seventy rooms, thirty-three house servants, and thirteen grooms, the other a $2 million villa compensated with furnishings worth $9 million. Fashions and social life reflected the same standard of the overpowering: the weight of the jewels, the expense of the costume, the dimensions of the ballroom, the extravagance in every detail. Even elite families who pretended to scorn the most brazen displays allowed themselves to be numbered by Ward McAllister, prime minister of high society: the Four Hundred officially quantified social quality. This was also the era when the very wealthy were transforming philanthropy into a type of purchase. Unprecedented sums bought a symphony orchestra or a library, a university or a church, some palpable proof of the donor's benevolence. Consequently, both the amorphous cause and the individual lost favor among philanthropists in an age of measurable return. Most evident in the major cities, these patterns were repeated in miniature across the nation.

Quantitative values received a good measure of support from religion, architecture, and literature. When the Episcopal Bishop William Lawrence devised an elementary equation between men's wealth and God's grace, he was only simplifying a message that prominent clergymen in every major denomination had been issuing for many years. The evangelical Josiah Strong illustrated how easily these values could become a habit of mind. Surveying the spiritual state of the nation in his popular tract, *Our Country,* Strong repeatedly phrased moral issues in a statistical idiom.

Records of church attendance, numbers of sinners, proper sums for donation, and the like—figures that presumably spoke for themselves—comprised the heart of his analysis. Quantity of results, not quality of belief, impressed Strong, as it also must have Dwight L. Moody, the extraordinarily successful revivalist. Late in the century huge tabernacles rose in city after city across the country to house the large, passive audiences this efficient agent of salvation fitted into his years of clockwork preaching.

Throughout the nineteenth century the dominant characteristics of American building remained an elaborate, massive eclecticism, "weird combinations of architectural souvenirs," as Lewis Mumford has described it. The frilly palaces lining Chicago's lake front for the Exposition of 1893 spoke that familiar language of beauty through size and display. Even the glimmerings of a new style appeared in strikingly large form. Henry Hobson Richardson's application of Romanesque principles to stately piles of masonry, John Wellborn Root's experiment with a functional interior in the design of a department store, and Louis Sullivan's remarkable integration of a huge steel frame with a grand yet restrained stone facing all relied heavily upon sheer size for their effect. Not until the early homes of Frank Lloyd Wright around 1900 did architecture begin to explore ways of separating the quality of the design from the quantity of the product.

Although serious fiction offered a more varied field, similar values crept in here as well. When writers first adapted naturalism to America, for instance, they turned automatically to the huge and the vast. Only the crowded canvas of the battlefield in Stephen Crane's *The Red Badge of Courage,* the endless carloads of wheat in Frank Norris' *The Octopus* and *The Pit,* or the numberless city faces in Crane's *Maggie* and Theodore Dreiser's *Sister Carrie* could express those implacable forces molding human life.

Crane, Norris, and Dreiser were merely giving singular form to the perplexity of a nation. As the network of relations affecting men's lives each year became more tangled and more distended, Americans in a basic sense no longer knew who or where they were. The setting had altered beyond their power to understand it, and within an alien context they had lost themselves. In a democratic society who was master and who servant? In a land of opportunity what was success? In a Christian nation what were the rules and who kept them? The apparent leaders were as much adrift as their followers. For lack of anything that made better sense of their world, people everywhere weighed, counted, and measured it.

3

Crisis in the Communities

THE GREAT CASUALTY of America's turmoil late in the century was the island community. Although a majority of Americans would still reside in relatively small, personal centers for several decades more, the society that had been premised upon the community's effective sovereignty, upon its capacity to manage affairs within its boundaries, no longer functioned. The precipitant of the crisis was a widespread loss of confidence in the powers of the community. In a manner that eludes precise explanation, countless citizens in towns and cities across the land sensed that something fundamental was happening to their lives, something they had not willed and did not want, and they responded by striking out at whatever enemies their view of the world allowed them to see. They fought, in other words, to preserve the society that had given their lives meaning. But it had already slipped beyond their grasp.

It was a strange assortment of symptoms that appeared rather abruptly during the mid-eighties. The Third Plenary Council of the Catholic Church in 1884 dedicated its hierarchy to a prompt expansion of parochial education. A few months later the Reverend Josiah Strong, in an alarming little book, *Our Country: Its Possible Future and Present Crisis,* whose sales would exceed half a million, called Protestant hosts to meet "the perils which threaten our Christian and American civilization." A "great uprising of labor" swept from the shipyards in Maine to the railroads of Texas, swelling membership in the Knights of Labor from 50,000 in 1884 to more than 700,000 in 1886. "Free government cannot long endure," warned the venerable Rutherford Hayes, "if property is largely in a few hands and large masses of people are unable to earn homes, education, and a support in old age"; and the young economist Richard T. Ely implored ministers to reach the wage earner before socialism engulfed him. In 1886 Grover Cleveland delivered the first Presidential message on labor.

At the same time Benjamin Tillman, "the one-eyed plowboy" from South Carolina's upcountry, was preparing to lead his people against both the white rich and the Negro poor. During these same months the gentleman reformer Henry Demarest Lloyd turned from a simple creed of antimonopoly toward some more radical solution for the nation's ills, and Henry George discovered that as a "single tax" on unearned rents his complex land program now received national attention. In 1887 rural alliances in the South and West verged on a grand expansion, a handful of bedeviled Iowans formed the anti-Catholic American Protective Association, and Edward Bellamy, a strange young man from Chicopee Falls, Massachusetts, was preparing the most popular utopian tract in American history.

These were the scattered events that announced a feeling suddenly acute across the land that local America stood at bay, besieged by giant forces abroad and beset by subversion at home. An important qualitative change in outlook had occurred within a few critical years. Emotions that had come and gone in earlier times now stayed to dominate men's thoughts. Once roused, the sense of emergency was self-generating. Matters that previously would have been considered separate incidents, or even ignored, were seized and fit into the framework of jeopardy, each reinforcing the others as further proof of an imminent danger. By the logic of anxiety, worries became fears, mounting until they had reached a climax in 1896.

Among the components of crisis, none found fuller expression than the belief that great corporations were stifling opportunity, and no one cried his resentment more persistently than the local entrepreneur. The dream that every American's birthright included a fair chance to win his pot of gold had, if anything, grown even more powerful in the expansive years after the Civil War. With prospects boundless, innumerable citizens of great expectation and modest means had enthusiastically entered the race for riches. The depression of the seventies only checked these hopes, as the proliferation of little companies, the extraordinary growth of branch railroads, and the passionate speculation in Western lands demonstrated early in the eighties. But now the tide appeared to be running out. Particularly with the mild depression between 1883 and 1885, the number of small-business failures increased sharply; the absorption of spur lines by the larger roads occurred as rapidly as new track was laid; and by the middle of the decade bad weather and bad judgment had pricked the Western land bubble. At least as important, limited projects brought limited rewards. Instead of opening doors into a magical kingdom, almost every small enterprise bound its sponsor into a bewildering complex of business relationships which seemed to restrict rather than extend his freedom.

From the perspective of that trap the basic distinction lay between individual enterprise and corporate wealth, between the scattered knights of private initiative and the soulless monsters of monopoly. An ingenious, persevering man who had won a personal fortune still belonged among the nation's heroes; sinister corporations that profited at the people's expense were the despoilers. A small businessman might praise Andrew Carnegie as the embodiment of the American success story and in his next breath condemn the "steel trust" as its corruption. Judgments like these represented a state of mind that people entered and left in unpredictable ways. Community boosters who had courted a factory for years would suddenly find it a tyrant and turn violently against it. "The people are in favor of building a new road and do what they can to promote it. [But] after it is once built and fixed," an official of the Illinois Central ruefully observed, "then the policy of the people is usually in opposition." Although another turn of the wheel, a new glittering prospect, could transform them just as quickly back into eager promoters, opportunities after the mid-eighties appeared ominously narrow and dependence so very deep. Ambitious men everywhere were rising up against an economy that extended too far beyond their ability to understand.

As the pace of industrialization quickened early in the eighties, the incomprehensible ways of the corporation were also alienating a multitude of wage earners. Rapidly losing control over their working lives, they knew only that decisions made somewhere else pushed them about like so many cattle. Industrial laborers who had sunk some roots tended to respond ambivalently. On the one hand, they sought to preserve the kind of decency typified by a neat white house and the respectful greetings of their neighbors; on the other, they inclined toward a vague class consciousness, a very general urge to find and join others like themselves. In towns where outsiders dominated the economy, the worker usually emphasized respectability. He was an acknowledged member of the community and his prejudices blended indistinguishably with those around him. But where local businessmen owned the factory and local leaders were still hell-bent on development, or in the cities where wage earners were increasingly isolated, the worker soon learned that he had been consigned to the dangerous classes, and he attacked the world above him that much more readily. In either case the laborer felt a system closing in upon him. He wanted power brought back into his own hands and some promise of alternatives—out to the land, up into business.

A revolution in the patterns of distribution was eliciting similar responses in a host of small towns. The primary significance of America's new railroad complex lay not in the dramatic connections between New York and San Francisco but in the access a Kewanee, Illinois, or an Aberdeen, South Dakota, enjoyed to the rest of the nation, and the nation to it. Much of that fundamental change came in two bursts of railroad construction, one following 1879 and the other 1885, which together produced more trackage than any comparable period in American history. Mainly feeders, these lines ran through countless, hitherto untouched small communities, pulling them into a broad system of transportation. Dependence arrived as abruptly as the connection was made, the one inherent in the other.

The years of explosive building were also years of chaotic rates. While shipping costs on balance decreased during the eighties, it often took a very discerning eye to recognize the long-range benefits. What the farmer and local merchant did see was an exceptionally erratic rate pattern, now up, now down, seeming to follow no logic beyond the caprice of a distant magnate. As a matter of course railroad executives compensated for a low return on competitive through traffic by adjusting their charges at all noncompetitive points. Sometimes month by month, almost always without notice, townsmen received insulting reminders of their utter helplessness before the fiats of an unknown czar. The railroads, in the cautious phraseology of the first Interstate Commerce Commission, had "determined at pleasure what should be the terms of their contractual relations with others . . . , [terms] which intimately concerned the commercial, industrial and social life of the people." Far more than a decade's averages, that feeling of impotence set the townsman's view of his enemy.

Changes in merchandising and finance proved equally a mixed blessing. As railroads incorporated large new areas into a regional or national market, the traditional methods of distributing goods collapsed. Jobbers who had carried their random assortments from town to town, bargaining at each stop, simply could not manage a sufficient range of territory or goods, and by the early eighties the trend was running quickly toward integrated wholesale houses that supplied a basic line of groceries and dry goods through standard contracts. The old procedure—expensive, uncertain, and inefficient—had at the same time been a human one. A glass of whiskey, a few stories, some haggling and promises, and the local merchant had returned to work certain he was master in his kingdom. Now he transacted most of his business from a price list. In return for lower costs and more reliable service, the storekeeper sacrificed a certain personal latitude, a certain sense of his own worth.

Customers were experiencing that lack of leeway at every turn. Though the prices they paid were dropping, the credit available to them was constricting, for few merchants could offer more flexible conditions than they themselves received. Only in purchasing expensive durable goods did the townsmen initially find credit no problem. Competition during the eighties led companies to entice buyers with astonishingly lax terms. But when the day of reckoning came, some stranger in the city read the ledger. Most important of all, the local banker was also being drawn into a tighter world of finance, where the notes he wished to rediscount had to express value in language a Chicago banker could appreciate. Neither merchant nor farmer could borrow on an informal basis as he once might have, nor could he expect his reputation or glib tongue to win a personal extension. The town banker might pass along lower interest rates, but as he felt the pinch of a stricter discipline, he passed that along too. In hard times, it could seem a cruel system.

Throughout most of the South pressures generated from the outside were matched by pressures generated from within. Small farmers and townsmen, often located in the relatively poor lands of the upcountry, emerged from Texas to Virginia during the eighties as a somewhat diffuse yet vigorous force demanding leaders of their own kind who would champion their own causes in their own idiom. Wooed but never wed by the political elites in their states, they had customarily awaited someone else's initiative. The immediate aftermath of the Civil War had actually strengthened these attitudes of dependence, and consequently the state constitutions that marked the end of reconstruction, rather than reflecting the special needs of the white farmer, again had invited the rule of self-perpetuating county cliques.

Yet the underpinnings of the old system had cracked. Upstart promoters and businessmen had already pushed their way to the top, and a growing number of whites found little that inspired awe or gratitude in this new leadership operating behind a facade of aristocratic names and military titles. The first waves of rebellion came early in the eighties. As disaffected Democrats or independents or even Republicans, younger groups of slight prestige challenged the oligarchies in several Southern states, insisting upon a more equitable tax system, broader services to the farmer, and certain restrictions on business. Usually inexperienced and simply unable to tap enough discontent, they were quickly defeated. Only the mercurial William Mahone's coalition of dissenters in Virginia won a major election, and they lost power after just one term in office. A far greater surge, however, rose in the second half of the decade, signaling the full-scale arrival of the countryside.

By chance a comparable movement was appearing in a northern stretch that extended from the industrial cities on the Atlantic to the Western wheatlands. The sons and grandsons of families who had poured into the United States during the late forties and early fifties, principally from Ireland and Germany, were also claiming a place of their own in American society. Where their fathers and grandfathers had generally turned inward before a hostile environment, the generation of the eighties, now reasonably well established, held their heads high and fought back. Eager to realize an explicitly American dream and at the same time keenly conscious of their heritage, they wanted broader opportunities, firmer security, and the right to select their own leaders. Politicians who had long recruited the "immigrant vote" through businesslike, bilingual brokers discovered that the nature of the vote was changing. A docile generation was giving way to a demanding one.

Moving roughly from east to west and from the cities into the towns, the process of ethnic maturation had already affected a number of Eastern centers by the early eighties. Against a backdrop of tension, Catholics of Irish descent had been elected mayors of Scranton in 1878, New York City in 1880, Lawrence in 1881, and Boston in 1884. By 1890 Irish names would dominate politics in sixty-eight Massachusetts cities and towns. Although these drives, like those of the Southern whites, often began through third parties, they almost always turned toward the Democracy, whose welcome markedly increased its vote in 1882 and placed the Republicans on the defensive for the balance of the decade. By the later eighties the movement had swept across the Midwest, leaving bitter conflicts in its wake. Particularly acute in Wisconsin and Illinois, they touched every state from Ohio to Kansas and the Dakotas. Because Democrats continued to offer the challengers a home, with seats of some honor, their militancy played a major role in the party's clear victories of 1890 and 1892. Sensitive and assertive, ethnic communities in quantity had come of age.

When the ambitious John Peter Altgeld, who had been brought from Germany as an infant, moved to Chicago in the seventies, he found a host of equally determined young men from immigrant backgrounds in a common search for wealth and place. As Altgeld succeeded in business and in Democratic politics, he continued to work most naturally with men of this kind. It was always easier to cooperate with George Schilling, the socialist labor leader, or with Chicago's Irish bosses than with the city's comfortable elite, even as he imitated the style of the rich. In 1890, on the eve of his greatest triumphs, he published "The Immigrant's Answer" to the current attacks against newcomers, one more round in a fight that had begun with childhood taunts of "little Dutchman." The last such helping hand he extended, a Governor's pardon for the German anarchists who had been convicted in ritual retribution for the Haymarket bombing, contributed to the rapid decline of his fortune later in the nineties. Altgeld fell as he had risen, a self-conscious, second-generation immigrant.

To a number of gentlemen, each portion of this general ferment merely supplied new evidence that a decent world where their word mattered, where their standards were honored and their families secure, was either rapidly passing or had already disappeared. These feelings of danger and defeat, which once again spread from the cities to the countryside, were by no means the monopoly of one particular group. They influenced patricians as different from one another as the kinsmen of John Adams and James K. Polk, as different as the men who retreated to their studies from such public figures as Morrison R. Waite and Joseph P. Bradley, Justices of the Supreme Court. But if diverse ways of life held them apart, common responses at least made them kindred spirits. Each considered the true and simple America in jeopardy from foes of extraordinary, raw strength— huge, devouring monopolies, swarms of sexually potent immigrants, and the like. Prominent families had experienced nothing like this since early in the century. Accustomed to a steady ripple of attacks, these men of breeding now saw a tidal wave that might sweep away all of legitimate society. Unlike some of their sons who would try to humble the bad men while preserving their means to power, these older gentlemen more often damned out of hand everything connected with the enemy, and in the process many of them retired behind dogmas too brittle to survive the coming decade.

The mild depression between 1883 and 1885 and the gradual decline in sections of agriculture commencing around 1887 neither created the crisis of the mid-eighties, nor ignited it, nor appreciably altered its course. Hard times merely supplied the harsh proof for truths already held.

The most significant characteristic shared by these many anxieties was the desire for community self-determination, and antimonopoly was its most common means of expression. An overwhelming majority of articulate Americans, including such studies in contrast as Thomas Cooley, the philosopher of corporate law, and Frank Parsons, the Boston socialist, or the precious intellectual, Henry Adams, and the stormy agrarian, Ignatius Donnelly, had committed themselves to some version of this vague creed. Seeming to appear from nowhere, the Sherman Antitrust Act of 1890, a brief law that outlawed monopoly in stern, sweeping, imprecise language, reflected that consensus. Although antimonopoly occasionally singled out a definite enemy

—some large corporation, a specific banking practice, a particular form of landholding—it usually served as a general method of comprehending the threats to local autonomy. Thus it would cover the whole range of railroad activities, from determining rates to influencing legislatures; all of American finance, from issuing currency to managing international exchange; and an entire scheme of land economics, from speculating in urban real estate to acquiring timber rights. Monopoly, in other words, connoted power and impersonality. It concerned the vast wealth, legal flexibility, and geographical scope of a major corporation far more often than a careful list of its procedures.

The railroads represented a partial exception to that rule. By the eighties they had alienated a remarkable range of Americans: the farmer saw them as the arrogant manipulator of his profit, the small-town entrepreneur as the destroyer of his dreams, the city businessman as the sinister ally of his competitors, the labor leader as a model of the callous, distant employer, and the principled gentleman as the source of unscrupulous wealth and political corruption. Because the roads affected their lives so directly, many of them compiled bills of particulars to prove their point. In various ways these demanded an end to preferential treatment for certain shippers, some arithmetic device to equalize rates, and greater publicity for the affairs of the railroads. Over the years their petitions accumulated in Congress, where John Reagan, once a local promoter of railroads himself, proved the most persistent agitator for rigid controls. The most effective pressure came from a group of New Yorkers, men of business and breeding who had once hoped that sins exposed in public would carry their own mortifying punishment but who now wanted national regulation. Not until the sudden increase of interest during the mid-eighties did the Senate set conscientiously to work. Then in 1887 Congress passed the Interstate Commerce Act, an evasive measure that ostensibly outlawed pooling and a number of discriminatory practices. Because the law did not seriously restrict the railroads, some executives actually welcomed it as a protective cover. Nevertheless, the mere passage of such an act through a Congress of the late nineteenth century indicated the breadth of antagonism toward the iron autocrats.

Antialien sentiments, cousins to antimonopoly, were almost as common and equally protean. In one guise they abused the immigrant in rising crescendo after the middle of the decade. Mixing contempt with fear, natives pictured the newcomers as dispirited breeders of poverty, crime, and political corruption, and simultaneously as peculiarly powerful subversives whose foreign ideologies were undermining American society. "The Roman Catholic vote is more or less perfectly controlled by the priests," wrote Josiah Strong, employing the popular stereotype of the individual Catholic as a mindless puppet. "That means that the Pope can dictate some hundreds of thousands of votes in the United States." What greater danger to a community's self-determination? Cries for a restriction of immigration and for stiffer naturalization laws accompanied the upsurge of nativism. Reflecting the new concern, Grover Cleveland became the first President of the century to give official mention to an "immigration problem"; and President Harrison followed soon after with a warning against disloyal aliens.

Fears of this sort did not depend upon the enemy's presence. Just as Southern voices swelled the chorus condemning Europeans who came to the Northern cities, so Americans thousands of miles from Utah mounted a savage attack upon the Mormon menace. With sudden efficiency the national government forced the church to capitulate on the issue of polygamy and to accept an outside civil authority.

Nor did the term "alien" necessarily mean foreign in a strict sense. Any distant, threatening power was alien to the beleaguered communities, and they labelled it as such. James Stephen Hogg, a friend of John Reagan with a similar background as a thwarted entrepreneur, rose to the Governorship of Texas by assaulting every available outside agency—insurance companies, major manufacturers, railroads, nonresident ranch owners, the national government—and by depicting each in turn as foreign to Texas. Around the mid-eighties town and country-

side in the Dakota Territory buried many of the differences that
had been dominating their politics in order to concentrate upon
two intruders, the railroads and the government in Washington.
A comparable spirit informed most of the campaigns for urban
home rule, an essentially negative program late in the nineteenth
century that sought to solve the city's problems by driving out
state politicians and industrial lobbyists. Precisely this suspicion
of outsiders enabled some wage earners to win wide sympathy in
their struggles against absentee owners. The brilliant publicity of
Henry Demarest Lloyd and the speeches of such politicians as
Altgeld rallied support for the depressed coal miners of Spring
Valley, Illinois, not by arguing the merits of their case but by
identifying the mineowner with Jay Gould, a symbol of all the
evils of alien monopoly.

Finally, the desire for self-determination encouraged the development of organizations that would express that spirit of
community autonomy. A natural impulse exaggerated by the
anxieties of the later eighties, it became a particular obsession
among the Southern white farmers and the Americans a generation or two removed from Europe. Just such organizations
represented the indispensable declaration of independence, the
essential proof of arrival. The process in the South followed a
fairly standard pattern. Moving first into a variety of farm
associations, small farmers and townsmen soon collected primarily within the Southern Alliance. At the same time, after a
few halting experiments with independent parties, they sought
control of the state Democracy. Where that succeeded, as it did in
South Carolina under Ben Tillman, they stayed; where it did not
they usually passed in large numbers into the Populist party.
Their fervent loyalty at each step became the trademark of the
Southern farmers' movement.

The case of the maturing ethnic groups was not as simple.
More scattered in the countryside, more intermixed with others
in a city, they found it much more difficult to establish and then
control their own organizations. Moreover, they faced much
deeper hostility from their neighbors. Partly for these reasons, the

ethnic groups placed a much higher premium on the organization itself. Rather than using it as a platform for reform, they
perfected its contents, its peculiar American Germanness or
Irishness. Nothing served them as well as their churches, largely
Catholic in the East with an increasing admixture of Lutheran
farther West; and out of these centers grew various supple-
mentary social and political clubs. Ward politics offered an
attractive alternative in several cities. It was no accident that so
many urban machines appeared just as Irish and German descendants were striving for an independent outlet. Where the
right machine did not materialize, third parties often did. Certain
labor unions and socialist groups also became their personal
organizations. In the strange way movements entangle, some
Protestant sons of Germans and Scandinavians in the Midwest
announced their arrival through the American Protective Association, the most voluble opponent of the Catholic sons of Irishmen.

A preoccupation with purity and unity served as the second
common denominator of the community crisis. Mingling with
the urge toward self-determination, it often showed itself first in
attempts to cleanse and combine at home. Prohibition, one of the
earliest expressions of this impulse, enjoyed the initial advantage
of a traditional Protestant respectability. Uneasy people could
turn here, as they had for generations, with assurance that in
attacking liquor they fought beyond question for the Lord and
the sanctity of the hearth. Early in the eighties, rabid prohibitionists began to appear in force here and there across the nation, and
before the movement had lost its vitality by the very end of the
decade, well over half of the United States had witnessed a noisy,
bitter debate with sharp political repercussions on the advisability
of outlawing drink. The greatest bursts of interest affected a rural
stretch from the Upper South into the Western territories. Most
of the states from North Carolina to Texas and Kansas held at
least one general election during which no other issue seemed to
matter; and when the Dakotas entered the union in 1889, both
were dry. In all, the enemies of liquor won few legislative battles.

But with a conviction that surmounted all obstacles, the prohibitionists effectively spread a disturbing gospel of the contaminated community.

During these same years the Women's Christian Temperance Union convinced most states to adopt prohibitionist propaganda as a standard portion of the public school curriculum. Just as naturally, anxious Americans looked to their schools as a bulwark of local defense, with increasing numbers insisting that public education infuse a new strength, a new cohesion, into the threatened community. Many demanded a renewed emphasis in the classroom upon Protestant doctrines. According to Josiah Strong, the schools had no alternative but to act as an arm of the Protestant churches "because immorality is perilous to the State, and morality cannot be secured without the sanctions of religion." Others concentrated upon the corrupting influence of alien textbooks, presumably foisted on the schools by some distant trust. Gaining momentum late in the decade and reaching its peak in the mid-nineties, a hectic campaign to instill patriotism through worship of the Constitution, the flag, and America's heroes engaged the energies of the Grand Army of the Republic and several recently formed ancestral clubs, including the Daughters of the American Revolution and the Sons of the American Revolution. As servants of the community, the public schools would simply have to inculcate its youth with a pure and narrow truth.

Like prohibition, protection of the common school served as a major line of battle with suspect ethnic groups, colliding headlong with the aroused sensitivities of Irish and German descendants. In fact, a fair portion of the concern for public education came in direct response to the new ethnic assertiveness. When the Third Plenary Council proclaimed the need for parochial schools, the prelates were reflecting as well as stimulating sentiments within Catholic communities. A number of priests, in spite of generally low incomes in their parishes, had already launched new educational programs, and worried Protestants, who were inclined in any case to see the parochial schools as centers of authoritarian indoctrination, interpreted these moves as an assault on democratic society. Nothing endeared the defrocked priest Edward McGlynn to anti-Catholics more than his praise of public education as "one of the greatest and most potent instruments for building up and maintaining one great, free, common nationality."

Both in the East and in the Midwest, where German Lutheran schools were also enmeshed in these conflicts, the opposition focused upon the sinister implications of foreign-language instruction. Demanding the compulsory use of English in all classrooms and sometimes adding the need for a general supervision of church schools, nativists brought the issue of parochial autonomy to a climax toward the end of the decade in Massachusetts, Illinois, and Wisconsin. Unquestionably the rising ethnic groups cared far more deeply than their vaguely distressed critics. In a flare of belligerence they fought off the threats in all three states and in the process contributed materially to the Republican defeats of 1890 and 1892 in Wisconsin and Illinois.

Although Americans might vacillate in their attitudes toward the immigrant, scarcely any of them by the mid-eighties still doubted the Negro's proper place. Treated as curse, clown, or barbarian, told by the Supreme Court to find his own social level, manipulated by employers and politicians North and South, he roused a few sympathetic voices only when he was most flagrantly abused. The quiet subordination that many whites found implied in Booker T. Washington's emphasis upon economic self-help would bring him spontaneous national acclaim in the mid-nineties. To some degree almost all whites found the Negro's presence both disturbing and convenient. In a loose, ostensibly egalitarian society, who could tell where the Negro might try to wander, how he might upset the order of things? At the same time, that diffuse society with its blurred hierarchies placed inordinate importance upon all visible distinctions. A marked man, the black became everyone's inferior by standards of either power or prestige. Only the poorer Southern whites had reason to doubt the serviceability of the color line. Often struggling in a net of mortgages, agricultural ignorance, and erratic prices, they had no guarantee of a lasting advantage over anyone. Beginning from the depths, Southern Negroes had risen markedly in literacy and property holding after the war, facts sometimes evident to the poorer whites and always easy to exaggerate. And as it happened, Negroes enjoyed a particularly rapid advance during the eighties, just as the first wave of farmers and townsmen was pushing toward a new independence.

The black man, then, represented an obvious target in the quest among newly arrived whites for place and purity. Yet the Negro, while politically subservient in almost every Southern state, remained a sufficiently valuable token in some to provide him with a tentative sort of defense. Perversely complimented by the white farmer's animosity, he was cynically protected by the white politician's ambition. The clearest expression of the assertive white's attitudes, therefore, came in those states where the Negro played a relatively slight role in politics and where relatively few hindrances slowed the agrarian drive for power. Precisely these conditions existed in Mississippi and South Carolina, and similar patterns emerged in the two states. Late in the eighties both extended the range and increased the severity of segregation, by 1890 both had effectively disfranchised the Negro, and particularly in Mississippi Negro education suffered anew at the expense of white. Moreover, both states were inviting a crude racism that previously had lain outside acceptable public bounds. By contrast with later decades there were still many restraints, still concerns about respectable rhetoric and policies. The arrival of the small farmers and townsmen, however, had battered the foundations. Regular additions to Jim Crow elsewhere in the South suggested that a trend had commenced, even though countless local variables kept its course uneven.

Where patricians in the South often resisted these harsh, formal controls over the Negro, their counterparts in the Northern cities tended to move in the vanguard attacking the urban masses. As Sambo, the Negro played a central role in the Southern gentlemen's tradition of leadership; relinquishing wardship over the Negro was an integral part of their defeat at the hands of *arrivistes*. In the North, on the contrary, most men of family and breeding regarded the city's strange hordes as primary enemies of the good society. They had crowded out the Yankee mechanic, who was now idealized as sober, industrious, and piously Protestant, and had replaced him with an alien culture; as a matter of course they had joined the bosses in debauching city government. By destroying a world where a gentleman could lead, they gave up any claim to his kindness. Around 1890 a significant number of Northern gentlemen, in league especially with urban ministers, set about the task of purification with a cold eye toward the center city. Vice and machine politics were their twin objectives. Repressive legislation would obliterate the former, and a combination of civil service and stern criminal prosecutions would destroy the latter. As Charles J. Bonaparte, the well-born president of Baltimore's Union for Doing Good, put it, that treatment would "rid our country thoroughly and once for all of these dangerous and noxious counterfeits of statesmen, and . . . thus make room for the genuine article, which we produced in good measure a hundred years ago. . . ."

The patrician's battle with the urban machine, projected beyond the city, was one part of a widespread demand to purify all political institutions. Directed particularly at Washington, it called for the redemption of government from its usurpers. Uniformly vague about the process of theft, differing over precisely who the impostors were and how best to overthrow them, all of these attacks did describe essentially the same result. A group of arrogant men had ensconced themselves in power and impudently used it for knavish purposes. Pretenders, in other words, had stolen the government from the people. The critics also agreed that an aroused populace could always remove the usurpers and, with minor exceptions, that removal alone would set democracy aright.

The oldest and most enduring of these protests exalted civil service as democracy's cure. By denying politicians the spoils of office, the argument ran, civil service would drive out the parasites and leave only a pure, frugal government behind. The nonpartisanship inherent in civil service would permeate politics, and as party organizations withered away, the men of quality now excluded by the spoilsmen and unscrupulous businessmen would resume their natural posts of command. The people in their communities would once again control a government that met the standards of "the Founding Fathers," as President Hayes dreamed it might. Led by principled gentlemen in the East and Midwest, the civil service movement had gathered enough general support by 1883 to produce the Pendleton Act, a weak law that effectively allowed each administration to classify public offices as it chose. Then after a pause in the mid-eighties, the drive revived to remain a small, insistent theme of reform. Throughout the century it retained that cleansing purpose. "While one of the main purposes of the [Pendleton] law is to improve the public service, yet this can hardly be considered its prime objective," the Civil Service Commission reported in 1891. "Its prime objective is to remove from American politics the degrading influence of the patronage system."

Far more significant, a distilled version of redemption was rapidly winning the allegiance of small-town America during the later eighties. The agrarian variation, largely indifferent to specific questions of patronage or bribery and openly hostile to the rule of a gentlemanly elite, struck directly at the heart of the government's operation. Rejecting the possibility of democracy in any extralocal setting, it denied the legitimacy of all formal political structures. Each one, from parties to legislatures, constituted an artificial barrier between the people and government, an antidemocratic mechanism which "lawyer-politicians" used as they, not the voters, saw fit. " 'We are your masters,' " an agrarian leader had Congress declare; " 'you are not ours.' " The only proper party was the people themselves; the only valid laws, according to the farm editor Milton George, were the people's truths phrased in the people's language. "The government is the *people* and *we* are the people" echoed from the Dakotas to the

Carolinas as thousands of rural Americans anticipated its literal realization.

Because most reformers conceived the world as an orderly affair where societies, like planets, normally functioned according to rational laws, they had customarily looked for that one gear askew, that one fundamental rule violated, as an explanation for America's troubles. Reset the gear, abide by the great law, and all difficulties would vanish. A crisis psychology accentuated this tendency: the more anxious the search, the more imperative that men penetrate to the root of the matter; the more serious society's predicament, the more grandiose the visions of perfection following that single correction. Solutions that already leaned toward revelation, such as Henry George's discussion of land monopoly, were pushed the final distance. As the single tax, George's program won a host of new and particularly zealous converts during the mid-eighties. At the same time, analysts reformulated problems to suit their solutions. "The Social Question," a term that covered subjects ranging from obscene literature and liquor to strikes and monopolies, suddenly emerged in 1885 as the most popular topic of the day, and in a debate of panaceas, Americans offered each other inclusive answers to the inclusive question. "All the great problems . . . ," the nativist Robert DeCourcy Ward declared, "the liquor question, the public school question . . . , are tied up with the one great problem of foreign immigration." Socialists, prohibitionists, inflationists, and many more merely substituted their chosen word for "immigration." Eighteen eighty-seven was an appropriate year for President Cleveland to rally his party behind a single issue, tariff reform. Brand Whitlock, the novelist who later served as mayor of Toledo, recalled that among his educated friends "the tariff question had seemed entirely fundamental" in the later eighties. Viewing all distress as an integrated series of causal connections, few found it irrelevant when the free trader told an audience of patricians, or the antimonopolist a gathering of labor leaders, that only his formula could stop government corruption or raise wages. Other reformers might disagree, but they understood. They also reasoned from a first cause.

Not everybody discovered his solution so easily. Some collected many answers on the chance that some one among them would prove to be the great corrector. In the late eighties and early nineties Frances Willard, famous as the leader of the Women's Christian Temperance Union, placed no more confidence in prohibition than she did in a number of alternatives. Always adding panaceas to her portfolio, she never lost faith that one of them would some day bring the Golden Age. Like others who yearned to understand the essence of man's difficulties, Willard gravitated to spiritualism, which enjoyed a considerable vogue during the eighties and nineties. Edward Bellamy borrowed liberally from the theosophists, who floated about his movement like covetous ghosts. For similar reasons such men as Josiah Strong, who explained America's heavy drinking by its location in a climatic "nervous belt," were attracted by the innumerable fads of pseudoscience. As a community of seekers, these people willingly explored each other's roads to utopia.

Probably the largest number of worried Americans looked for peace and unity in Protestantism, the most natural of all reservoirs for hope. Although most denominational spokesmen offered little comfort, some, who tended to lie along the edges of Protestantism, did respond. Each started from the premise that bitter conflict, on the streets or in men's hearts, was un-Christian. "The state of industrial society is a state of war," the young Congregational minister Washington Gladden lamented in 1886, and religion must act as the great peacemaker. At that point the Christian reformers diverged. The most respectable among them, including a few well-placed in their denominations, tried to reconcile profits and ethics within the existing framework, modified only by some stimulus to man's finer instincts. Usually they spoke to the rich and well-born, on the assumption that these of all Americans longed to serve their God. Some exhorted businessmen to treat their customers, competitors, and employees as

Christian brethren, promising that economics tempered with love would gain them earthly as well as heavenly rewards. Others supported experiments in model capitalism for tenement houses and factory life. Again, they presented a distinctly industrial message, with a 6 percent return one of its essential components. Still others organized forums through which men of many backgrounds could gather, discuss, and then bury their animosities in mutual understanding. Ministers of this general persuasion saw themselves as catalysts and arbiters. Aggressive as philosophers, they would nonetheless have to preserve a perfect social impartiality, a beacon for the nation's ultimate reunification.

More angry, more immersed, and more marginal, another Protestant group rejected any truce between capitalism and Christianity. Because capitalism by its nature engendered strife and hate, only a new order could bring peace to the land. What these men envisioned was a sudden mass awakening that would draw Americans into a communion of cooperation and love. Shading imperceptibly from this handful of radical ministers, an assortment of sectarians and independents preached roughly the same doctrine under any of a dozen names. One of these men, Henry Demarest Lloyd, describing himself as "a socialist-anarchist-communist-individualist-collectivist-co-operative-aristocratic-democrat," unconsciously labelled a movement. While in most cases they denounced all churches, they simultaneously reflected a deep and essentially Protestant commitment. "The new religion— *man the redeemer*," Lloyd glowingly scribbled, ". . . *this divinity of democracy—the creative will of the people* which is to be substituted for the old God."

Despite the moderating efforts of such men as Gladden and Richard Ely, Christian capitalism and Christian socialism remained fairly distinct camps. Where Christian capitalists accepted socioeconomic divisions as a necessary part of God's plan, the socialists were almost pathologically hostile to classes, even as a means to the cooperative commonwealth. "We say, let there be revolution," declared the romantic Episcopalian W. D. P. Bliss. "Let us to arms. Let us sing the Marseillaise. Only let it be a revolution that shall go to the bottom of the question. . . . Let it be an uprising of not the third or the fourth or the fifth estate, but of all estates, of all God's children against the slavery of Mammon." When Laurence Gronlund offered Americans their first popular treatise on Marx in 1884, he omitted the class struggle. America, he believed, had a uniquely benign destiny. "My understanding of the true 'class consciousness' is that one should be opposed to all classes," wrote Lloyd. "My 'class consciousness' is an anti-class consciousness." No group better exemplified the longing for national unity.

The presumed passing of the frontier subtly wove a thread of uneasiness through many of these late-nineteenth-century themes. Under all circumstances the abrupt termination of a century's preoccupation would have commanded national attention. But as numerous writers demonstrated, the sweep westward lent itself just as readily to self-praise as to self-doubt. Early in the eighties the conquest of the Plains had served as evidence of America's virility, the fulfillment of one destiny promising grander ones to come. It was the perspective of the threatened community that turned victory into the preface for defeat. When anxious Americans paired the congested cities with dwindling opportunities along the frontier, urban centers seemed that much more turgid, and the prospects of an explosion that much more ominous. Advocates of immigration restriction cited the scarcity of free land as one more reason why the nation could no longer leave its doors open. How could newcomers who were never exposed to the democraticizing influences of the farm and the village learn the American way? For the first time Malthusian theories of overpopulation gained a significant following. Henry George's denunciation of land monopolies made that much more sense. An inclination to protect natural resources appeared in discussions of the land laws, hardening demands that the railroads, already regarded as thieves of the best land, now return every acre they could not justify. Both parties committed themselves to the revocation of all lapsed land grants, and in a vaguely worded law Congress gave at least token response in 1890. An inchoate urge toward conservation—at least toward prudence—strengthened the attacks against speculators, alien owners, and wealthy land grabbers.

In the land of enterprise, these were unfamiliar broodings. Expansive questions about where the nation was going had elusively given way to pensive ones about where America was and who its people were. Very often this taking of stock placed the West in a position of special prominence. Likening it to "an infant" that would "one day be a giant, in each of whose limbs shall be united the strength of many nations," Josiah Strong declared that the many dangers besetting America concentrated here with singular intensity. The battle for civilization's future, he announced, was already raging throughout the West, with liquor and materialism, alien ideologies and alien religions, holding the initial advantage. In more measured language, the historian Frederick Jackson Turner sketched a process by which successive frontiers had continually rejuvenated the nation through infusions of individualism, daring, and democracy. Now, he said, the frontier had closed. His underlying purpose, as David M. Potter has written, "was to explain the differentiation of the American from the European," to examine, in other words, the unique qualities of the American character, an involvement that was assuming far less healthy forms among nativists, purveyors of patriotism, and theorists of race destiny.

Like so many free-floating particles, groups of worried citizens tossed about, attached themselves to a cause, then scattered again. Many crusades attracted them; none seemed able to hold them fast. Among these mildly adhesive movements, three of the most important—the Knights of Labor, Edward Bellamy's Nationalism, and the farmers' alliances—illustrated the ways of late-nineteenth-century reform. The Knights of Labor, originating in 1869 as a tiny league of blacklisted Philadelphia garment workers, began an essentially new life after the depression of the seventies. Reorganized as a national association in 1878, it rose to prominence and fell into decay under the leadership of Terence V.

Powderly, its Grand Master Workman from 1879 to 1893. Shrouding its meetings in secrecy for many years and always setting great store by the comforts of ritual, the Knights of Labor never outgrew its initial posture of defense. The enemies listed in its platform—big corporations and great fortunes, unlimited immigration and large landholders, banks and railroads—comprised a standard array of threatening forces for any antimonopoly program. To meet those giants, the Knights constructed an organization around dozens of autonomous local groups. These District Assemblies, which were gatherings of all laborers regardless of skill or sex, remained the effective units of power throughout the Knights' history. Expulsion, the last resort in an efficient centralized system, was really the sole means of control available to the national officers.

The Knights of Labor, in other words, was a collection of local associations designed partly to re-create and partly to protect a sense of community among its members. The community core—the District Assembly—would develop according to its own social logic. It did not have exact physical boundaries, for no lines could define a community; and it excluded only those who manipulated money and corrupted morals, for all honorable men, laborers "of the hand or of the brain," properly belonged to the healthy community. As a reminder that these communities were ultimately parts of a united society, the leaders designed an organization of architectonic symmetry which rose to its apex in the Grand Master Workman. Ineffectual as a means of responding to the economic needs of the workers, it served an entirely different purpose. It was the geometric replica of a philosophical principle, and contemporary reformers, who also conceived of organization as an embodiment of the ideal, appreciated it precisely for that archetypal quality.

Avowedly a moral movement, the Knights sought an ethical substitute for the capitalism they believed was destroying opportunity, equality, and brotherhood. As the eventual replacement for an evil system, the leaders of the Knights placed their hopes in producer and consumer cooperatives, the economic expression of the community spirit. In the meantime, they advocated the abolition of national banks, clearing the way for a currency issued "direct to the people"; the nationalization of the railroads, transforming them into society's avenues; and an end to alien land ownership, reopening farms for honest laborers everywhere. Powderly in particular deplored the strike as a fruitless, barbaric practice. Instead the national officials counselled discussion and negotiation, even the advice of an impartial outsider, and in time they accepted the boycott as an appropriate means of community persuasion.

This combination of philosophical radicalism and decent daily behavior constituted a petition for membership as respected citizens in a moral American society. Certainly those ethnic groups, especially of Irish background, who had captured portions of the Knights behaved as if their organizations were a personal plea for recognition; the antagonism of many Catholic clergymen to the Knights represented the special hostility of a rival for these people's loyalty. When the anarchist Albert Parsons claimed with some justification that "the foundation principle of socialism, or anarchy is the same as the Knights of Labor, viz., 'The abolition of the wages system' and the substitution in its stead of an industrial system of universal cooperation," the leaders of the union recoiled. "He is a true Knight of Labor," Powderly declaimed, "who with one hand clutches anarchy by the throat and with the other strangles monopoly!" Powderly courted the company of such people as Henry George, whose dislike of exclusive trade unions led him to befriend the Knights; Frances Willard, another supporter who some said secretly loved the handsome labor leader; and the respectable agrarians in the farmers' alliances.

In that setting success proved the Knights' undoing. Early in 1885, a time of high tension among wage earners, Jay Gould made a tactical retreat before the Knights on his Western railroads, giving them the semblance of an astonishing triumph. Impatient workers by the hundreds of thousands poured into the organization. These angry immediatists, demanding a quick return on their membership, came faster than the staid officials could even count, let alone control, and then proceeded to set their own policies. Distressed and confused, Powderly changed overnight from the eloquent spokesman into an indecisive, quarrelsome leader who followed orders with counterorders, accepted then cancelled charters, and generally made a fool of himself and his organization in a desperate effort to contain the rabble and save the Knights' good name. Victory had made a travesty of Powderly's dream. As he denounced radicals and subverted the strikes of his own districts, substantial Americans and members alike called this fumbling man a megalomaniac. A quick succession of defeats, including one in 1886 at the hands of the crafty Gould, sent membership tumbling, with urban workers the first to leave. Powderly never understood that they needed a workaday sustenance for their visions. By the early nineties, the Knights of Labor had declined into a sedentary organization composed mostly of small-town Americans. By the standards of late-nineteenth-century reform, Powderly and his colleagues had been rational men mangled by an irrational world.

Many of the elements in the program of the Knights found pleasant, plausible form in Edward Bellamy's extraordinarily popular utopia, *Looking Backward*. A novel only in the loosest sense, Bellamy's book won its huge audience not as fiction but as a simple, logical essay combining so much that the discontented already accepted as gospel. The worried reader of the late nineteenth century, transported into the year 2000 through a genteel Bostonian, Julian West, discovered what he knew only too well about his own day: that America was verging on catastrophe as "riches debauched one class with idleness of mind and body, while poverty sapped the vitality of the masses by overwork, bad food, and pestilent homes." Through the alchemy of righteousness, Americans would rise from the dust, cast off the oppressive system, and fashion a rational society where peace and goodwill reigned among men. In one of history's odd communions, an introvertive mystic, frail and tense, who suffered from delusions of omniscience touched millions of troubled hearts in farmhouses and shops and corner offices across the land.

"The solidarity of the race and the brotherhood of man," declared Dr. Leete, West's guide to utopia, "which to you were but fine phrases are, to our thinking and feeling, ties as real and as vital as physical fraternity." This essential unity, the law of human nature, assured society's flawless operation without the intrusion of bankers, politicians, and lawyers. Each man worked in a useful, suitable vocation from maturity to middle age when he retired to cultivate his tastes. Middlemen vanished. A system of finance, "the clumsy crutch of a self-made cripple," simply had no function; "all estimates deal directly with the real things," Dr. Leete explained, "the flour, iron, wood, wool, and labor, of which money and credit were for you the very misleading representative." Because the government, which had replaced private owners in industry, oversaw the distribution of labor and goods, a later generation would find ominous hints of totalitarianism in Bellamy's message. But his contemporaries understood. Government returned to the people in a society attuned to the moral laws quite literally eliminated government as a distinct institution. In the unlikely event that legislation was needed, an instantaneous expression of public opinion by telephone shaped the statute; and if some officeholder acted in a capacity other than tabulator, an immediate recall removed him. What did an administrator do in a society that ran, as the Englishman William Morris said, "by a kind of magic"? By the same token, laws emanating from men's hearts would of course require no judiciary. Nor did the citizen of Chicopee Falls violate the canons of local integrity. Utopia would be divided into a multiplicity of self-sufficient, balanced social groups that elected their own editors and ministers. These ideal communities, in turn, would be held together by the overarching "principle of fraternal co-operation." Here lay the true meaning of America, Bellamy believed, and he not only entitled his dream "Nationalism" but placed patriotism among the cardinal virtues of the new order.

In this purified, unified, and democratized utopia, Bellamy had provided anxious Americans with a hope brilliantly suited to their temperaments. Fellow visionaries like Lloyd and Willard recognized him at once as a major prophet, and the less philosophical, ranging from well-born reformers in the East to agrarian agitators in the South and West, also showered him with praise. Nationalist Clubs appeared everywhere, followed soon after by a journal with Bellamy as editor. No one really tried to give these associations coherence. To Bellamy they represented one more proof that the wellsprings of brotherhood were flowing fast and that utopia lay just ahead. Once again, organization reflected an inner spirit; like the District Assemblies of the Knights, each Nationalist Club acquired its own character and set its own goals. Spiritualists captured a good number. Respectables in the Eastern cities used them to attack the monopolist and the Irish boss, and in the West they served primarily as another forum to denounce banks, railroads, and distant politicians. Then as Bellamy inclined toward Populism, his Eastern adherents fell away; his followers in the West, often Populists already, blended into the larger agrarian crusade. The grand uprising of yesterday just disintegrated, and Nationalism had run the natural course of reform.

The alliances, a broad movement that attracted about three million members in the South and West, grew from the same ideological roots as the Knights of Labor and Nationalism. Designing men in control of an evil system had disrupted America's unity and impoverished its good citizens, the alliancemen charged. Now the just were mobilizing. "The masses of the Northwestern States, the Southern States and the Western States will be arrayed on one side, and on the other will stand the plutocrats and monopolists of the Northern and Eastern States. There will be but two parties—the people against the plutocrats." With "God and right on our side," the issue could scarcely remain in doubt. Corporate nabobs, bankers, lawyers, and a variety of speculators and middlemen would certainly be purged, and many alliancemen also visualized the new world as dry and white. Prohibition played an especially important role in the Dakotas, Texas, and Mississippi; antagonism to the Negro, extending as far west as Kansas, most deeply influenced Mississippi where Frank Burkitt, the leader of the state alliance, also championed constitutional disfranchisement, and the Carolinas where one prominent newspaper exhorted agrarians under the banner *The Caucasian*. A Negro spokesman, departing North Carolina in the late eighties, singled out the alliance as a particularly "oppressive institution to the colored laborer."

A society reunited and cleansed in this fashion could then operate democratically. Quick to demand limitations upon the power of the existing government, alliancemen planned to introduce elaborate programs once it had been redeemed. Enthusiastic agrarians talked of direct government through the initiative and the referendum replacing rather than merely guiding the suspect legislatures; the nationalized railroads, as one example, would become truly the instruments of the people. The same kind of assumptions controlled their plans for financial reform, always an area of intense interest. The subtreasury scheme, a brief sensation early in the nineties, proposed a network of public warehouses at which for a nominal charge farmers might store their durable crops in return for legal-tender certificates equal to the current market price. Because the farmer could remove his crops for sale if the price rose, the plan did appeal as a shrewd expedient. But its authors clearly anticipated that it would supplant the entire system of currency and credit. At one stroke they would eliminate the national banks, the market in futures, the commission merchants, and the private warehousemen, and in their place a simple people's currency would satisfy every need. "EUREKA! Key to the Solution of the Industrial Problem of the Age," declared the Southern Alliance's major journal. Translating the law of nature by way of an incorporeal government would destroy the "power of money to oppress." Similarly, silver inflation, which eventually obsessed the agrarian leaders, and Jacob Coxey's proposal to issue $500,000,000 of legal tender as payment for building roads, which a Populist Senator sponsored, were expected not to help but to cure by miraculous transformation.

In almost every instance, these reforms followed an identical catechism. God had meant man to enjoy the fruits of his own labor in his own locality; powerful, invisible agencies—the great corporations, the wizards of finance, a ring of political bosses— had learned ways of growing fat off the rights of others; reform must release the community from their grip. That inward pull accounted for the alliancemen's strong interest in cooperatives, which continued until too many failures finally disillusioned them. As in the case of the Knights of Labor, cooperatives meant control brought home, a moral union of work, product, and exchange. Within that framework, certain varieties of antialienism thrived naturally. Each enemy, whether the American Tobacco Company or a British land company, the Cotton Exchange in New York or Liverpool, the magnates of Wall Street or of Lombard Street, fell into a common category. On other occasions the agrarian was perfectly capable of differentiating between the United States and the rest of the world; here the distinction was immaterial because wherever the giants happened to live they were equally strangers to rural America.

When Powderly prepared a joint statement with alliance officials late in 1889, he did not take exception to a single portion of the agrarian program. They simply saw the world through the same spectacles. Effortlessly Bellamy was incorporated as a major philosopher of the movement, and by the early nineties a constellation of additional satellites had clustered about the agrarians: Lloyd; Willard; Gronlund, who found his version of Marxism reflected in their program; a number of Christian socialists; and many more.

Here finally were the people on the march. Even more important to its future than numbers alone, the alliance movement concentrated so heavily in the wheat, cotton, and tobacco lands that its members often constituted a standing majority in their counties, an immediate if raw form of power no other discontented group could match. The Southern Alliance had already attracted such men as Charles Macune, an opportunistic nomad who guided its rapid expansion between 1887 and 1889. Both in the North and in the South other ambitious men drew near as the ranks swelled, and a concerted move into politics became almost unavoidable. Beginning even before 1890 in some localities, this culminated in the formation of the People's or Populist party, a national force by 1892. As a final gesture to the era of evanescent organization, the elaborate structure of local, state, and regional alliances rapidly melted away. Many, though by no means all, of their members simply shed one coat to don another as warriors in the Populist crusade. With that decision the agrarian protest underwent a basic transformation. The special loyalties aroused by the major parties, the specific requirements of day-to-day politics, the particular discipline imposed by the existing rather than a utopian government, all remolded it to fit another environment. While the ideology of the alliances moved onward through Populism, that confident feeling of a whole countryside marching in unison was soon lost.

The sweep of reform represented by these movements sought to preserve individualism and democracy, as their adherents understood the terms, by protecting America's communities. In no sense did the reformers expect to realize their program by way of its antithesis; that is, by constructing a huge apparatus for centralized direction. As Lloyd explained, "To say that socialism is governmentalism is as if one were to define the farmer as a rake. The rake is only one of the tools of his work," and it had neither life nor purpose apart from its master, that hoary symbol of democratic individualism. Each proposal attempted to place power in the hands of small, familiar groups under the dual assumptions that it had once resided there and that a good society required its return. Such was the rational plan of God and nature, and upon its fulfillment all the shadowy enemies of the people would vanish like so many phantoms of the night. Nor did these reformers want to force America back into a bucolic paradise. Very few of them despised machinery or pined for a world without factory goods. They simply saw no conflict between popular community control and modern technology, and they fully anticipated all the advantages of Bellamy's utopia in the cooperative commonwealth of tomorrow. What they did reject were the current means of America's industrialization—the corporations, the systems of credit and distribution, the alterations in political power. In trying to destroy the lot of them, they planned a revolution without quite realizing it and, as it happened, lost at every turn.

4

The Fate of the Nation

BY THE EARLY NINETIES the movements of community protest had generated their own nationwide crisis. Men from all walks of life, already shaken by an incomprehensible world, responded to any new upheaval as an immediate threat. They had no alternative, they felt, but to select an enemy and fight. Many of them had no natural line of battle, and much of the nation's story between the mid-eighties and mid-nineties concerned the nature of their forced decisions: whom they would oppose and how they would fight. For the officials in America's rising urban-industrial system, however, the choice was automatic. The target of almost every reform movement, they mobilized to secure their power, and in the process they raised a second standard—the standard of suppression—around which frightened citizens might rally. The two camps never even found a common ground for debate; in fact, neither really sought to communicate with the other. In the end this dialogue between the deaf only delayed the establishment of a new order.

Anxiety, like the common cold, was a most egalitarian malady which in many respects ran the same course wherever it struck. Men in formal authority, equally disturbed by their sprawling, impersonal society, also reached out for that essential, elusive mastery. Like the protectors of the community, they also underwent a basic shift in outlook which converted incidents into series, giving their worries that same cumulative, self-fueling quality.

Yet the differences were just as significant. Because many of the men in power tried initially to ignore signs of upheaval, they tended to enter the crisis spiral more slowly. Once they did, they moved through it that much more swiftly and savagely. Moreover, their themes of distress, while also phrased in the language of individualism and unity, had a distinctive ring. In the baldest sense, they came to fear that in a democratic society the people might rule. Individualism, except as a mode of implicit contempt for the scattered sheep below, almost always referred to the rights of an elite to retain what they held and to acquire more; cohesion meant an imposed order, one that would necessitate a sharp-edged enforcement. Rather than anticipating the good that would eventually arise from crisis, they wanted to quash all disorder now, to forestall catastrophe by fitting society into a safe, sturdy mold. "Law" and "property," the fundamental terms in their rhetoric, connoted a whole complex of social, economic, and political privileges. Finally, they responded more ingeniously on the whole than the leaders of apocalyptic reform. In a narrow and often coarse manner, they constructed some instruments that would outlast the period of crisis and serve as a basis for their expansion in the years ahead.

Champions of the community seemed to materialize everywhere all at once, swinging broadly at their enemies from the very beginning. Among the men in power, by contrast, an acute anxiety appeared first in the major cities and concerned issues immediately at hand. An urban leadership, already uneasy over the strange population swelling about them, reacted to the "great uprising of labor" in the mid-eighties as if an army of swords had been unsheathed. With incredible exaggeration, they interpreted the Knights of Labor as disciplined mass sedition and the brief epidemic of local labor parties in 1886 and 1887 as a preface to political revolution. References to an American Reign of Terror and a domestic version of the Paris Commune were now heard everywhere, and the most discussed wonder of modern science was the dynamite bomb, symbol of mob terror.

While the alarm spread rapidly through the cities, it penetrated the countryside more gradually. Both in the West and the South local oligarchs generally belittled the first indications of discontent around them, even attempting in many cases to maintain friendly relations with the challengers. That lag had vanished by the end of the eighties, however, and by the early nineties specific worries both in the cities and in the countryside had grown into generalized fears. Now danger lurked everywhere. Farmers and wage earners, dissenting ministers and angry editors, immigrants and ideologists, peaceful petitioners and armed strikers, all blurred into visions of a society unhinged. The wells of panic, once tapped, flowed continuously.

Appropriately, the first significant changes in policy came from an urban elite. As labor disturbances swept across the country during the mid-eighties, employer associations organized in response. Such leagues had long been common during crises. In the past, however, they had dissolved as soon as the immediate danger passed; now a number of them remained as standing weapons against their employees, and more arrived in each succeeding year. Most of these associations promised mutual assistance to any firm facing labor difficulties. Some also invested in strike insurance, a novel policy introduced just for these anxious times, and a few attempted the systematic suppression of all unions throughout their plants. Seldom well-coordinated, these groups still marked an important departure, particularly at a time when distrust and uncertainty were undermining almost every other form of joint action among corporations.

Spreading to include the whole of the slums, the new concern affected other urban leaders just as deeply. Who could tell when someone might grab the torch and march? An explosion in May 1886 next to Haymarket Square in Chicago raised precisely that specter. Workers, aliens, radicals, mobs, and dynamite all had coalesced in one incident. A local strike had stirred resentment;

German anarchists had called a meeting of protest; then when the police tried to disperse it, a bomb had risen out of the shapeless crowd, killing one and mortally wounding a half-dozen more. Immediate punishment was imperative. In the absence of a culprit, the state sped eight available anarchists through the processes of justice, convicting seven to die. Sanctity of human life had certainly not been the issue; within a few hours after the event the police had indiscriminately killed at least as many as the bomb. Nor had inviolability of the law; substantial citizens demanded death, not due process. Behind this insistence upon reprisals lay the assumption that fundamentally the masses could understand only the bared fist, that without the authority of an indisputable force—always visible, always ready—chaos would reign.

This time the sense of jeopardy did not subside quickly as it had after the riots of 1877. Haymarket was an indicator, not merely an incident. In order to bring that naked power close at hand, wealthy citizens of Chicago donated the land to establish Fort Sheridan and Great Lakes Naval Training Station. Private subscriptions elsewhere built and filled city armories. Efforts to strengthen local police, militia, and the United States Army, specifically as a bulwark against radicalism, were supplemented by a host of vigilante groups, usually called "law and order" leagues, with the rusty rifles of the Grand Army of the Republic much in evidence.

Because the effective use of force depended upon timely government orders, prominent citizens now paid closer attention to politics. Like the spokesmen for reform, they thought of government, properly constituted, as a passive agent in society's smooth operation, and they regularly complained about interfering politicians and disruptive legislation. Yet if their ideal government had no more free will than Bellamy's mechanical state, it did contain noticeably more substance. To correct the malfunctionings of natural law, men of authority envisaged not just one grand change—the adoption of a single tax or a subtreasury system—but an indefinite number of lesser repairs. These acts did not fall into sequences; that is, they were not the components of a continuous policy. Each stood alone, the particular remedy for a particular ill. Consequently a day-to-day diagnosis, a mood of the moment, would determine their quantity, type, and extent.

Although men of power were sprinkled through both parties, an increasing interest in the national government inclined them toward the Republicans, whose organization in Congress made them somewhat more attractive in times that might require decisive action. As the party of tariff protection and as the party generally more favorable to Federal spending, it had simply drawn more of those clear-eyed lobbyists who were the chief legislative disciplinarians, and in a broad sense its members had acquired a certain habit toward coordination. The Democratic party, on the other hand, always felt the centrifugal pulls of an especially large agrarian constituency and the almost morbid Southern resistance to an initiating central government. In addition, both the newly assertive Southern farmers and the maturing ethnic groups were now contributing their disruptive influences. By the early nineties, at the peak of their popularity, the Democrats in Congress defied anyone to harness their energies.

As long as Grover Cleveland remained in or near the Presidency, that inclination toward the Republican party did not significantly alter the balance in national politics, for much of the growing interest in the national government centered upon the chief executive, whose control over the veto and the troops gave him special importance in a troubled time. Cleveland and his close associates, who came from a thoroughly respectable section of the Democratic party, reflected that same deep concern for property, law, and order which was obsessing substantial citizens everywhere. A forceful man, he could be relied upon to resist radical legislation and to intervene promptly wherever the need arose. Harrison, the Republican who held office between Cleveland's two terms, commanded far less of that respect.

Yet above even the President, it was the Supreme Court that received the most solicitous attention. To the degree a general government policy existed in the years following reconstruction,

Federal courts had usually supplied it. Disorganizing change during the late nineteenth century had encouraged exactly the kind of broad, outlined guidance the judiciary could provide, just as it had inhibited a more detailed, daily direction through either legislation or administration. Moreover, the other two branches had regularly invited the judiciary to assume greater responsibilities. The leading judges of the late nineteenth century saw themselves as major policymakers and framed their important decisions with that purpose in mind.

Samuel F. Miller and Joseph P. Bradley, the dominant members of the Supreme Court until the nineties, were experiencing the same uncertainties that beset equally able men throughout America. Along with several of their colleagues, they were deeply disturbed by the deterioration of a familiar society. They worried about the irresponsible power of great corporations, especially about the financial wizards behind so many of them. "Modern Shylocks and Railroad Smashers," Bradley disgustedly called them. Consequently in the seventies the Court had on several occasions reaffirmed the right of state and local governments to regulate industry as essential to the public welfare. But while they opposed monopolies and manipulators, they also wanted the avenues of national commerce open to legitimate business, and that in turn led them to protect interstate corporations from what they considered excessively obstructive local regulation. They too regarded property as society's keystone, and they too revered law and order.

The result of these mixed attitudes during the eighties was to discourage precise declarations and leave a great deal to the discretion of the lower courts, including those of the states. Rather than abdication, it represented the cautious response of policymakers feeling for solid ground, a search that was naturally affected by the anxious climate of the later eighties. In general, the judiciary expressed its rising apprehension by a greater sensitivity to the claims of private property, a gradual shift toward defense, and, above all, the preparation of exceptionally broad rules of surveillance. In the area of corporation controls, **for** example, it had long been assumed that at some extreme point state regulation could deprive a company of its property without due process of law, in violation of the Constitution. For years, however, that remained a theoretical consideration, and the Supreme Court continued to treat due process solely as a matter of legal procedure. Then around the mid-eighties, worries about social stability began to cast shadows on business regulation that had once been considered a proper exercise of the community's police power. A time of trouble invested property with much higher importance, and in 1890 the Court officially reserved the right to invalidate any state action that set injuriously low railroad rates. When it saw fit, in other words, the Court could determine what was a reasonable and what an unreasonable return on capital, a vast, new province for judicial review.

With even greater vigor, lower courts were following a parallel route in labor law, a subject the Supreme Court had as yet largely left alone. Injunctions against strikers and demonstrators, for instance, had for some years been granted in cases of immediate danger to physical property. Out of the turmoil of the mid-eighties and the fantasies of an irresistible union power, the meaning of both danger and property expanded into huge misty concepts. By the later eighties Federal courts were issuing injunctions to protect intangible as well as tangible property from potential as well as actual danger, rulings that essentially commanded a group of workers to avoid any hint of a disturbance. Just as they could determine the degree of business regulation commensurate with a proper return on capital, so the judges, a case at a time, would demarcate "the allowable area of economic conflict" between employer and employee. Both realms left the judges peculiarly free from any prior restraints in deciding extremely complicated social problems.

As long as the Justices of the Supreme Court believed that they were merely strengthening an outer wall, they could afford such large, gray areas of discretion. But many substantial citizens, growing frightened more rapidly than a majority of the Court, found that leeway intolerable. Lacking controls from above, a judge on the Court of Appeals in West Virginia could uphold state regulation of the coal industry because "the public tranquility and the good and safety of society" demanded it. The same sweeping logic they were employing, in other words, could be used to exactly the opposite conclusion. Other courts might demonstrate great resourcefulness in preserving order, as one did in 1892 when it used an obsolete statute on treason to demoralize the workers at Homestead, Pennsylvania, but the men in power were furious that such crucial matters should depend upon jerry-built law. Seeking the security of rigid, inclusive rules, an increasing number of them, including many prominent lawyers, undertook to extract that kind of certainty from the Supreme Court. The rationale for judicial intervention was now well developed. As soon as five Justices shared the feeling that the outer wall had been breached and the inner one was cracking, they could act with dispatch all along the line.

These attempts to tighten social control were never coordinated into a general campaign. Almost all of the employer associations remained local leagues that rarely communicated with one another. The same usually held true for those who tried to discipline the legislature, stiffen the executive's will, and win strict rulings from the Supreme Court. The movements were also crude, with a penchant for the bludgeon rather than the rapier. Yet whatever their failings, they enjoyed incalculable advantages of power. To the degree that anyone could marshal society's resources, these men sitting in or around the seats of authority qualified. Together they comprised the citizens whose goodwill and enterprise seemed essential to a community's prosperity, most of the strategic officeholders in government, and the best legal talent. They constituted the explorers in a new national power. They were the ones whose positions in finance and distribution placed countless Americans in an attitude of dependence; whose corporations could maneuver simultaneously around several city councils or state legislatures, playing one against the others and confusing the lot; whose positions in the major parties most closely approximated national leadership. And while they duplicated each other's efforts, at least they were not working at cross purposes.

As if to frame the pending struggle, rural politicians had been gerrymandering the cities during the same years that an urban elite was fashioning a system of national power. Certainly the rebels from the towns and countryside would have preferred to fight where they felt at home, in the very communities they were striving to protect. But this much they had already learned: to free the community they would have to free the nation. All of the community movements assumed that a natural, local society required the destruction of unnatural, national powers. As the Populist platform suggested, government would again become a function of men's everyday lives only after direct democracy had dissolved a distant, corrupt government; technology would serve the communities only after nationalization had removed an oligarchy of railroad, telegraph, and telephone companies; power would belong to the people only after a silver currency, a decentralized postal savings system, and subtreasury notes had replaced Wall Street and the national banks.

The attempt to accomplish these goals through a political party exposed a second hard truth: thousands of Americans whose locus of power, range of vision, and emotional involvements were narrowly local could not by fiat merge into a national organization. Even by the loose standards that the Republicans and Democrats had set, the Populists scarcely functioned as a party. Some men had criticized the Southern and Northern Alliances for dallying so long in their moves toward political cooperation. The wonder was not that they had experienced difficulties joining in a common cause but that regional associations had ever existed to negotiate, because beneath the trappings of conventions and candidates decentralization ran riot. As in the case of the reform movements that preceded it, the Populist party expressed its commitment to local autonomy by an almost anarchic organizational independence.

On another level, important differences in tone and emphasis also separated the two concentrations of Populist strength: the

South, roughly following the coast from North Carolina to Texas; and the West, including both the wheatlands from Iowa to the Dakotas and the mountainous mining states. One of these was the sharper line between town and countryside in the South, where tenantry, poverty, and ignorance more often turned the farmer's bitterness within his own community. A tendency rather than a rule, it still invested portions of Southern Populism with the harsher qualities of a civil conflict. The marginal life of many Southern Populists also increased their feelings of precariousness. There the fervor and the apocalyptic vision, the insistence upon wholesale changes and the resistance to compromise, all acquired an exaggerated character.

The railroads figured much less prominently in Southern Populism than they did in the West, where overland transportation was the equivalent of survival. Not only did Western Populism take root in newly developed areas with spare service and erratic rates, but it thrived particularly where enthusiasm for railroad projects had been running high to the very eve of the third party's formation. In Kansas, community assistance had flowed quite heavily into more roads until 1890, and on a smaller scale localities in Minnesota, Iowa, Nebraska, and the Dakotas had also been sinking their funds, and hopes, in fresh enterprises. The arrival of Western Populism, in other words, very often marked that breaking point between eager promotion and outraged disappointment, exemplified in South Dakota by the two-year interval between a statute encouraging local aid to railroads and a constitutional prohibition against all forms of public subsidy. While farmers and townsmen had sometimes clashed over details, both had usually agreed upon the necessity of building roads, and both readily joined forces against an alien captor. In general, Western Populism demonstrated much more the qualities of cheated development, gathering whole communities into a mutual pact against the enemy; whereas Southern Populism, appearing in a more settled and somewhat less expectant region, expressed more that grinding resentment over daily oppressions which often divided communities.

These differences directly influenced the decision to form a third party. In the newer sections of the nation, all party organizations tended to lack fiber. The high proportion of recent arrivals, the factional confusion surrounding schemes for development, and the mere absence of many customary arrangements held politics in a fluid state. Party loyalties had a meaning somewhat different from the one that existed in more stable parts of America. Particularly if a man swung between regularity and independence rather than between the two major parties, he might wander in and out of his party several times without either losing his identification with that party or seriously jeopardizing his community standing. Thus the move to Populism seemed as often a tactical maneuver as a religious conversion. In the South, by contrast, the firmer social mold and deeper political traditions, reinforced by the threat of Negro power, meant that the decision to enter a third party might determine a man's future in his community, cutting off old friends and casting him out of respectable society. Only the impetus from the newly assertive whites carried large numbers into such a revolutionary camp. The dialogue between West and South on political independence became a study in unintentional deception.

Atomized in one sense and divided in another, Populism exposed still another set of weaknesses in its relations with the broader world of reform. At the beginning of the movement, there seemed every reason to anticipate an irresistible expansion among the discontented, particularly throughout rural America. As if to encourage these prospects, more and more politicians in the Old Northwest joined those from the South and the Plains in condemning monopolies, financiers, railroads, and the rest of the alien intruders. Yet in the midst of this dissent, the Populist party served more often as a reference point than as a rallying point. To the north and east of its main strength, more mature rural societies with less pressing resentments rejected independence in favor of somewhat milder rebellions within the major parties, and as Democrats or Republicans they became political opponents of the Populists instead of their loose confederates. That defining process had even sharper repercussions inside Populism's heartland where discontent was so pervasive that citizens might face three political versions of the same general protest. Here partisanship turned neighbors and ideological comrades into keen political competitors. Time and again men who had cooperated toward common goals now expended their energy inflating the differences between each other.

Sometimes they simply fabricated the differences. Reputable and disreputable alike divided about equally among the three parties in the West. Even in the South, where class lines assumed greater significance, the upper stratum of Populists still included its portion of such honored names as Colonel Leonidas L. Polk, kinsman of a President, who had he not died in 1892 might well have been a Presidential candidate in his own right. The basic continuity in several states as Populist and non-Populist administrations succeeded one another merely underlined these striking similarities.

Nevertheless, the decision to stay or go did tend to express differing inclinations toward the industrial world. By and large, those who retained entrepreneurial ambitions continued to find a more congenial home in one of the major parties. Somewhat more prone to hedge their commitments against a rosier tomorrow, they preferred to cry havoc from the safest available base. The Democratic Governor James S. Hogg of Texas exemplified that cautious cast of mind. So close to the Populists on a great many political issues, he never ceased to work for a modern Texas booming under the auspices of Texas capitalists, and he fought the new party on these as well as on strictly partisan grounds. His later plunge to riches in oil was a perfectly consistent extension of the old dream under bright, new circumstances. The same was true of William Jennings Bryan, whose antagonism toward an impersonal industrialization always sounded Populistic with a difference. He too wanted to destroy the national banks—but carefully preserve the state banks, thereby enhancing their powers over currency and credit; later, he too wanted to nationalize railroads—but only the primary trunk lines, prudently leaving the question of intrastate roads in limbo. By contrast, prominent Populists appeared a bit more like the indiscriminate opponents of all modern business.

The maturing ethnic groups also tended to shy away from Populism. As suspicious as they were of outside interference, they seldom found much satisfaction in a broad reform program. It was sufficient to fight specifically for their own leaders, their own rights, and their own opportunities. Only a very few politicians, such as Altgeld of Illinois, appealed with equal success to these narrow sensitivities and to the more common feelings of community crisis. Moreover, the process of climbing upward gave the major parties two additional attractions. They were more respectable, more the appropriate berth for solid citizens, and they generally offered better prospects for a lasting, substantial influence. If one or another of the major parties welcomed the arriving groups, they seldom looked further. In fact, they often displayed a particularly deep partisan pride. In Minnesota, for example, where the sons of the Irish had already risen to power within the Democratic party and Scandinavian descendants were claiming a share of the Republican leadership early in the nineties, not even a magnetic name like Ignatius Donnelly could draw many into the Populist ranks.

Populism met an even colder reception among the gentlemanly reformers in the cities. Seeking a future more attractive than bloody industrial conflict, these men had attacked the great corporation and opposed at least its crudest maltreatment of customers and employees. Their influence had helped to deter the promiscuous use of troops against strikers, and their funds had supported missionary work among the city's poor. Some in the mid-eighties had even smiled upon orderly trade unions and upon a mollifying Catholic Church. In all, they had tried to find a way of removing the monopolists on the one hand and of civilizing the masses on the other. Yet a strain of fear that barbarism would never die ran through all of their proposals. Jacob Riis, journalist and aspiring gentleman, caught its spirit in a parable of slum life that appeared in *How the Other Half Lives* (1890), a widely read book addressed to the upper-class conscience.

A man stood at the corner of Fifth Avenue and Fourteenth Street the other day, looking gloomily at the carriages that rolled by, carrying the wealth and fashion of the avenue to and from the big stores down town. He was poor, and hungry, and ragged. This thought was in his mind: 'They behind their well-fed teams have no thought for the morrow; they know hunger only by name, and ride down to spend in an hour's shopping what would keep me and my little ones from want a whole year.' There rose up before him the picture of those little ones crying for bread around the cold and cheerless hearth—then he sprang into the throng and slashed around him with a knife, blindly seeking to kill, to revenge.

As the sense of crisis mounted, that knife gleamed ever brighter. Upper-class opposition to unions and strikes stiffened. Immigrants acquired ominous hues of red and black. In the mid-eighties the patrician economist Francis Amasa Walker had welcomed the newcomers to a growing young country. Shortly he began to question their economic value and soon after their social effect. By the early nineties he had proposed a major rationalization for restriction, arguing that because native Americans had refused to produce children in competition with such a fecund rabble, immigration through a Gresham's Law of Race was rapidly debasing the nation.

Such fears were far advanced by the time Populism arrived. Many gentlemen had already turned their backs on moderation, and many others were effectively paralyzed as reformers. Populism simply rephrased the issue before them. Here was a concrete embodiment of the anarchy they dreaded, readily identified by women cursing at farmers to "raise less corn and more *Hell*" and by sympathetic Senators vowing to stick Grover Cleveland's "old fat ribs" with a pitchfork. In the past they had freely disdained both the uncouth masses and the new industrial kings. Now, in response to an immediate danger, they felt they had to choose, and without hesitation the large majority embraced the monopolist for the duration of the crisis. Save civilization first; otherwise there would be nothing to purify. In its essentials the same reaction was occurring among gentlemen in the towns as well.

Populism, in other words, acted as reform's precipitant. Against it, the movement no one could ignore, others tested their purpose and crystallized their attitudes. Where some substance of power existed, as among the more active local entrepreneurs, the arriving ethnic groups, and the urban patricians, the outcome hurt not only the new party but reform generally. Where that toughness was largely absent, the decision scarcely mattered. Philosophical radicals without an organized following, National- ist Clubs without independent strength, and well-wishers like Frances Willard, without political authority even in her own Women's Christian Temperance Union, could contribute very little to a party's cause. The greatest potential seemed to lie with the millions of wage earners, a popular mass that by the logic of reform theory should have flocked to the Populist standard. Actually some labor leaders did give indications of sympathy, despite the widening chasm between urban and rural lives. But once again disorganization blighted these hopes. A rapid differen- tiation according to industrial skills and job stability, an espe- cially heavy flow of immigrants, and bitter rivalries among the unions left wage earners peculiarly formless early in the nineties. The dying Knights of Labor, the infant American Federation of Labor, and a few, frail socialist unions had little to offer even if they had not quarrelled over the proper course. Across the nation the scattering furies of reform were disarmed before the battle.

The weaknesses were by no means obvious at the time. On the contrary, Populism appeared to gain strength with each election. Following some minor successes in 1890, the party won almost 10 percent of the Presidential vote in 1892, as well as several state victories in the West; two years later its total vote rose by nearly 50 percent, and for the first time it captured a Southern state. To friend and foe alike these surface advances spoke for themselves, an augury of far greater changes. The softness beneath—the insubstantial organization, the invitation to mercurial leadership, the utter confusion in local tactics, the dearth of funds, the barriers to expansion, the tremendous burden of fighting a political battle from the outside—escaped men of every persua- sion who had wrapped their minds in a catastrophic vision.

By the summer of 1893 a major depression had spread over the land. Although even a downturn as severe as this one did not significantly alter the nature of conflict, it carried a far more jolting impact than had the milder decline of the eighties. Loosening tongues and feeding fears, it added a sharp sense of urgency to the debates. The very presence of entire agricultural districts impoverished, of perhaps one-quarter of the cities' unskilled without jobs, of over six hundred banks closed before autumn, meant concrete evidence for everyone's predictions of disaster. The depression worked on men's nerves until some resolution to the general crisis became imperative.

Later, people would realize that the nineties had remained surprisingly free from violence. At the time, men who were so certain of an eruption saw volcanoes under each puff of smoke. In 1894 when thousands throughout the North and West responded to Jacob Coxey's call by gathering in ragged bands for a "petition in boots" to Washington, substantial citizens prepared to throw up the barricades. While newspapers nervously ridiculed their thin ranks and eccentric commanders, armed groups met the marchers almost everywhere they stopped. It was only a policemen's drill. The unemployed pilgrims, proud of their peaceful, democratic cause, did not make trouble even under provocation and finally dispersed out of hunger and futility.

The Pullman strike of that same year offered a far better test of how well prominent citizens had mobilized since the mideighties. Pinched employees who lived in the manufacturer's company town just outside of Chicago initiated a widespread, enthusiastic attempt among railroad workers to humble the Pullman management—or at least to do something—as depression enveloped them. Under the direction of the American Railway Union, led by Eugene V. Debs, an orderly and quite effective boycott of Pullman cars paralyzed traffic in and around Chicago, the hub of the nation's railroad system. The program of suppression began at once. When Governor Altgeld refused either to break the strike or to invite the national government to do so, Richard Olney, Cleveland's arrogant Attorney-General, took charge on the ruse of protecting the mail. Confiding to a member of the railroad managers' association, who served as a special Federal attorney in the crisis, that "the true way of dealing with the matter is by a force which is overwhelming," Olney neutralized the leaders of the union with a sweeping injunction and brought troops from Fort Sheridan to protect railroad property and, if necessary, to run the trains. Leaderless and cowed, the laborers soon drifted back to work. The basic new machinery—an employers' association, an alert national executive, strategically placed troops, and an amenable judiciary—had combined to crack the boycott and smash the union.

These agencies of control, as dynamic as the fears behind them, moved on to more advanced lines. Within a year after the Chicago boycott the Federal judiciary had taken three large steps toward that precise defense of property substantial citizens had been urging upon it. First, a lower court, sitting in the shadow of the conflict, anchored the labor injunction to the Sherman Antitrust Act. A strike that interfered with interstate commerce, the presiding judge declared, was a conspiracy in restraint of trade. Furthermore, to continue striking in face of an injunction automatically made criminals of its leaders because a strike by its very nature damaged property. Then in 1895 the Supreme Court removed the threat of that same Sherman Act from almost all major corporations by a tortuous distinction between manufacture and commerce: monopolies of manufacture fell beyond the scope of the law, the Court decided, because "however inevitable" their influence upon interstate commerce, they were not literally vehicles of commerce themselves. The last case involved the legality of a modest income tax which Congress had appended to the Wilson-Gorman Tariff Act of 1894. By broadening the word "income" with the reverse of the logic that had narrowed "commerce" just weeks before, the Court found the law a violation of the Constitution's prohibition against direct taxes.

Unquestionably, recent additions to the Court—Chief Justice Melville W. Fuller and Associate Justices David J. Brewer and Rufus W. Peckham—had smoothed the transition to an explicit defense of "order" and "property." Like their acidulous mentor, Justice Stephen J. Field, these men openly sought to destroy what Field had called as early as 1883 "the agrarian and despoiling spirit." Nationwide discontent had brought *"Looking Backward . . .* nearer than a dream," Brewer warned, and the Court must meet the assault with an iron resolve. The greater "the threatened consequences of popular or populistic wrath may be," the eminent lawyer Joseph H. Choate had told the Justices during the arguments on the income tax, the greater the Court's obligation to strike down radical laws. As Fuller's decision indicated, the income tax ruling had repulsed "an attack upon accumulated property by mere force of numbers."

Despite this unusual thoroughness, the Court was still functioning in a familiar capacity as an exponent of principle and a maker of general political policy. The national executive, on the other hand, responded to the mounting pressures by pushing into strange territory. Ordering soldiers to quell a disturbance was not itself an innovation. But where Hayes in 1877 had sent troops reluctantly at the behest of local officials, Cleveland overrode Governor Altgeld in 1894 and managed the Chicago boycott as peculiarly the national executive's problem. Blunt attacks suited the President's temper. Impatient with ambiguities, Cleveland conceived his task as the application of elementary ethics to a number of discrete executive problems. The right answer always came promptly to him, and he pressed it vigorously, growing even more stubborn under fire. His capacity to isolate each issue, combined with such self-assurance, enabled him to pursue one simple truth far beyond normal limits without either sensing a contradiction or intentionally setting a precedent.

In one instance, these qualities led to a major break in executive practice. Like most of the men who trusted him, Cleveland abhorred the thought of adulterating the nation's gold currency with quantities of silver. In 1878 and again in 1890 representatives from the Western mining states, joined by others who regarded silver as a more democratic—and a more abundant— money, had enacted laws that obligated the national government to buy certain amounts of the cheaper metal, ostensibly as a supplement to gold. After purchasing what the law required, however, successive administrations had withheld most of it from circulation, simply subsidizing the silver industry with payments in gold. Even before his re-election Cleveland had determined to end this nonsense, a resolve the panic of 1893 merely hardened. To the cheers of his admirers and howls from the growing number who looked upon silver as salvation, the President undertook to dictate the repeal of the act of 1890, an unprecedented invasion of Congressional prerogative. Once set, Cleveland would not swerve. Not only did he make repeal a matter of party loyalty, but to overcome the powerful sentiment for silver among Western and Southern Democrats he used patronage as his primary means of coercion, a second basic departure from political custom. For decades patronage had only required assistance to a party faction around election time; now Cleveland was demanding votes on a particular bill. With the aid of the Republicans, he prevailed. An overriding compulsion to save civilization had transformed the conservative Cleveland into a startling innovator.

With the challenge met, Cleveland subsided into the traditional role of President. He could have accomplished little more in any case, for the Democratic party was crumbling beneath him. Discontent in the West and South had turned a large majority of the party into belligerent defenders of the community. Ethnic tensions deepened in the East and Midwest as the sons of Germans and Irishmen were grasping more and more power from a previous leadership. At the same time two calamities struck the party. The depression, so harsh in human terms, cut sharply into its support; and Cleveland, so obtuse in human affairs, disabled himself as a party leader. Firmly planted on the unpopular sides of community protection and ethnic advance, he responded to criticism with characteristic stubbornness, trampling upon everyone's sensitivities until he was the most hated Democrat in the land. Moreover, he had used most of his reserve power in the battle for repeal of silver purchase, and his later attempts to discipline rebellious Democrats had little effect upon men whose requests had already been denied or who felt they had already paid for the favors. With dissension and resentment rife, the Democrats became the minority party in 1894.

The broad political rebellion that deposed Cleveland raged simultaneously on many fronts. Particularly in Populist territory the same local chiefs who repudiated the President faced a similar threat in their own bailiwicks. The new party seemed on the verge of devouring the Democracy in the West. In the South the claim that Populism was tomorrow's party of the people sounded just plausible enough to spread panic among the established leaders. Here, however, the Democrats enjoyed an inestimable advantage: they controlled the machinery of government. Fighting for their stake in society, they set about the task of counting the challengers out of every election, protected by majorities in the state legislatures and a friendly judiciary. Republicans to a lesser degree used the same techniques in the West. Although voting frauds permeated politics in the late nineteenth century, making a crude joke of those who debated why a party had won this or that hairbreadth victory, the grim, methodical work of the nineties belonged in another category. Exemplars of community virtue joined hands with hacks to prostitute the democratic process in the name of a higher civilization, claiming as so many did during those years that however sordid the means the end would glorify them. Above all else, the crisis mentality demanded results.

Tightening rings of control expressed in terms of power the generally pathological state of a nation. In an increasingly mixed society what men did and saw and thought and dreamed had been diverging farther year by year. Yet until the eighties mutual ignorance, even mutual intolerance, had tended to separate people whose paths seemed not to be crossing anyway. Despite the undertones of suspicion, in other words, American society had contained more diffusion than conflict. The members of the New York Supreme Court who praised the sweated laborer's tenement home for "its hallowed associations and beneficent influences"

were inexcusably blind but not systematically inhumane. The
eminent economist who explained strikes on the "one-sided
reading" of the workers was fatuous but not sinister. The balance
began to tip during the mid-eighties as larger and larger numbers
came to believe that people they could neither trust nor understand were pressing upon them. Feeling crowded, persecuted,
hated, they turned to face that enemy. Ignorance and intolerance
now mattered a great deal. When Theodore Roosevelt advocated
"taking ten or a dozen of [the Populist] leaders out, standing . . .
them against a wall and shooting them dead," he was both
benighted and vicious. By the mid-nineties fears had deepened to
the extent that other men's guilt came embedded in each new
event, and once incidents carried their own meaning, communication between opponents effectively ceased.

In place of communication, antagonists confronted each other
behind sets of stereotypes, frozen images that were specifically
intended to exclude discussion. Reinforcing the faithful's feeling
of separateness, the rhetoric of antithetical absolutes denied even
the desirability of any interchange. If as so many substantial
citizens maintained the issue was civilization versus anarchy,
who would negotiate with chaos? If as so many dissenters
claimed the alternatives were the people and the plutocrats, who
would compromise with Mammon? In such a simplified world
like always attracted like; good and evil flowed irresistibly to
opposite poles. By the same token, virtue and vice reproduced
themselves. In one camp men miraculously shed their sins, while
in the other they invariably spawned new, often covert ones—
immoral recreations, private bestialities, and the like—that suited
a diabolic ideology. The established leaders in urban-industrial
America properly believed that their opponents would destroy
them, or at least their functions, if they could, just as the protectors of the community accurately sensed the existence of a league
of unrestrained power such as the one that operated during the
Chicago boycott. Both then assigned the enemy a monolithic
consistency and machinelike organization, invested it with a
conspiratorial design, and imputed to it an almost supernatural
potency. Honors for distortion divided about equally.

The mediator simply could not function. A well-intentioned citizen like Frederick Jackson Turner, who tried from the middle ground of Wisconsin to explain the radical West to the respectable East, had to await a saner day. Such men as Arthur Pue Gorman, who had premised his career upon compromise, could find almost no one who cared to negotiate. As the Democratic party fell apart, Gorman and a few others hurried helplessly to and fro, frustrated, angry, and now obsolete in a time that could no longer use their skills. It was a world of strange choices that finally placed Gorman, the urbane manager of Cleveland's first campaign, in William Jennings Bryan's agrarian camp, an awkward and lonesome observer. Words that had once had a common, albeit vague meaning had acquired the blacks and whites of mutual recrimination. When Cleveland and Altgeld debated the events surrounding the Pullman strike, they spoke in private vocabularies. To the Democratic President "Federal government" represented the natural, responsive agent of law and order, and "business" the corporate protectors of social stability. To the Democratic Governor "Federal government" referred to an alliance of monopolists and bosses bent upon wholesale oppression, and "business" the legitimate pursuits of average men thwarted by that alliance. "Republic" meant restraint of the masses to Cleveland and a local bulwark against national aggression to Altgeld.

At the center of each rhetorical cluster lay the symbols of finance. Over the last decades of the century banking and currency had come to hold a mysterious meaning apart from the rest of the economy. They comprised the inscrutable science. Unlike the bulky power of manufacturing and commerce, finance functioned invisibly. With fugitive slips of paper, men in hidden offices seemed capable of moving the universe. At the same time, finance appeared the most fundamental of all the nation's business. It dealt with money—the core of the matter— and in the end everything else must revolve about it. This was simple logic in a society that relied so heavily upon wealth, raw wealth at that, as its differentiator. No doubt finance chilled more hearts than it warmed. Vast and mystical in scope, it worked itself into almost every discussion of corruption and iniquitous riches and alien power; that is, of all the eerie, evil forces besetting the community. The masters of Wall Street "engage in no commerce, no trade, no manufacturing," wrote Justice Miller in the bitter perplexity of an old-fashioned man. "They *produce nothing.*" Yet they seemed to control everything. By the nineties a "Foreign Syndicate," always standing far back in the shadows, explained each strike and each foreclosed mortgage to men like Henry Demarest Lloyd. Their feelings of impotence before such a phantom accounted for the extraordinary popularity of *Coin's Financial School* (1894), a short tract in favor of free silver in which the common sense of an untutored youth confounded the greatest magicians of finance.

Spokesmen for the community, therefore, were the first to gravitate toward a single, inclusive monetary answer to the people's woes. Gathering strength from the late seventies onward, then arriving with a rush, the unlimited coinage of silver had far surpassed all other reforms in popularity by the mid-nineties. If ambitious mine owners subsidized the campaign, the natural attractions of the panacea explained its overwhelming success. Money was power; conspirators had controlled the nation by dictating the type and quantity of legal tender; a people's currency would send power along with money back into the communities. However elaborate the argument might grow, that syllogism still underlay an entire movement. In their negative fashion, the silverites were the true advocates of hard money. Deposit credit had scarcely touched much of agrarian America, and hating that incomprehensible system, they would destroy it. Gold represented all of the legerdemain, the omnipotence, of an amorphous enemy. When Julian West dumbfoundedly exclaimed that "a cartload of gold will not procure a loaf of bread" and Dr. Leete's daughter replied, "Why in the world should it?" visions of evil banished and truth triumphant thrilled thousands who had sought comfort in *Looking Backward.* The solution was that simple and complete because it was that fundamental.

The obsessive commitment to gold, developing somewhat more

slowly, served in part as a defensive response, a reply in kind, and
to that extent it lacked the fiery enthusiasm aroused by silver.
Even after the panic of 1893, a small circle of political and
financial leaders, fearing instability above all, contemplated an
international agreement that would have allowed silver a controlled, subordinate place in America's monetary system, a pit-
tance perhaps but far greater recognition than the agrarians
would have accorded gold. Yet in the end the faith in gold
proved equally irrational. Just as susceptible to simplistic answers,
substantial citizens eventually attributed about the same godly
powers to their metal. Meeting the enemy's argument on its own
ground, they looked upon free silver as anarchy's spearhead. Gold
was the shield of a civilized life; in fact, it represented a fixed
scheme of things in which all values, epitomized by the intrinsic
worth of their dollars, would never change. When the Cleveland
Administration negotiated privately with an international syndicate in 1895 for the sale of bonds to save the gold standard,
infuriating the silverites, men of wealth and place everywhere
declared that the President and J. P. Morgan were pulling society
back from the brink of disaster.

As in the case of the more general demonologies, these central
symbols—silver and gold—did bear some relationship to the
interests of their champions. Currency, which in the absence of a
sophisticated credit system played an inordinately important part
in the rural economy, was not only too scarce in the agricultural
regions but was doubly dear because of the inequities of the
national banking laws. Moreover, as the nation's investment
capacity reached a new level of maturity early in the nineties,
gold did constitute a special form of power for a handful of
financial magnates, men with a surplus at their disposal who laid
the basis for broad, new controls in the industrial economy
through securities they purchased with gold. Populists could
scarcely have dreamed of anything more insidious. Similarly,
advocates of gold had reason to predict that free silver would
disrupt international exchange. The status quo did offer a better
safeguard to their privileges than any abrupt change. And in the

way passionate movements carry their own fulfillment, emotions on both sides helped to substantiate everybody's worst fears. The louder the agrarians agitated for silver, the more hastily investors withdrew their funds from the cyclone area, further contracting credit in the countryside. The more often prominent citizens told each other that the silver craze was destroying confidence in the economy, the more confidence they destroyed, further deepening the depression.

In a remarkable testimony to the habits of democracy, a decade's accumulated bitterness ultimately flowed into a single national election. Primarily the agrarian dissenters selected that as the battleground. Throughout their protest they had drawn upon the most respectable portions of their tradition. They had gathered in orderly groups for peaceful purposes, and they had turned to politics in part because it expressed their sense of a proper American dignity. They had never armed themselves as, in effect, the best families in the cities had done, nor had they rioted even when no one could have checked them. An occasionally ferocious imagery derived from the traditions of evangelicalism, as did the general orientation toward cataclysmic thought. The very essence of their Armageddon was its bloodlessness. Refusing to acknowledge class divisions, they had insisted that a whole people would rise up and by the simple act of emerging set the world of natural law aright. Perhaps they were trapped within their own democratic ideology. In any case, they looked toward the national elections of 1896 as the irresistible means to an inevitable conclusion: Right could not fail to triumph at the polls. Their substantial opponents gladly accepted ballots in preference to barricades. Their very lack of faith in the masses suggested that votes, after all, could be won with proper care. Consequently, men who could scarcely communicate with one another tacitly accepted the fall elections as the final, official test between them, the ritual war of good against evil.

So in 1896 the battle of stereotypes became the Battle of the Standards, silver versus gold. Although the Republicans, meeting first, couched their monetary plank in somewhat evasive language, largely because the veterans of compromise still exercised some power in that party, the dominant sentiment in the convention clearly favored pure gold. The Democrats, on the other hand, issued an unequivocal call to arms. Delegates from the South and West, easily controlling the convention, ran free and unlimited coinage of silver to the top of their mast and invited the people to separate from the plutocrats for the coming struggle. According to their symbolism that was precisely what happened. A bloc from the Western mining states led by Henry Moore Teller of Colorado had already walked out of the Republican convention. An irate group of Gold Democrats now planned to nominate its own candidates. Then while the two major parties were undergoing purification, the Populists met to decide their role in the final contest.

The officials of the new party had scheduled its convention last so that Populism would arrive as a climax of truth and sweep the field. Equally appropriate, the Populists soon discovered that they had almost as many alternative plans as delegates. Since the silver movement had worked its wonders with special effect in Populist territory, a great many of them read the Democratic declaration as an adoption of the Populist cause—which it certainly was not. Both practically and idealistically, therefore, they felt a strong obligation to join the ongoing silver crusade. At the same time, a good number of these same people recoiled at the prospect of entering the Democracy. Some hoarded the power they could only hold in a third party; others, particularly from the South, had painfully left that party and could only return now as beggars; still others believed that on grounds of precedence and superior virtue the Democrats must join them. Finally, a few rejected the silver panacea, almost always because they favored other, equally sweeping solutions.

With a logic peculiarly their own, the party first selected a Populist candidate for Vice-President, the fiery Tom Watson of Georgia, and then nominated Bryan, the Democratic candidate for President. Again, the maneuver had almost as many meanings as interpreters—a token act, a guarantee of independence, a shrewd tactic to steal the Democratic standard-bearer, a move premised on some secret promise from the Democrats, and so on. Whatever their hopes, the practical effect was suicide, a final act of organizational self-destruction from late-nineteenth-century reform. Except in a few pockets of the South the Populist party soon lost its identity, and the Democracy absorbed all who were willing to come.

On the surface this completed the realignment, with each camp now fully manned. Of course in a nation of multiple suspicions and conflicts, that was pure myth. Tammany Hall had no closer affinity to Carolina Populism than the Republican farmer in Iowa had to the Republican magnate in Wall Street. Under the stress of crisis many Americans had joined with their enemies to champion irrelevant causes in a manner that could not possibly last beyond the moment. Nevertheless, both as individuals and as politicians, the two Presidential candidates did reflect something of the struggle at hand.

William Jennings Bryan, whose electrifying oration on silver at the national convention had convinced the uncertain Democrats to nominate a man of thirty-six, came out of the beleaguered communities of Nebraska. He understood the powerful pull of village values because he felt it; and he predicated a career on the assumption that a sufficient number of voters would respond in the same way if only the call were made clearly enough. His public life was devoted to translating a complicated world of affairs he barely comprehended back into those values he never questioned. As an ambitious politician with fair organizing talents, he fought steadily for power and place, yet as an especially honorable man, he compromised less than any of his equally prominent contemporaries.

William McKinley, who was practically assured of the Republican nomination months before the convention, listened carefully and pondered long before he acted. As honest as Bryan in personal affairs, he leaned much more heavily than the Great Commoner upon his party's balance of opinion, duly adjusted for political influence. If dominant voices cried gold, he would not resist them even though he cared relatively little about the matter. His specialty was tariff policy. If money from the corporate rich poured in incredible quantities to support his campaign, he would not resist that either even though no party could emerge the same after such lavish attention. Where Bryan would speak for the towns against any party faction, McKinley would quietly respond to the factions with the power. Less a leader, he was a far shrewder analyst and a more skillful organizer than the Nebraskan. McKinley of Ohio suited the party of greater tensile strength.

In a long American tradition of political slander, very few campaigns have matched this one in scurrility and in sheer emotional release. As the contest progressed, with Bryan undertaking an unprecedented schedule of speeches throughout the land, the Democrats showed the greater confidence and therefore took slightly higher ground. Even then, they simply read their opponents out of American society. Leading Republicans slipped further and further into panic. Likening the silver crusade to anarchism, Jacobinism, and mob rule by the torch and the club, they drummed endlessly upon a central theme: the Democrats had issued "a declaration of war against civilization." Manufacturers threatened unemployment, mortgageholders eviction, and preachers damnation if Bryan were elected. That man, the New York *Nation* would say just after the struggle, had spread more terror without actually taking a life than anyone else in history.

By any reasonable standard, Bryan should have been canonized in every city club across the nation. Succeeding where everyone else had failed, he and his Democratic colleagues had engineered one of America's great political coups. With honeyed words, no compromise, and a David to lead them all, they had captured the Populist party, the country's most puissant symbol of fear since the Civil War, and now contained its remnants within a heterogeneous major party. Of course they had done so as a strategic necessity, a matter of survival in Bryan's region. Still, they had accomplished what many had thought impossible. Instead of hailing him their hero, substantial citizens at once turned their venom upon the conqueror, claiming that he was the conquered. "The Democratic party," the chilly aristocrat Henry Cabot Lodge wrote that September, " . . . has passed completely into the hands of the Populists," and Bryan, backed by fiends like Altgeld and fools like "Sockless" Jerry Simpson, was their spokesman.

Fear proved highly profitable for McKinley's campaign manager Mark Hanna, who himself was immune. Throughout the fall he received a flood of donations and then systematically assessed more among the nation's important businessmen, many of whom had never before involved themselves seriously in politics. By such a thorough entwining of their need for political service with the Republican need for campaign funds, Hanna and these agitated contributors inaugurated one of the most significant arrangements in modern politics, which would set broad but firm boundaries around the Republican party as it acted in national affairs. At the time, however, Hanna concentrated upon turning dollars into votes. Spending perhaps twenty for every one by the Democrats, functioning with a far better integrated party beneath him, and demonstrating a skill no Democrat could match, he methodically covered the nation. Wherever Bryan's train stopped for half an hour, Hanna's influence—the posters equating McKinley with prosperity, the liberally financed workers, the propaganda adjusted to changing local conditions—preceded and followed him. Charm and enthusiasm alone had severe limitations. The Democracy, already the minority party saddled with a depression, suffered the fate of a poor, diffuse organization. It held the devoted but won too few converts. With a 5 percent margin in popular votes—the largest since 1872—and a clear victory in the electoral college, McKinley triumphed that November.

"Thank God!" breathed the New York *Tribune*. By a silent compact to accept the people's verdict—and by men's need to be relieved of such extreme tension—the war had ended, and an extraordinary deflation spread across the land. Participants debated the preceding months like so many dispersing spectators.

The effect upon the reform movements that had risen in the eighties was devastating. Formally and feebly, some of the challengers promised to try again, but everyone felt it: the fire lay in ashes. Populism was dead. Campaigns that had been growing around it withered. After capturing four Western states between 1890 and 1896, the movement for women's suffrage lost both its cohesion and its thrust. Prohibition seemed no more than a passing fad. Certainly no one could have predicted much of a future for the Anti-Saloon League, quietly established in 1895. In the cities reform unions had practically disappeared, and Christian radicals spoke in muted tones. Although many strange alliances were broken, men who had sided with one set of opponents to stop another had not only drained their energies but had usually destroyed their rationale for reform in the process. Among Eastern and Midwestern respectables the old antimonopoly creed would never truly recover.

A full corps of reform's spokesmen, stunned and disheartened, now passed from the scene. Tom Watson turned inward to brood. A number of radical Christians and socialists looked sideward with a sudden interest in a few, short-lived experiments in cooperative community living, an almost pathetic reversion from macrocosm to microcosm. "This is the frictionless way," Frances Willard said in 1897 of a colony named in her honor, "it is the higher law, it eliminates the motives for a selfish life; it enacts into our everyday living the ethics of Christ's Gospel. . . ." But Willard then disappeared into spiritualism's private sanctuary. Another momentary convert, Henry Demarest Lloyd, was soon searching abroad for better models of a cooperative system. Bellamy failed to stir the nation with a sequel to *Looking Backward,* and a subdued Josiah Strong, who had once likened the end of the nineteenth century to the time of Christ's birth, now contemplated the twentieth with vapid optimism. Terence Powderly gratefully accepted a government post from the Republicans.

This remarkably abrupt, clean removal of old causes and old champions left thousands adrift. The near unanimity greeting the

Spanish-American War of 1898 was largely a tribute to America's unique receptivity on the morning after. What a pleasure to believe that this, after all, was the real fruition of the years of turmoil, a culmination in unity and world destiny. Only a very few of the established reformers like the durable Bryan and Eugene Debs, martyr of the Pullman boycott whose future as America's premier Socialist lay ahead of him, fought their way back; and even most of these landed somewhere along the edge of the movements that followed.

The Democratic party would show its scars for years to come. It remained poor. The ample funds that the suave New York businessman William B. Whitney had collected for Cleveland's campaign in 1892, although strictly a fund in behalf of one man's candidacy, still suggested how well the Democracy might have competed for political capital, perhaps even sharing the liaison with corporate wealth which the Republicans came to monopolize. Bryan's nomination destroyed that at a stroke, not only on the national level but in state and city politics throughout the East and Midwest. As a corollary, the silver campaign marked an important, long-range shift in power within the party. In large measure the men associated with Cleveland and gold had already been overthrown in the Midwest before 1896. Then during and after the election many traditional Democratic leaders in the East retired before the combination of agrarian dominance at the top and ethnic challenge at home. In such cities as Boston, Albany, and New Haven, the late nineties brought a final conquest by the Irish bosses. In sum, these changes increased the party's decentralization by destroying the rudiments of an integrating national force and by strengthening numerous little bastions of autonomous power.

Every advantage lay with the Republicans: willing, wealthy donors; able managers; a good general cohesion; a majority of the votes; and almost a surfeit of respectability with the addition of many Cleveland Democrats. Intraparty struggles had filled the Democracy with suspicions and grudges; the Republicans enjoyed a legacy of cooperation and success. Their party even returned to competitive strength in the Western mining states, the one significant center of desertions in 1896. Yet in another sense 1896 did plant the seeds for a later conflict within the Republican party. When Chief Justice Fuller changed his allegiance from Democrat to Republican, it counted immediately. He automatically belonged to that circle of officials whose views always received a thoughtful audience from a party's leaders. But when George Record, a young lawyer from New Jersey, also turned his back on Bryan and the Irish bosses, no one noticed. Record and many more like him—young, ambitious, and reform-minded—unobtrusively swelled the ranks of a new Republicanism that was soon pushing its way up the party's ladder.

The most dramatic extension of power had been made by the national judiciary, which now more or less completed the pattern it had been developing since the eighties. In 1898 the Supreme Court announced one more precise formula, a very generous device for protecting railroad income from the effects of state legislation. In general, however, the courts had managed to avoid ironclad rules in spite of the pressures for exactness. Through such extremely flexible doctrines as due process, equal protection of the law, liberty of contract, and the public purpose of a tax, judges at every level preserved their freedom to intervene when, where, and how they wished across a domain of imperial scope. Justice Field, unrepentant authoritarian to the end, thought his philosophy of reaction was now enthroned. "This negative power," he exulted upon his retirement in 1897, "is the only safety of a popular government." But Field had misread the results. Rather than wedding the judiciary to a particular ideology, judges had set themselves apart as social guardians. Yeasayers as much as naysayers, they would determine which political policies to stop and which to let pass as their sense of society's safety changed.

More slowly, a culmination of quite another sort was occurring throughout the South. The movement for greater controls over the Negro had hardened into an insistence upon a formal caste system. In large measure Jim Crow followed a route marked by the newly assertive Southern white farmers and townsmen. Their inclination toward official discrimination, continuing as long as they worked within the Democratic party, momentarily became a casualty of Populism. Trapped by the need to maintain a party and win elections, Populist leaders had made a variety of businesslike compacts with local Republicans, arrangements that involved a good portion of the dwindling Negro vote. Although a handful of Populists now envisioned a grand league of the dispossessed, white and black, nothing other than tactics had changed for the great majority. Many, in fact, were still proclaiming that "this is a white man's country" as they pursued the politics of expediency. For a time, however, the third party could scarcely recommend Negro disfranchisement.

The Populists gained very little but abuse for their efforts. Usually they found the independent Negro vote too small to matter. In fact, the districts where Negroes concentrated had tended to return overwhelming Democratic majorities, a function of the dominant party's efficiency in buying or merely stuffing in the ballots necessary to win. With the demise of Populism, the need to bend a natural inclination disappeared, and the arriving whites again turned on the Negro, this time with a vengeance born of frustration. Their own party destroyed and their enemies still at large, they struck out at the one threat of old still within easy reach. Under any circumstances the renewed drive against the Negro would have had a jagged edge. Changes inside the movement of white farmers and townsmen made it an especially brutal campaign.

Initially a middling class had dominated that movement for independence. Striving for recognition as much as for power, they had tried to preserve a homespun dignity. Speakers in their Sabbath best and leaders with a claim to education continued to hold honored places in the cause, even if some plain farm words now and then were a necessary ingredient. But the new self-consciousness was contagious. Men a notch below the original participants and a notch below that listened and pondered and then entered into the spirit. The drawing power of the movement

acted so gradually, and the people involved shaded so imperceptibly one from another, that the effects of this deepening
process usually did not show from year to year. By the new
century, however, the changes over two decades were glaring and
fundamental. Instead of a measured if salty rhetoric, spokesmen
for the arriving whites bawled the language of the saloon; instead
of ten-point programs, they sprayed out the everyday feelings of
the sharecropper and millhand; instead of Sunday respectability,
they thumbed a nose at the mighty. Shifts in leadership traced the
outlines of this evolution. In Mississippi, it ran from Frank
Burkitt to James K. Vardaman to Theodore Bilbo, in South
Carolina from Ben Tillman to Cole Blease. Though Tillman, for
example, had eagerly sought the votes of the poorest whites on
his way to power, once in office he not only failed to defend the
mudsills' rights; he eventually advocated their disfranchisement
when Blease, vulgar and shrewd, rallied them against a false
prophet. These changes were well advanced as the movement for
Jim Crow revived after 1896. The attempt at a decent tone and
some semblance of rationality gave way to an unvarnished, crass
racism.

Its demands met little resistance. There were some whose sense
of justice, or propriety, rebelled at the crudeness, and there were
others who resented the inconvenience and expense of an elaborate segregation. Still, none of the Southern whites could champion Negro equality, and few of them had any stake in his right
to vote. Actually, the victors of 1896 who had commandeered
blacks at election time saw attractive possibilities in disfranchisement. Almost any barrier to Negro voting short of a bold
exclusion by color would simultaneously block the poorest whites
as well. Poll taxes, "understanding" tests, and complicated regis-
tration procedures could provide an invaluable defense against
the truly formidable threat from the hills. Consequently, established politicians often seized leadership in the movement, trap-
ping the champion of the disinherited whites in a net of his own
making. How could he push the blacks to the bottom without
pulling his own followers after them? In state after state, the

mixed appeals of disfranchisement carried the day, and comprehensive discriminatory regulations soon covered the entire South. As for the lowliest white, he depended, as usual, upon what men with what sympathies controlled the electoral machinery. His friends could always qualify him; his enemies would now find it much easier to turn him away.

The viciousness with which Southern farmers and townsmen attacked the Negro after 1896 told a story of the community's failure. Its members in the South and elsewhere suddenly felt stripped before their enemies. Never again would an agrarian movement demonstrate that simple confidence in the people's ultimate triumph. Although many in the countryside would now fit themselves into the new urban-industrial world, many others retired behind an inner defense, that much more grim, more withdrawn. The growing importance of a hard Protestant fundamentalism and the narrow zeal of a later prohibitionist campaign would express much that same sense of vulnerability which poisoned human relations in the South.

However cathartic the climax of 1896 had been, traces of uneasiness remained in the victors as well as the vanquished. If from below the business magnate could never serve as quite the same pure model of success, from above the masses could never seem quite so sheeplike. They would bear a close watch. Although the organized efforts to contain Catholicism and restrict immigration largely collapsed after the mid-nineties, in part because the arriving ethnic groups had won enough to ease their ambitions and too much to be recaptured, newcomers never again met the widespread public indifference that had sometimes greeted their predecessors. Along with that lingering suspicion of immigrants came an increasingly elaborate race theory, designed to cover all peoples, and the spread of a cold, formalized anti-Semitism. Throughout America a residual fear had shrunk the outer limits of optimism.

5

A New Middle Class

As the island communities disintegrated, certain Americans sought to transcend rather than preserve them. Particularly in the cities, where so many could not avoid a deep and continuous involvement with the larger world, a variety of people groped for some personal connection with that broader environment, some way of mediating between their everyday life and its impersonal setting. One index to their concern was an almost obsessive interest in "class," as if here alone was a concept big enough to encompass the problems they faced.

During the eighties and nineties only a few urban aristocrats achieved very substantial results. In the battles for social position between the beleaguered old families and the nouveaux riches, both increasingly sought advantage beyond their cities, usually through marriage. Intermarriage tended to draw separate aristocracies into a single group; and in order to demarcate this national upper class new modes of identification such as a common educational experience in an exclusive boarding school and then in one of a select set of Eastern colleges assumed far greater importance. Aristocrats, in other words, made peace with an impersonal world by extending their familiar pattern of life. For most Americans, however, the task was much more complicated. In the process of relocating themselves, they were forced as well to redefine their environment.

Little noticed in the heat of the nineties, a new middle class was rapidly gathering strength. Although the political crisis at the end

of the century certainly affected its members, it distracted more
than it involved them. The issues were confusing, the idiom of
debate uncongenial, the atmosphere unsettling. Deeply concerned
in their own way by the condition of American society, they
would pose another set of questions in a new language and by
their zeal and optimism help create a fresh climate.

In part, the new middle class was a class only by courtesy of the
historian's afterthought. Covering too wide a range to form a
tightly knit group, it divided into two broad categories. One
included those with strong professional aspirations in such fields
as medicine, law, economics, administration, social work, and
architecture. The second comprised specialists in business, in
labor, and in agriculture awakening both to their distinctiveness
and to their ties with similar people in the same occupation. In
fact, consciousness of unique skills and functions, an awareness
that came to mold much of their lives, characterized all members
of the class. They demonstrated it by a proud identification as
lawyers or teachers, by a determination to improve the contents
of medicine or the procedures of a particular business, and by an
eagerness to join others like themselves in a craft union, professional organization, trade association, or agricultural cooperative.

Around 1900 these men and women were still minorities
within their occupations. Moving near the mainstream of urban-
industrial development, they welcomed it in a manner that the
dissenters of the eighties and nineties had found impossible.
Rather than a threat, the new order promised them release. At a
minimum it provided outlets never before available for their
talents. Usually it offered them respectable and profitable positions as well. In time, they became sufficiently secure to look
beyond the day's work and try to locate themselves within a
national system. Thus scientifically minded farmers studied marketing and suggested novel experiments in government assistance, social workers set their profession in an inclusive urban-
industrial framework, and teachers experimented with ways of
relating public education to a whole society. Outgoing and
enthusiastic, they were self-conscious pioneers. If they were too

diverse to feel cohesion as a class, a remarkable degree of interaction did nevertheless occur among them. Similar spirit, similar experiences, even roughly similar aspirations, drew them together far more often than chance alone could have explained.

The exceptional vitality of the new middle class derived in large measure from the very personal benefits its membership bestowed. Early in the nineteenth century, widespread hostility toward privilege in a land of opportunity, and pell-mell expansion in a land of weak communication, had combined to destroy the traditional standards surrounding most occupations and to isolate those few who still maintained a high degree of skill. If, in a democracy, every man could manage every task, no one acquired prestige from any job; and if, in a sprawling country, men of similar talents did not know of each other, they could scarcely act together. Regardless of occupation, therefore, most people had found their place within the categories of a small community where criteria of wealth and ethnic characteristics predominated.

As this society crumbled, the specialized needs of an urban-industrial system came as a godsend to a middle stratum in the cities. Identification by way of their skills gave them the deference of their neighbors while opening natural avenues into the nation at large. Increasingly formal entry requirements into their occupations protected their prestige through exclusiveness. The shared mysteries of a specialty allowed intimate communion even at long range, as letters among the scattered champions of public health demonstrated. Finally, the ability to see how their talents meshed with others in a national scheme encouraged them to look outward confidently instead of furtively. As much as any other trait, an earnest desire to remake the world upon their private models testified to the deep satisfaction accompanying this revolution in identity.

No part of the process came with such force or exercised such profound influence as the one in medicine. A respected if scientifically imprecise occupation in early America, the practice of medicine had once been reasonably protected by state and local licensing laws. During the second quarter of the nineteenth century, equalitarianism and decentralization had broken this monopoly, as it was called, so that by mid-century almost anyone could, and a great variety did, enter what had once been a profession. Doctors of the people—allopaths, homeopaths, eclectics, and later osteopaths—roamed the land at will. In the seventies, Charles Macune practiced medicine from the same intuition his father had used spreading the Gospel; and a decade later the upright Leonidas Polk set out to make his fortune with a bottled cure for diphtheria. Those who bewailed the passing order found few sympathizers; precursors of the modern doctor specialized in harsh remedies and feeble results.

Rumblings in Europe during the sixties turned into the roar of revolution after 1876 when Pasteur and Koch proved that a specific micro-organism caused a specific disease. Within two decades scientists had isolated the sources for a vicious array of man's enemies: typhoid, malaria, leprosy, tuberculosis, cholera, tetanus, diphtheria, and plague. Equally spectacular discoveries followed in parasitology, one area where Americans made important contributions, as doctors around the turn of the century traced malaria, yellow fever, typhus, and Rocky Mountain spotted fever to the mosquitoes, lice, and ticks that carried the bacteria to humans. In most cases, immunizations appeared soon after. Piling higher the riches, antiseptic surgery also spread throughout the nation's better hospitals during these same years.

Too far from the centers of early discovery, the United States did not feel the full impact until the nineties, when the new medicine arrived in the major cities and fanned out rapidly from there. Although quacks and nostrums continued to thrive on the ignorance and the desperate hopes of millions, they would fall farther into the shadow land with each decade. After the introduction of diphtheria antitoxin during the nineties, no more honorable men tried to cure it from a bottle.

Doctors responded by organizing and proselytizing. Since 1846 a handful had used the American Medical Association as a forum for complaints and scientific information. Yet despite stirring in a

few specialties, no substructure of local medical groups under-
pinned the AMA as late as the eighties. Those that did exist had
neither strength nor scientific consistency. Then in the nineties
doctors rushed into local organizations, modernized them, and
infused them with a fresh militant spirit. Feeling the pressures
from beneath, the AMA reorganized in 1901 as the capstone of
these associations, and utilized its new energy to encourage even
more complete organization. Membership in the AMA, which
had been 8,400 in 1900, leaped to over 70,000 by 1910. A decade
later 60 percent of the nation's doctors had joined. The organizations immediately demanded modern scientific safeguards limiting entry into their field, with doctors as the gatekeepers. Local
governments readily complied. Now a medical profession existed,
and its champions turned to their slower brethren, attempting to
re-educate older doctors and reorient older medical schools. At
the same time, "like religious men . . . who believe in their own
vision . . . and wish to go among others," the new doctors
descended upon the cities and towns with a scientific gospel.

One natural expression of that gospel was public health, which
in effect became a profession within a profession. Prior to the late
eighties, public health had constituted little beyond a few ineffectual boards and the loan of private medical facilities in time of
catastrophe. During the nineties, a cadre of the new doctors
transformed this field into a distinct branch of medicine which by
1912 had its own professional school in the Massachusetts Insti-
tute of Technology. In contrast to its subordinate role in research,
the United States led the world in translating modern medicine
into public policy.

The prototype of these missionaries was Dr. Hermann Biggs,
who raised the city and then the state of New York to pre-
eminence in public health. After studying with William H.
Welsh, America's statesman of the new medicine, Biggs went
abroad and witnessed the revolution in the laboratories of Koch
and Pasteur. Joining New York City's board of health, he
introduced diagnostic tests for cholera in 1892. Two years later he
experimented with diphtheria vaccine and in 1897 shocked the

city's physicians with an ordinance requiring them to report basic information on cases of tuberculosis. A pioneer in the treatment of the "white plague," he was a founder of the National Tuberculosis Association. Over the next two decades, he labored to purify water and milk supplies, introduce a variety of medical services to schoolchildren and the poor, and extend the efficiency of quarantines. Appropriate to the new professional canons, his counterpart in Providence, Charles V. Chapin, criticized Biggs only for failing to stop private practice entirely and devote all of his time to public health.

The fall of infant mortality from 273 per 1,000 in 1885 to a third of that by 1915 expressed in statistics what millions showed in outpourings of gratitude. These officers were public heroes, as a group of Cornell students verified by selecting Biggs the University's greatest alumnus over a field of prominent financiers, lawyers, and educators. During Biggs' tenure in New York, Charlie Murphy, chief of Tammany Hall, declared public health beyond politics. In fact, the whole family of medical professions had suddenly risen from the depths to a position of exalted prestige.

In certain formal respects, the history of lawyers paralleled that of the doctors. Early in the nineteenth century educational and apprenticeship requirements had still restricted the practice of law in many parts of the East. As in medicine, deprofessionalization moved apace in the second quarter of the century, when democratized, decentralized admission to the bar demolished practically all standards. Training passed from the colleges to a convenient law office, and along with thousands of others, John Peter Altgeld, an indifferent student, passed the bar examination after reading for a few months in his spare time. A great many practiced law as a sideline. With the exception of bankers, no group late in the nineteenth century stood in lower public repute. Officially excluded from the farmers' alliances and the Knights of Labor, they were widely attacked—often with justice—as shysters and cheats.

Contrary to the story in medicine, however, an elite of legal experts had always enjoyed a lucrative market. It was these men, partly to honor themselves, partly to work for higher standards, who in the seventies began organizing city and state bar associations, capped in 1878 by the American Bar Association. What started gradually became a flood after 1890. The expanding need for carefully trained lawyers shifted education back to the classroom, where in the better schools the quality of instruction rose rapidly and the curriculum came increasingly to include work in economics, government, and sociology. The professional zeal of these faculties helped to establish new goals of excellence for a generation of students. When New York in 1894 adopted a central examining board of skilled lawyers to control admission to practice, a host of states quickly followed, and the framework of professionalism was set. By 1916, 48 state and 623 local bar associations had grown from the total of 16 in 1880.

The best law schools and bar associations could never maintain the same degree of discipline as the leading medical schools and associations. The law always remained a looser, less esoteric occupation. Yet by the nineties a sense of professionalism had undoubtedly captured a significant number of relatively young lawyers, eager to see their work as a science, alert to ways of using their specialized knowledge, and far more aware than their predecessors of the social implications of the law.

If the greatest public need for professionalism was in medicine, the greatest occupational need was in teaching. Ridiculed over the nineteenth century as Ichabod Cranes and fussy schoolmarms, teachers embodied the apparent paradox of exceptionally low prestige in a land that acclaimed universal education. Actually there was no paradox. To most Americans of the nineteenth century, universal education referred only to the bare rudiments, a basic version of the three R's, which countless people were qualified to teach. Few could live on the teacher's starvation salary, few saw opportunities for advancement, and therefore very few—often the Ichabod Cranes and futile old maids—devoted a life to it. Far more often teaching was a way-station, for a James A. Garfield and a Henry M. Teller in search of careers and for young ladies in search of husbands.

The main lines of educational development late in the century ran downward from the universities and upward from the primary grades, meeting at the high schools. The expansion of higher education after the Civil War steadily increased the pressure on the schools beneath it. Harvard's diversified undergraduate curriculum and elective system, an experiment soon copied by other institutions, reflected the rising interest in a more precise, utilitarian college education, and this goal in turn required a broader base of preparatory schools committed to a more exact training. Leading academicians sought to shift that burden from the private schools, which traditionally had prepared college students, to the public high schools. In the seventies, institutions such as the University of Michigan certified the best public schools as an incentive to reform; then beginning in New England in 1884 and reaching the Northwest by 1918, special accrediting agencies set the standards. In their new preparatory role, the high schools grew and improved gradually during the balance of the century.

At the same time administrators were seeking programs for elementary education that would serve the industrial city. In a decentralized agrarian society, instruction had become what each of a thousand communities cared to make of it. Usually that meant little more than rendering a free people literate. The city, on the other hand, required some formal means of organizing its schools, and a great many of the jobs in an urban-industrial market demanded skills well above a rudimentary level. Ambitious administrators such as Superintendent William T. Harris of St. Louis attempted to resolve these problems through an ordered curriculum in eight grades of increasing difficulty. One purpose of the reform was to build a ladder that would then rise beyond the primary grades, and administrators insisted upon cooperation from the high schools in making a connection. By 1900 America for the first time showed the outlines of an educational system.

Pressures outside the schools, however, continued to mount. Educational reform was not keeping pace with the demand for greater skills at all occupational levels, and a variety of interested citizens combined to insist that public education make such training more and more generally available. Where only six states had compulsory attendance laws in 1871, virtually all in the North and West had acted by 1900. The movement for vocational education, especially manual training, gained momentum during the nineties and spread in the new century until in 1917 it received Federal assistance in the Smith-Hughes Act. Systematic critiques disparaging the schools began to appear in popular journals early in the nineties, and organizations of ambitious parents formed a national congress in 1897 which called for better quality and wider opportunity in education. Most of the campaigns centered upon the high schools, demanding that they broaden their goals and enlarge their services. With a rush after 1900, that is exactly what they did. Renovating their curriculum to suit a modern industrial society, the high schools acquired a rationale and life of their own in the next twenty years. From 1890 to 1910, both teachers and students increased more than fourfold, then more than doubled again in another decade.

Teachers who had watched the school administrator monopolize benefits from the reforms of the late nineteenth century were determined to take advantage of this latest ferment themselves. They faced three major challenges: to enhance the prestige of their work, to counteract excessive mobility, and to protect a peculiarly vulnerable occupation from outside interference. As the most important part of an elaborate program, they insisted upon the requirement of specific professional training for every position in the public schools, a principle forty-two states had accepted by 1911. With invaluable assistance from teachers' colleges and accrediting associations, they interwove a new science of pedagogy into the expanding curriculum, thereby encouraging further professional prerequisites. The battle for stability also included demands for tenure and for precise salary scales with regular increments. Finally, the teachers supported professionalized school administration, nonpartisan school boards, and definite procedures for promotions, all to discourage meddling by powerful outsiders. A tangle of regulations and rituals that would appall a later generation of critics meant professional self-preservation at the turn of the century.

Around 1900 a variety of organizations, ranging from Margaret Haley's militant Chicago Teachers' Federation to quiet discussion groups, were nourishing and being nourished by the new spirit. But it was not until 1905 that the National Education Association, long the vehicle of administrators and college educators, felt the surge of the public school teachers. With the election as president of Ella Flagg Young, Chicago's milder leader, the balance of power in 1910 tipped toward the teachers and the new science of education. The professionalization of teachers would continue to run about a decade behind that of doctors and lawyers.

Comparable experiences affected smaller numbers in scores of other occupations. In journalism, for example, a growing number who entered by way of college were distressed by the stereotypes of crude inquisitor and callous purveyor of sensation. The alternative image of romantic adventure exemplified by the dashing Richard Harding Davis served little better, whatever its secret attractions. Some of the new journalists followed the usual route to professionalism, attempting an exact definition of the field and encouraging the development of separate technical schools. Another group gravitated toward the monthly magazines, where they saw unrealized opportunities for expert journalism. As muckrakers and social analysts, many would fulfill critical functions for their new-middle-class audience. In both cases, they were men with a mission, seeking ways to use what they regarded as a scientific method of reporting.

Social workers, who as one of their leaders remarked made a "mutual discovery of one another's existence" during the first years of the twentieth century, acted first to dissociate themselves from philanthropy and establish themselves as a distinct field within the new social sciences. Beginning with local leagues in Boston and New York, they had formed the National Federation of Settlements by 1911 and soon after captured the old National Conference of Charities and Corrections, renaming it the National Conference of Social Work. Also early in the century, they moved from ad hoc classes of special training to complete professional schools within such universities as Chicago and Harvard. After 1909, the *Survey* provided them with a spokesman. So it went with architects, a variety of public and private administrators, and many more: definition, professional associations, and specific academic training.

The universities played a crucial role in almost all of these movements. Since the emergence of the modern graduate school in the seventies, the best universities had been serving as outposts of professional self-consciousness, frankly preparing young men for professions that as yet did not exist. By 1900 they held an unquestioned power to legitimize, for no new profession felt complete—or scientific—without its distinct academic curriculum; they provided centers for philosophizing and propagandizing; and they inculcated apprentices with the proper values and goals. Considering the potential of the universities for frustration, it was extremely important that higher education permissively, even indiscriminately, welcomed each of the new groups in turn.

The universities became virtually the exclusive home of several other professions whose early history could be read as an increasingly refined self-consciousness among members of the old American Social Science Association. During the eighties the American Historical Association, the American Economics Association, and the American Statistics Association broke away from the parent group; the American Political Science Association and the American Sociological Society followed in 1903. Along with psychology, which preferred classification with the behavioral sciences, each of these represented a highly articulate discipline, jealous of its identity, zealous to spread its scientific message, and influential in the lives of countless members of the middle class.

A case apart, yet generically similar, was the entry of a select group of women into public affairs. The most noisy manifestation of the new spirit accompanied the drive for women's suffrage, which after a dormant period burst forth under fresh leadership in the second decade of the century. An equally well-publicized part of the process was the trickling admission of women into such professions as law and medicine, where token integration gave many of their male colleagues a warm sense of paternal tolerance. The most important advances, however, occurred in those few professions which women gradually, quietly, came to dominate.

Behind the entire movement had lain an implicit yet basic question: what public tasks would women seek and which ones would men allow them to fill? The answer grew out of the traditional image of women as tender mothers, angels of mercy, and keepers of the morals, an answer that found its fullest expression in two professions increasingly identified with women —teaching and social work. In such areas as these, men responded to the well-trained, dedicated woman with considerable deference. "An Ella Flagg Young as Superintendent of Schools in Chicago and a Katherine B. Davis as Commissioner of Charities in New York," read a typical male comment, "can render services of a kind that few men are equipped to give." Men usually did not feel threatened until women's activities pushed past the stereotype. They seldom did. Such women as Lillian Wald, the nurse who pioneered in social work, indicated that they too found works of mercy and child care "natural" to their inclinations. More than the logic of slum life led the settlements to devote such a heavy proportion of their energies to children— their health, their recreation, their rights to a decent education and to freedom from hard labor. Even the few women in law and medicine specialized to an exceptional degree in such fields as juvenile crime, pediatrics, and humane extensions of public health. They followed these paths not because they were necessarily more moral or humane, or even ofttimes because they were mothers, but because they were women, both as they and as men

defined them. Tacit, mutually accepted limits accounted for their
remarkably smooth arrival into a professional middle class.

Various economic groupings, a part of the same trend toward
specialization, also served roughly the same purposes of identification. Among businessmen they took the form of a great
quantity of associations, most of which appeared rather suddenly
around 1900. In contrast to the gatherings for isolated promotions, complaints, or emergencies that had dotted the nineteenth
century, these were durable organizations with continuing programs. Local chambers of commerce and boards of trade comprised the largest number, attracting a middle level of successful
businessmen who had survived the business cycle and technological change. Particularly in the major cities, businessmen often
belonged as well to organizations more directly reflecting their
self-consciousness as specialists. With ever finer precision, these
functional associations multiplied after 1900. What began simply
as a group of bankers would subdivide into commercial, savings,
and investment bankers; what was originally a grocers' league
would split retail and wholesale; and so forth throughout the
business world.

As organizations specialized, their members also gathered more
often into groups with a particular cause. Hundreds in the
various manufacturing associations, for example, doubled as
members of the National Association of Manufacturers, either to
lower the tariff or to destroy the unions. Loyalty to the large
organizations complemented the local or trade attachments of the
more confident businessmen, especially those from the major
cities who could not and did not wish to avoid increasingly broad
involvements. With roots more firmly planted in a definite area
of the economy, thousands early in the twentieth century sought
some embodiment of all American business. The United States
Chamber of Commerce, founded in 1912, became the national
spokesman for these newly organized, ambitious business groups.

For an elite of skilled wage earners, the craft unions provided
an even more important means of location. As long as the

craftsman enjoyed respectable standing in his community, he had felt little pressure to form a permanent union. Like the successful businessmen and lawyers who had belonged simply to the community's upper class, the skilled worker identified with a broad stratum of independent, largely self-employed citizens. As late as the eighties, he most often used the terms "labor" and "workingman" to designate all honest men, not a determinate category of industrial wage earners.

The seventies and eighties also contained evidence of a changing outlook. Where technological innovation threatened without demolishing special skills and where the effects of a national economy impinged upon without absorbing the craftsmen's independence, trade unions began to grow. As the migration of laborers increased during the eighties and nineties, strings of autonomous locals found that they could not manage a number of complex jurisdictional problems. Because they required a general arbiter, locals grudgingly, erratically, granted national headquarters degrees of control over their craft, spreading from the supervision of union cards to bargaining with employers. Although powerful locals continued to rebuff outside interference, the trend was clear. The ability of the national unions to survive far better during the depressed nineties than during the prosperous eighties attested to their basic social and psychic values.

Most of these unions came to maturity soon after the depression of the nineties. National officers, rather than using the union as a springboard to better jobs as their predecessors so often had, now linked their future with the organization, a going concern that absorbed all of their time and special talents. The apparent "class" consciousness of such men as Samuel Gompers actually represented no more than a generalized version of this extreme craft and organizational consciousness. One index to the strength of the new spirit was the weakness of the American Federation of Labor, to which almost all of the skilled unions belonged. In the early years of the AFL, infant unions had looked to it for legitimacy, guidance, and whatever concrete assistance it could muster. Occasionally its officers had played a determining role in a particular union's policies. But as the crafts consolidated their power, the AFL's influence over them declined accordingly. The more impressive President Gompers seemed to a public that watched the Federation's expanding membership, the less effect he could have on actual union activities; the more he appeared the statesman, the more he was, in fact, the servant.

The most striking aspect of maturity was the development of a new business unionism. Where that term had once connoted the efficient management of a union's affairs, it now implied a full interpretation of organized labor's position in industrial society. Above all, it contained a binding set of business values—the inviolability of contracts, the inevitability of industrial concentration, the practical sovereignty of management in the making of general industrial policy—which fundamentally conditioned the nature of the labor movement. Correlatively, it expressed a passionate urge toward respectability. Sensitive to their slender hold within the middle class, a number of leaders such as Gompers and John Mitchell of the coal miners responded to every slight as an affair of honor, almost crudely dissociated themselves from radicals, Negroes, and most new immigrants, and somewhat after the fashion of Booker T. Washington wooed doubters by appearing to ask so little that no decent citizen could deny them. Finally, business unionism carried the obligation that union executives become technical experts in their particular industry. If the crafts did not always adjust quickly enough to a shifting technology, they were at least alert to its basic importance.

The irony of America's first truly self-conscious wage earners locating themselves by business values in a business system was repeated in agriculture—with even fewer reservations. No occupational group experienced a more difficult transition than the farmers. Long accustomed to think of themselves as "the people," they could scarcely comprise a distinct segment at the same time. As the rhetoric of innumerable agrarian movements illustrated, they had habitually viewed the nation in either-or terms. Either a man belonged with them by some dependence upon agriculture or by the analogy of honest work; or he fell beyond the pale. When Bryan classed the farmers, along with all citizens of respectable enterprise, as the nation's real businessmen, he was not seeking a place in the sun for his constituents. He simply gave the benediction of Americanism to those whose lives followed the farmer's—the people's—way. What greater affront to this tradition than the creation in 1889 of a cabinet post for agriculture, as if the government needed a Department of American Citizens!

The first to detach themselves least resembled the yeoman of the American tradition. They were the well-to-do commercial farmers, interested in scientific agriculture and expert management and often indistinguishable from the town's landowning merchants and mortgage-holding bankers. Nevertheless, no group within the new middle class relied so heavily upon outside leadership. Dispersed, partial heirs to that Jeffersonian tradition, and beset by conflicting agrarian reforms, they waited in large measure until others showed them the way. Some guidance came from farm journals—"carrot improvement" sheets, a Populist disgustedly labelled them—which preached better farming techniques and tighter organization both out of zeal and out of a shrewd business sense. More came from those professional advocates of scientific agriculture who late in the nineteenth century moved back and forth between the land-grant colleges and the first Federal bureaus of agriculture. Only a handful in the eighties, they led the battles for the Hatch Act in 1887, which placed a network of Federal experiment stations under the aegis of the land-grant colleges, and the second Morrill Act in 1890, which finally guaranteed the colleges adequate financing. At the same time, they were gathering converts among commercial farmers through their work in animal and plant diseases, breeding, and soil depletion.

Early in the new century, signs of a new consciousness showed everywhere. Hardheaded marketing cooperatives, usually with close ties to state schools and departments of agriculture, rose and prospered. Where the earlier cooperatives had dreamed of sur-

mounting the profit system or returning business from evil men
to the people, these sought a lucrative place, often a monopoly,
within the existing system. In 1903, Seaman Knapp, who had
been a leading lobbyist for the Hatch Act, took practical demonstrations of scientific agriculture into the Southern fields to
counteract a plague of boll weevils. Always careful to work
through local elites and most successful where the least tenant
farming existed, his demonstrations quickly gained supporters
not only in the Southern towns but also among business firms
that sold in a farmer's market. By the second decade of the
century, the same community leaders in towns North and South
were hiring permanent county agents to demonstrate and educate. A local leadership then collected around these agents in
farm bureaus which multiplied, mounded into state federations,
and in 1919 formed the American Farm Bureau Federation. Here
the firm business values, the new vocabulary of marketing and
chemistry, and the exaggerated repudiation of the Populist heritage emerged most clearly, an official declaration of these farmers
as agricultural businessmen instead of "the people."

Under any circumstances a reordering process of this scope and
force would have had a powerful impact upon American society.
What heightened its significance was the compression of its most
vital phase in both time and space. Almost every group within
the new class experienced its formative growth toward self-
consciousness in roughly the ten years from 1895 to 1905. There
had been important preliminaries before the mid-nineties in
medicine and law, among skilled workers and business groups,
just as there was still much of a basic sort to accomplish after
1905 among teachers and commercial farmers. Nevertheless, for
numbers sufficient to warrant talking of movements, that decade
around the turn of the century was the critical time of revelation
and cohesion.

These groups, moreover, not only concentrated in the cities but
generally appeared first in the older, larger, and more industrially
developed ones, mostly in the Northeast. The waves of arrival

were admittedly uneven: particular groups such as the social workers and teachers in Chicago, particular individuals such as Judge Ben Lindsey of Denver, or even particular events such as the tidal wave at Galveston that led to an important experiment in administrative government, might alter the pattern. And the major cities certainly did not hold a monopoly on the new middle class. Obviously commercial farmers did not live there, nor did impressive, if scattered numbers of the new businessmen, unionists, lawyers, doctors, and journalists. Yet not only did the older cities lead in most respects—medicine and public health, modern bar associations and educational legislation, assertive new business and women's groups—but they continued to attract more and more outsiders in the process. Isolated academics, hopeful young journalists, professional architects, experts in administration, and many others gravitated here where opportunities beckoned and where they could find enough of their own kind.

This clustering meant considerably more than an arithmetic difference. It drew together groups undergoing similar experiences and sharing similar values and interests. As the professional secretaries who moved among their organizations discovered, members of the new middle class spoke a common language and naturally, easily, they began to encourage each other's efforts toward self-determination. In Chicago, for instance, the architect Allen B. Pond designed uniquely functional settlements for Jane Addams, who aided Margaret Haley in achieving professional status for teachers, who joined with John Fitzpatrick, progressive president of the Chicago Federation of Labor, in championing the rights of wage earners. Every major city produced comparable patterns. Moreover, they increasingly met each other in broad areas of mutual concern. Joining doctors in the public-health campaigns, for example, were social workers, women's clubs, and teachers who specialized in the problems of youth; lawyers who drafted the highly technical bills; chambers of commerce that publicized and financed pilot projects; and new economists such as John B. Andrews, whose exposure of "phossy jaw" among the workers in phosphorus-match factories remains a classic in the history of industrial health. Greatly enriching the movements, such pools of talent also returned inestimable benefits of morale and insight to the participants.

These men and women communicated so well in part because they were the ones building a new structure of loyalties to replace the decaying system of the nineteenth-century communities. As members of the new middle class found their rewards more and more in the uniqueness of an occupation and in its importance to a rising scientific-industrial society, the primary differentiators of the nineteenth century weakened proportionately. They lost that appreciation for fine gradations in wealth and its display, that close emotional involvement in differences between English and Irish, Swedish and Bohemian. The compulsive identification with a political party also waned. Although they usually retained the party label of their fathers and some traces of the old feeling, they tended to subordinate that loyalty to new ones drawn from their occupation, its values, and its policies. Joining an occupational organization was a defining as well as an identifying act. Just as a political party had once done, now the occupational association supplied many answers, hopes, and enemies far beyond the range of their immediate experience. Where a shift in party allegiance had once been treason, it became not only possible but in some circles popular, opening the way to various forms of nonpartisan and interest-group politics.

If partisanship declined, therefore, political involvement certainly did not. During the earliest stages of self-consciousness, the strongest political ambitions concerned occupational autonomy. For such groups as doctors, lawyers, and teachers, that entailed legal sanction for their own standards of entry and proficiency. Accredited members of the group—a board of doctors or lawyers or teachers—would administer the laws, passing upon the qualifications of applicants and adjudging any violations within the profession. The academic professions, by controlling degrees and jobs, enjoyed similar privileges without the need for legislation. Business and farming groups, however, discovered that effective self-regulation required more than an empowering statute. With

increasingly elaborate plans for stable prices, coordinated marketing, and reliable, expensive data, they looked as well to a variety
of government bureaus and agencies that would provide the
technical services their specialized needs demanded. In almost
every case, these groups depended upon the government for the
means of independence from all intruders, including the government itself.

The forces of occupational cohesion were at the same time
forces of general social division. Most obviously, they widened the
gap between the major cities and rural–small town America. In
part, the new middle class only helped to formalize differences
that had been developing for years. Professional teachers, for
example, were improving a modern educational system that had
scarcely touched the rural areas, especially in the South. Even
more important was the matter of communication. Proud of their
specialties and comfortable only with others who shared their life,
the new class lectured to but seldom talked with country folk. To
rural Americans the strange language, the iconoclasm, the threatening values of these articulate urbanites, came to represent
much of that conglomerate danger, the sinful city.

As usual, the men in the countryside overlooked the many
ways in which this new class was also sharpening differences
within the cities. In the poorer wards where a keen sense of
nationality continued to determine antipathies and alliances,
neither the bosses nor their constituents could understand the
ways of the new class. They seemed like so many mugwumpish
ingrates lacking even an elementary morality in political matters.
The very rich on their part found little to their liking in the
behavior of the new class. Attacks from far below, however
irritating, merely verified their low opinion of the ignorant, weak,
and envious. It was quite another matter for otherwise respectable lawyers and businessmen to add their cries. The wealthy
could seldom distinguish between traditional assaults upon them
as monopolists, manipulators, and oppressors, and new ones
accusing them of backwardness, waste, and crudity. As Thorstein
Veblen's biting comments on barbarism and conspicuous con-

sumption suggested, the new professional challenged their rights to prestige as much as their place in the economy. Fortunately for the new middle class, the basis for a league of their opponents, wealthy and poor, urban and rural, did not exist.

For a time the most bitter conflicts generated by the new class were intraoccupational. To the many who fell outside the main lines of urban-industrial change, that urge toward professionalization and an exact definition of role seemed irrelevant. They still viewed their problems within the framework of a community rather than an occupation. While city bankers discussed methods of rationalizing banking procedure and modernizing financial laws, country bankers talked of recapturing independence from the cities and assuming the role of confessor and adviser for all the townspeople. Sometimes inert in the face of change, sometimes hostile to the strange innovations abroad, thousands from the countryside resisted the new ways in their occupations. Others fought their opponents face-to-face. It was an eminent general practitioner, his reputation ostensibly at stake, who led the attack in New York against diphtheria vaccination. Battles between labor reformers and craft unionists, charity and social workers, the Non-Partisan League and the American Farm Bureau Federation, echoed through these years.

That confident, driving quality which infuriated their enemies covered far more uncertainty than the new middle class ever recognized. None of these people broke cleanly from his past. If old values of ethnic background and wealth diminished, the feelings invested in them were too powerful to destroy. As they declined, they went underground to emerge again in other guises. A precise ethnic consciousness gave way to a more generalized racialism, presumably with scientific foundations. Careful comparisons of income were replaced by vaguer concerns about the moral and social implications of extreme wealth and extreme poverty. Certainly those social workers who made a public display of their adopted poverty had in no sense freed themselves from that kind of involvement. This was transmutation, not emancipation.

Members of the new class announced their bold visions too loudly and exposed too often the shadows on their own bright faith. Children of urban-industrial America, they looked proudly upon their cities. "The Hope of Democracy," Frederic C. Howe called them, holding the precious contents of a great civilization. Yet· in the next breath Howe pined for "the freer, sweeter life which the country offers." Almost worshipful of a nebulous, exhilarating something they called "science," they still purchased and praised quantities of simple romantic literature. Seeking a new urban leader for modern America, many gave their hearts to a man almost invariably pictured in a cowboy hat, Theodore Roosevelt.

Nevertheless, these men and women did represent a new society. They had enough insight into their lives to recognize that the old ways and old values would no longer suffice. Often confused, they were still the ones with the determination to fight those confusions and mark a new route into the modern world.

6

Revolution in Values

WITHIN a relatively isolated community, it made sense to think of society as numbers of individuals. Year after year townspeople watched each other labor and idle, save and spend, help and cheat, attend church and frequent saloons. Encouraged by maxims from the Bible and the almanac, they judged their neighbors with a clear conscience, and as democratization levelled many social distinctions, a single standard had generally sufficed for all. If more prudence was expected of the minister and more charity of the rich man, no sharp divisions set some apart with moral privileges greater than their fellows. Nor had these townsmen any reason to doubt the infinite extendability of their principles. Just as providence blessed the godly man and disaster punished the sinful, so cities, nations, whole civilizations, rose and fell according to their record along the same scale.

What had served to explain a community-centered society proved increasingly inadequate to comprehend America late in the nineteenth century. As more people clustered into smaller spaces, it became harder to isolate the individual. As more of a previously distant world intruded upon community life, it grew more difficult to untangle what an individual did and what was done to him, even to distinguish the community itself from the society around it. Now a perverted world was enabling men to perpetrate monstrous hoaxes in the name of the old morality. It had been natural enough to account for business success and failure in terms of individual virtue and vice; it was quite another matter to permit the corporations ill-gotten profits because the Supreme Court adjudged them "persons" within the meaning of the Fourteenth Amendment. Yet from inside the traditional value system, the Court's logic was maddeningly difficult to break. No just God had given Rockefeller his money, whatever the man said. Yet for those who had customarily thought of wealth as a token of grace, rearguing the case brought only frustration. An increasing number felt the same frustration when they heard the familiar, personalized virtues of a simple government from the very men who seemed to gain by the government's restraint.

Most Americans, too preoccupied to square theory with practice, merely patched together makeshifts from the old and the new. When that architect of a vast and impersonal business empire, J. P. Morgan, pronounced "character" the basis for all of his transactions, he signified not that he was a liar but that he could still live at peace with his inconsistencies. For those who worked systematically through the problems of social theory, however, the contradictions grew to be more than they could manage within the traditional system. If they also salvaged as much of the familiar as possible, they at least tried to recast the village values in a modern framework.

From the seventies through the First World War, the nature of social change dominated their inquiries. How did society move from there to here and beyond? How did a society in motion hold its members together? With few exceptions, the individual, who absorbed earlier and later generations, received only perfunctory attention. Much like their contemporaries on the Court, theorists concerned themselves with the rights and needs of the individual only when they could not avoid him. Engrossed in the sweep of impersonal forces, they could not tarry long with one man.

By the late seventies, the theory within which men would maneuver for the balance of the century was already more or less complete. Appropriate to the age, it was impressive for the spread of its canvas, the simplicity of its principles, and the dehumanization of its contents. All men, the theory read, applied themselves in the search for wealth and found rewards according to their ability. A few, the highest types of their race, discovered more effective ways to combine land, labor, and capital, and drew society upward as the rest reorganized behind their leaders. The large majority, possessing no more than ordinary talent, divided a fund that was fixed by the requirements of the dearer resources, land and capital. The weakest simply disappeared. Meanwhile, government maintained order, conducted some public services at minimum cost, and above all did nothing to disrupt the laws of free competition. The society that abided by these principles slowly and steadily progressed, enjoying an ever superior utilization of its resources and an ever improving race winnowed by competition.

Frankly economic in conception, the neat rules and inexorable results of this classical theory had a stark character that bothered many Americans even at the height of its acceptance in the eighties. Consequently, many of its popularizers softened the edges. John Fiske, for example, tied the system to God's cosmic destiny and held out the promise of a more benign world later in the process of social evolution. Others, such as the industrialist Andrew Carnegie, offered immediate relief: society's fittest would channel their surplus into philanthropies that guaranteed the greatest good to the greatest number. But William Graham Sumner, a giant among these men, kept the faith pure. Besides demolishing all half-hearted adherents—humanitarians, protectionists, imperialists—who would bend the theory out of pity or ambition, he contributed in *Folkways* (1907) a brilliant explanation of how the gummy weight of custom and habit held society to an imperceptibly gradual progress.

Not even Sumner avoided a second anomaly that increasingly crept into the classical theory. More and more subject to attack after the mid-eighties, its proponents responded by emphasizing the system's fragility rather than its strength. If a handful of unions exacted wages beyond the allotted fund, they would drive capital in unnatural directions and stop all progress; if government assisted weak enterprise at the expense of the strong, it would jam the delicate mechanisms of trade; or if philanthropy coddled the poor, supporting dishonorable men and corrupting honorable ones, it would reverse the evolution of the race. The slightest deviation, in other words, might overturn the entire structure. By imputing such power to a few errant men, the theorists mocked the grandeur of their own fundamental laws.

An amalgam of many ideas, the classical theory owed its largest debt to the economists in the school of Adam Smith, particularly David Ricardo. Charles Darwin's evolutionary hypothesis, refracted in the writings of Herbert Spencer, gave powerful authority to the economists' world of pure competition and, more important, supplied a sense of growth and collective improvement that progress-minded Americans had missed in Smith and his followers. Still, the heyday of social evolution was several years away, and the theory's exponents made it as much a part of Newton's mechanical world as of Darwin's organic one. When the economist David A. Wells called the coinage of silver "a violation of the natural laws of supply and demand, and an attempt to provide for the survival of the unfittest," he demonstrated how easily Darwinian rhetoric could echo the hallowed principles of economics. Most important, the theory, for all of its harsh qualities, drew upon a rich tradition of village values. Equal opportunity for each man; a test of individual merit; wealth as a reward for virtue; credit for hard work, frugality, and dedication; a premium upon efficiency; a government that minded its own business; a belief in society's progressive improvement; these and many more read like a catalogue of mid-nineteenth-century virtues.

The mores of the town set within a simple, yet scientific frame: that proved a formidable combination to challenge. Still, the classical theory seemed to systematize rather than resolve the very contradictions between values and practice that were bedeviling so many Americans. Consequently the first group of opponents, who had gathered in numbers by the mid-eighties, launched their criticisms by pointing to the obvious. Irrefutable proof lay at every hand, they claimed, of brutal developments which instead of condemning, the current theory condoned. Believing in an imminent cataclysm, they argued that the same evidence demonstrated great changes occurring now, not after a thousand years of gradual evolution. Yet whatever their emotional leanings, their reasoning was bound by virtually the same premises as the classical theory. Unable or unwilling to destroy it as a piece, they sought some loophole that would allow American society to make its sudden leap into heaven instead of hell.

A few fashioned technical escapes. Henry George, for example, reworked the classical relationship between land on the one hand and capital and entrepreneurship on the other. In *Progress and Poverty* (1879), George explained how all inequities in wealth, power, and privilege stemmed from the right of a few to monopolize the rising value that society as a whole bestowed upon land. The man who had held property next to Fort Dearborn sat in a chair while society created Chicago around his plot and transformed him into a millionaire. If society claimed its own by returning the unearned value on land to all the people, injustice would disappear. The correction of this one great flaw, George believed, would bring social progress into concert with nature's laws.

Others escaped through transcendental means. Without George's daring or his skill in economics, the Reverend Washington Gladden, a founder of the Protestant Social Gospel, remained even more tightly strapped within the classical theory. He stood in awe of the traditional economic laws, praised Herbert Spencer's ethics, and predicted disaster if the government interfered further in society's operations. Yet what he saw did distress him greatly. "Competition," he wrote in *Applied Christianity* (1885), "is of the nature of warfare," and warfare, brutalizing all participants, devastated the moral order. Unable to find even that one crack which freed George, Gladden had no choice but to step outside the system, leaving it intact behind him. Especially upset by the barbaric struggles between organized labor and capital, he called upon employers to rediscover Christ's law and, without tampering with the wages-fund or vitiating character through charity, take their employees as brothers into a partnership which shared both adversity and prosperity. In the same fashion, without a technical answer to monopoly, he advocated a boycott against gifts of its "tainted money." The grand solvents of love and brotherhood would quickly usher in a new Christian age.

Still others simply concentrated upon rereading the evidence. What Gladden would insert from the outside, Edward Bellamy and Henry Demarest Lloyd found latent within the system. Appalled by the viciousness of industrial competition, both men became convinced, as Bellamy wrote in the late eighties, "that the dawn of the new era is already near at hand, and that the full day will swiftly follow." For Bellamy, tomorrow would bring the nationalist state he described in *Looking Backward* (1888), where "the principle of fraternal co-operation . . . the only true science of wealth-production," would receive perfect embodiment in a people's economy supervised by an immaterial government. "The machine which [the government functionaries] direct is indeed a vast one," explained Dr. Leete, Bellamy's spokesman in the novel, "but so logical in its principles and direct and simple in its workings that it all but runs itself. . . ." When "supply is geared to demand like an engine to the governor which regulates its speed," all the waste, inequalities, and corruption of the late nineteenth century would dissolve. Society would have leaped beyond competition into a perfect, self-operating state under pure natural law.

Lloyd, who like Gladden began by calling for a "new conscience" among employers, rapidly moved to the position where he, too, saw a "new order" swelling in hearts across the nation. Although Lloyd never approached the exactness of his associate Bellamy, the contours of his utopia were the familiar ones: cooperation replacing competition, nationalization under an invisible government, a classless society living by the Golden Rule; the reign, in other words, of truly just social laws.

Apocalyptic in vision, perfervid in spirit, and sweepingly moral in rhetoric, these dissenters spoke in the tradition of Protestant evangelism. Although Lloyd and Bellamy had left their churches, they had done so out of the strength, not the weakness, of their convictions. Instead of timid official Protestantism, they demanded, in Lloyd's words, "a church which will worship God . . . through a mediator, Mankind, which, having suffered all and sinned all, can sympathize with all and will carry all the weak and weary ones safe in its bosom." "But 'if we love one another God dwelleth in us,' " quoted Bellamy's Dr. Leete, explaining the arrival of utopia, "and so men found it." When George came to the climax of his message, he discarded the concrete world of economics to preach the application of Christ's law to human affairs.

These men, representing a wide range of Social Gospellers, Christian socialists, and romantic Marxists, addressed themselves to what was widely regarded as the crisis of a moral civilization. Repelled by the dominant characteristics of their day, they gravitated naturally back toward the life of the town, and sometimes in strange disguises, they sought to preserve that world in modern America. An abstracted individual, their social atom, was the ultimate object of salvation. It was he whom George would release from the grip of monopoly and Gladden would lift from beneath big business and big labor. The higher the socialism, Lloyd announced, the freer the individual, a maxim Bellamy transposed into a utopia where everyone automatically lived by the village virtues. Their Christian individual was an upright, property-owning, unobtrusive citizen, the same person, in fact, whom William Graham Sumner courted as "the forgotten man." To a cautious rebel like Gladden, such an emphasis came easily, but even an apparent radical like Lloyd agreed. When utopia arrives, he said, "it will be the middle class that will survive and will furnish the human material for the new order."

Despite the considerable skill such men as George and Lloyd demonstrated in analyzing particulars, the broad vision clearly dominated their thought. Means mattered very little. Even

George made no substantial effort to relate his economic reforms to his Christian end. When Bellamy was asked how to accomplish the Nationalist program, he replied that society should nationalize first one thing and then another and then another. The process that he described as "a melting and flowing forth of men's hearts toward one another, a rush of contrite, repentant tenderness, an impassioned impulse of mutual love and self-devotion to the common weal" defied more precise explanation. Basically all of these theorists offered a feeling, an ethic, and a hope.

As the sense of crisis waned late in the nineties, so did the impulse toward this particular variety of utopianism, and at the very end of the century another group of critics collected for a final attack inside the classical framework. More learned, more catholic in their interests, and more sophisticated as theorists than a George or a Bellamy, they tended to speak as self-conscious specialists, one to the other. None wrote a bestseller to match *Progress and Poverty* or *Looking Backward*. Their theories culminated and combined two of the most important themes in late-nineteenth-century social thought, biological organicism and philosophical idealism. Although they repudiated Spencer's literal application of such Darwinian rules as the struggle for survival, they were captivated by their own more general biological orientation. "Since all organic cohesion is conditioned by growth," the sociologist Franklin H. Giddings explained, "a policy of ceaseless activity is necessary . . . [for] any political cooperation." "Cities have personalities just as men have," said the urban reformer Brand Whitlock, and so did groups, races, states, and nations. Seeking a new social science in Europe, these specialists had in the process brought back a great deal from the philosophies of Georg Hegel and Auguste Comte, ideas reinforcing their belief that social units possessed a separate, independent existence.

The major theme in this phase of dissent was an historically rooted sense of progress by stages. Blending organicism and idealism, these theorists described how society as an entity had evolved step by step from lower, simpler forms to higher and more complex ones. In each succeeding stage Intellect, or Rationality, exercised greater dominance over the material, an Idea came increasingly to control the involvements of the workaday world. Emphasizing society's life apart, they almost always capitalized their basic terms. Certain in their own way that great things were near at hand, they pictured progress as an ever accelerating movement. Advanced industrial societies were marching through the last stages to a final goal inherent in and predetermined by the process of social evolution itself.

Although descriptions of this orderly progress varied in form, their substance remained constant. In *Dynamic Sociology* (1883), the pioneer Lester F. Ward analyzed society's evolution in four stages. Following the anarchic conditions of natural man, society formed loose aggregates, then congealed into national states, and finally achieved universal integration. In the penultimate stage the state was assigned extensive powers in order to prepare society's collective intelligence for the arrival of world unity. The theory of another pioneer, the economist Richard Ely, required seven steps, with society currently hurrying through the fifth and sixth, industrial competition and industrial concentration, to reach its destiny in industrial integration, essentially a Christian cooperative commonwealth.

The most popular number, however, was three, perhaps because Comte had discovered that many stages over half a century before. Around 1900 Simon Nelson Patten explained how society, after a long history under a scarcity or Pain Economy, had recently achieved a surplus or Pleasure Economy. As soon as race intelligence caught up with economic progress, society would pass to its climax of self-direction, cooperation, and altruism in the Creative Economy. An articulate group of urban reformers, represented by Frederic Howe, also discovered three steps in the evolution toward the Free City of Free Men: an initial state of growth and exploitation, then the struggle over such specific reforms as home rule and the municipal ownership of transportation, and finally emancipation through a collective city sense. Typically, Howe found the signs in 1905 extremely encouraging:

"Democracy, rather than class or business interest, is becoming intellectually organized." "When within this [urban aggregation]," he continued, "out of its common interest and common need, conscience is born and responsibility awakened; when will power and intelligence are civic forces, focussing on a united purpose and a definite ideal; when in addition to self-consciousness and family-consciousness there arises a city consciousness . . . then . . . does the city spring to life."

During these same years Henry Adams, whose exquisite disillusionment would charm a later generation, and his brother Brooks, whose blunt catastrophism impressed his own, privately fashioned from these same materials an anti-utopia that sent society to its doom as it diffused energy at an accelerating rate and ultimately disintegrated.

Superficially far freer of classical theory than the utopianists who preceded them, these advocates of a predetermined progress actually remained well within its bounds. Surveying the field of Herbert Spencer's critics, Thorstein Veblen shrewdly remarked, "[They] stand on his shoulders and beat him about the ears." By their emphasis upon biological organicism, they infused much more forward movement into their systems, which Ward and Patten proudly called "dynamic" in contrast to the "static" classical theory. But they mistook differences in speed for differences in kind. The sociologist Edward A. Ross, who told Anglo-Saxons to stop blaming each other as individuals for the sins of social custom, deviated from the basic principles in *Folkways* only to the extent that he believed custom could evolve rapidly and Sumner did not.

As specialists, many of these theorists enjoyed greater success when they attacked those portions of the classical theory which fell within their particular province. Patten, an especially talented critic, adapted the law of supply and demand to include the altered values such goods as cardboard and corn flakes or cigarettes and Sen Sen acquired in combination and in the process assigned a new significance to the consumer. Yet among his many debts to classical theory, he retained the imaginative entrepreneur directing social progress as duller workers organized behind him; and much like Ross, he broke the bonds of "Social Heredity" only by assuming it had a beneficent destiny. Giddings, who contributed fresh ideas to social psychology, experienced as much difficulty as Washington Gladden in explaining how laborers might benefit beyond the iron law of wages. Each pushed an arm, and no more, through the wall.

In certain respects, these idealists bore an even closer resemblance to the utopianists of the eighties. Indeed, at certain points the groups merged. When the evangelist Walter Rauschenbusch, in *Christianity and the Social Crisis* (1907), described the stages of evolution that had brought society to the verge of Christ's commonwealth, he stood so close to Lloyd that no set of categories could possibly separate them. Yet if a common territory lay between these approaches, important differences in orientation, spirit, and method still held most in the two camps apart. The idealists' feeling for history was at the same time a sense of development, an appreciation for stately change, which the now-this, then-that conception of the earlier utopianists utterly lacked. Relatively unaffected by the emotional crisis of the late eighties and early nineties that had overcome such men as Gladden, Bellamy, and Lloyd, the idealists were much more moderate in tone. Although they, too, heralded a bright new day, they pictured it emerging naturally, almost gracefully, in a happy grandeur. The earlier image of God's world bursting from the rubble of conflict was foreign to all but a very few like Rauschenbusch.

The most significant difference in the long run concerned modes of analysis. A flexible multicausation now replaced the tight single causation of Gladden's new conscience or George's single tax. The idealists were genial eclectics, welcoming all manner of explanations for the ways of their everyday world and bundling them together with little regard for consistency. In Frederic Howe's hands, for example, the single tax joined dozens of other solutions in a conglomerate of cures for the city's ills. These theorists, who showed a renewed respect for inductive analysis, cared deeply about solving the specific problems of their time. Perhaps they never reconciled a highly variable, shifting analysis of the particular with a rigidly organic conception of the whole society. Perhaps they accepted ideas indiscriminately. Nevertheless, these very qualities made room for a new interest in contingencies and relationships.

In part their involvement with daily problems proceeded from a belief that man in the higher stages of social evolution could control his own progress, an assumption that caught them in a dilemma they never resolved. Vaguely they argued that as evolution lifted social intelligence, it raised man's abilities to the level of conscious power over himself and his environment. But they never reconciled human control with a predetermined progress. How could man's mind affect social movements that were tied by their very nature to a particular destiny? Teleological theory produced another contradiction as well: how did arrival at the ultimate stage—the Christian Commonwealth, the Creative Economy, the Free City—magically release men from the laws of growth and change, the previously binding rules of an organic evolution? The same theorists who gave social development an impressive historical dimension envisioned a day when men would miraculously step outside of history.

These philosophical problems might have remained only curiosities for the specialist except for the extensive influence analysis by stages exercised over all of their thought. To these men stages were far more than a convenient device. They represented a cast of mind, an inclusive orientation, which in large measure became their prison. Development in stages was the social law, and each man found his bearings through it. That law explained where society was at a particular time, what specific events meant, what men should do, and where their actions would take them. But what happened when society failed to abide by the rules? What if it changed in another direction, in ways totally unanticipated in the idealist's system? His scheme could not encompass movements sideways or backwards, and his commitment to one pattern, by which he understood his world, denied him the right to alter those stages so that they suited novel circumstances. Always threatening, this trap grew especially dangerous as the theorist felt that final step at hand, the purpose of centuries of evolution almost fulfilled. A wrong turn here might topple the entire structure. An approach for sunny days, it left its adherents peculiarly defenseless before such a debacle as the First World War.

Perhaps it was providential, then, that this system also proved vulnerable in another, quite different respect. Eclecticism, as it turned out, was an invitation to subversion. The idealists, so confident of their ability to attach almost any particular explanation to their conception of progress, increasingly adopted a new and interrelated set of ideas which in time combined to form an alternative to the very foundations of their, or any other, system. This, in sum, did constitute an intellectual revolution. Certain they had launched a victorious assault on the classical theory, the idealists contributed to its defeat largely by leaving their own rear unguarded.

The ideas that filtered through and eventually took the fort were bureaucratic ones, peculiarly suited to the fluidity and impersonality of an urban-industrial world. They pictured a society of ceaselessly interacting members and concentrated upon adjustments within it. Although they included rules and principles of human behavior, these necessarily had an indeterminate quality because perpetual interaction was itself indeterminate. No matter how clear the evidence of the present, a society in flux always contained that irreducible element of contingency, and predictability really meant probability. Thus the rules, resembling orientations much more than laws, stressed techniques of constant watchfulness and mechanisms of continuous management.

Gone were the constructs of philosophical idealism. The bureaucratic approach had no use for stages of social development or collective intelligence, and its exponents spelled their terms with small letters. Of particular importance, institutions ceased to live apart from the human beings who comprised them. The political state, independently alive and occasionally exalted by the idealists, now acquired meaning only as a mode of human behavior, and cities no longer had personalities. Labor and capital, fuzzy entities in earlier systems, rarely appeared in bureaucratic analysis. When they did, they designated definite groups of employees and employers who could, if necessary, be seen, felt, measured, and weighed. The Labor Question and such counterparts as the Immigrant Problem and the Money Issue had enabled men like Washington Gladden to ask the inclusive questions and supply the inclusive answers. The idealists had then transformed them into detached essences; the Race Question, for example, always had a separate existence. Bureaucratic thought pared all of these back to their human components and subdivided them into recognizable, everyday problems.

Gone also was the commitment to biological evolution with its interminable organic analogies. Even the historical dimension largely disappeared, leaving just enough of the past to provide a running start into the present. In place of the organic images, bureaucratic analysis preferred mechanical ones, though they were markedly different from those in vogue before Darwin. Instead of likening society to a clock's simple gears in perpetual motion, men were now thinking in terms of a complex social technology, of a mechanized and systematized factory. The later analogies had the fluidity of calculus, not the order and balance of plane geometry. Once social change could be expressed by a single line—the imperceptibly rising one of Sumner, the sharply angled one of Bellamy, or the rapidly inclining one of Patten. Now change was interaction and adjustment, forming elaborate and shifting multilinear patterns.

On the surface, bureaucratic ideas continued the reign of traditional village values. The new orientation actually seemed to revitalize the ways of the town after idealism had partially submerged them. Once again frugality, promptness, foresight, efficiency, and many more familiar virtues sat enthroned within a system. But the morals of the farm town had moved to the industrial city. Generations of Americans, for example, had honored efficiency as know-how or Yankee ingenuity or the better mousetrap. In this sense efficiency had referred to an individual, concrete solution. Now it meant an approach to a fluid social process. In fact, the self-sufficient farmer, that jack-of-all-trades, began to appear more a relic than an ideal citizen. Gradually, haltingly, the bureaucratic sense was transforming yeoman into yokel.

"Science," the basic word that every school of thought claimed and worshipped, also altered in meaning to accommodate the revolution. In all varieties of classical theory, science referred to a grand design whose fundamental principles men could comprehend and apply. If the idealists showed a new respect for minute investigation, they eventually subordinated their findings to the laws of a broad social evolution. Bureaucratic thought, on the contrary, made "science" practically synonymous with "scientific method." Science had become a procedure, or an orientation, rather than a body of results. When it still did connote exact truths, it referred to something very specific—the doctor's microbe—not to the laws of a world order.

The changing implications of statistics illustrated this transformation. When Carroll D. Wright, whose social views approximated those of Washington Gladden, became America's first commissioner of labor statistics in 1873, he had expected to complete his work in one great investigation. He would gather all pertinent data and retire. Even afterwards he had defined his task as the intensive illumination of single problems. Then around 1900 a younger generation replaced Wright's, abandoned the isolated studies of select issues, and substituted a continuous flow of statistics covering a wider and wider range of subjects. The meaning of data had fundamentally changed. Earlier theorists had examined society assuming an infinite number of one-to-one relationships: a cause produced an effect, a law covered an action, a reform led to a result. Now society was "a vast tissue of reciprocal activity . . . all interwoven to such a degree that you see different systems according to the point of view you take." If, as the political scientist Arthur F. Bentley wrote, "no group has meaning except in its relations to other groups," if all groups "move forward by their interactions, and in general are in a state of continuous pressure upon one another," then cause-and-effect relationships would be as intermingled and as fluid as society itself. That would require a radically new approach to social analysis.

Just as pronounced a shift occurred in the treatment of human personality. From the original classical theorists through the idealists the individual was described in terms of inherent and competing faculties. Herbert Spencer had called them Egoism and Altruism; Gladden rephrased them as self-love and benevolence. The challenge each theorist faced was how to encourage the good faculties and not the bad. "Human nature has antagonistic elements," said Patten, "and the natural man is buffeted about and often destroyed by opposing forces springing from his inner self. . . . Virtue is real; but so is sin. To strengthen the one and to weaken the other is the source of all progress. . . ." Despite some borrowing from recent European philosophy, faculty psychology as Americans employed it was rooted fundamentally in the Christian tradition of God and the Devil struggling for man's soul. Spreading from psychology throughout social theory, these dualisms—competition versus cooperation, want versus plenty, the material versus the intellect—diffused a religious aura over the whole. Gladden simply made a host of major premises explicit when he declared, "Jesus Christ knew a great deal more about organizing society than David Ricardo ever dreamed of knowing."

The bureaucratic orientation did more than sweep away faculty psychology and its Christian dualism; it obliterated the inner man. The focus had shifted from essences to actions. The new ideas concerned what men were doing and how they did it. As Arthur Bentley said, the individual was meaningless as a unit for investigation; only men's social behavior deserved analysis. Along with faculty psychology went most of the involvement with heredity and race. Public education reflected the changing psychology rather promptly. From anywhere inside the classical system, education meant mental discipline. Schools should train the good faculties, give them muscle in their fight against the bad. Now education implied the guidance of behavior in harmony with social processes. If destruction of the faculties eventually cleared the way for modern psychology, its most immediate beneficiary was social engineering.

Arriving around 1900 and gaining momentum after 1910, the bureaucratic orientation did not reach its peak of success until the nineteen twenties. Partly because its climax lay in the future, partly because its ideas lent themselves to piecemeal adoption, the bureaucratic revolution came rather quietly, almost surreptitiously, in the years before the First World War, with very few clear-voiced champions. Consequently, its influence often appeared first in shadows and corners, as the shifting emphasis within almost every significant social movement demonstrated. In the mid-nineties, the National Municipal League promised that the application of a few elementary rules would enable "good citizens" to elect honest men and pass "good laws"; a few years later their rules had become encased in a fairly elaborate administrative apparatus; by 1915 the League concluded that an even more detailed program for expert government could not "in and of itself produce good results. The most that any plan can do is to provide an organization which lends itself to efficient action. . . ." By degrees the philosophy of urban political reform had moved from simple moral principles guaranteed by the proper forms of government to complex procedural principles advanced by the proper administration of government. Over the same years, other civic reformers gradually replaced the City Beautiful, balanced and orderly, with the goal of the City Useful, harnessing energies to serve fluctuating needs. Here as elsewhere, the word "plan," which had once referred to a complete and fixed program, came to mean an hypothesis and an approach.

A similar transformation occurred in social work. The original settlement workers had entered the slums and served the poor as moral acts. Over time, as the careers of such people as Jane Addams and Lillian Wald illustrated, they became increasingly immersed in the endless, interrelated problems of a whole city's life. By the war many settlements had grown into centers of efficient procedure and expert management. Casework in the nineties had meant a personal concern for an individual's spiritual and material elevation; two decades later it meant the scientific analysis of a life in process. In the same way, philanthropy had also concentrated upon the act, the gift to a good cause; then the arrival of foundation philanthropy presaged the shift toward a continuous application of funds for less determinate objectives.

Concepts of the law underwent a comparable, if more complicated transition. In place of fixed rules in the spirit of Newton, Oliver Wendell Holmes, Jr., offered the alternative of an organic law, evolving in general concert with social custom. The insertion of growth alone, however, did not essentially modify the traditional majesty of the law. A sharper, though largely unformulated break came early in the twentieth century with a variety of attempts to gear law to indeterminate process. The most successful was the growing body of administrative law, a direct response to the government's new discretionary powers. In the same vein, the faint introduction of "sociological jurisprudence," which would adjust legal decisions to inductive, social evidence; the establishment of specialized juvenile and domestic courts, as much involved in counselling and mediating as in pronouncing law; the classification and differential handling of criminals; and the development of probation for adults as well as juveniles; all bent the law toward an adjustment to contingencies.

The new social sciences, obsessed with teleological thought at the turn of the century, also migrated slowly toward bureaucratic ideas. In a witty, opinionated book, *The Process of Government* (1908), Arthur Bentley presented all disciplines with a model of bureaucratic analysis that stripped every vestige of philosophical idealism from the study of fluid group interaction. Charles A. Beard offered more popular versions of the same approach. By the war, members of the "Chicago School" of sociology had developed stray ideas from earlier writings into their own version of indeterminate group relations. John B. Watson, the father of

American behaviorism, proclaimed the revolt of the psychologists in 1913. Positing little more inside the individual than an elementary box to manage stimulus and response, Watson would investigate men's actions to discover a "purely objective" method for the "control of behavior."

Another young specialty, scientific management, had been born in the midst of modern industrial complexity. First systematized by the engineer Frederick W. Taylor in the nineties, it sought the largest output from workers with the least waste and cost. Still, as Taylor conceived it, scientific management was an interlocked pattern of rigid rules, laws for the world of the factory. Not until the eve of the war did a new generation introduce major revisions. Then under the guidance of Robert G. Valentine, the emphasis began shifting from laws to orientations, from efficient rules for individuals to efficient attitudes among groups, and from a superimposed system to arrangements developed according to the requirements of a particular factory.

Even pragmatism, which at first glance looked like the perfect philosophical rationale for bureaucratic thought, underwent significant changes before it joined with the new approach. A revolt in its own right from idealism, pragmatism, like scientific management, carried relatively little traditional baggage. By treating truth as a process instead of an essence, and knowledge as the continual testing of hypotheses against life's facts instead of the inculcation of fixed truths, it seemed to offer just the fluidity required by the new orientation. Yet the pragmatism of William James, its great exponent, bore only a loose relationship to bureaucratic ideas. As an introspective person sensitive to man's private needs, James was primarily concerned with the individual's psychic state, not his social adjustment; and as an aristocrat, he obviously favored the exceptional individual at that. Bureaucratic thought and pragmatism met only after John Dewey had transformed it into a theory that made individuals the plastic stuff of society.

Dewey might have been the great spokesman whom bureaucratic thought so badly needed except for an abiding commitment to the goals of idealism. A theorist of great power and scope, he made important contributions to subjects ranging from epistemology to education. He despised all dualisms, particularly those justifying instruction by drill, as if learning were a form of calisthenics; and he fought all superstitions, particularly those implying man's helplessness before an incomprehensible universe. Throughout his writings ran a limitless faith in the scientific method as the means for freeing people of all ages to learn through exploration and through social experience. One day, he believed, that freedom would create a pure, rational democracy. In fact, Dewey's vision was so clear and so simple in its fundamentals it could not accommodate the endless group interplay, the contingencies, the perpetual management, that lay at the heart of the bureaucratic approach. His ideas formed a completed, unitary system more congenial to Hegelian idealism than to the pluralistic, fluctuating harmonies of bureaucratic thought.

Aside from a few relative unknowns such as Arthur Bentley, the men of the early twentieth century duplicated this same general pattern of engrafting new ideas upon old. No one would have cared to say then, and no one is able to tell now, how at a given time these competing, intermingling ideas balanced against each other. If the bureaucratic approach eventually prevailed, that was a matter for the future. After predicting an ultimate stage for urban reform in 1915, Benjamin De Witt then wrote, "There is no panacea for municipal ills . . . [and] any attempt to remove inefficiency and waste must be continuous." Jane Addams could smile in 1910 at the earlier furor over "tainted money" and talk knowingly about administrative efficiency, yet she still discussed "the social question" and anticipated with other settlement workers the coming "nationalization of good." Louis D. Brandeis, lawyer and Justice of the Supreme Court, whose career in so many ways exemplified a new bureaucratic professionalism, experimented in sociological law, flexible business regulation, and scientific management without taking his eyes from a utopia of rational individuals competing through small political and economic units. Gifford Pinchot, who directed bureaucratic programs for the management of the public domain, continued to view his world in clear and simple moral terms. Speaking for most of his colleagues as well, he declared that "the Conservation question is a question of right and wrong," democracy and privilege, the people and the interests, God and the Devil.

Although Thorstein Veblen, the most brilliant mind of his time, seldom spoke for anyone other than himself, his intellectual wanderings provide one more example of how men of this era often thought in strange theoretical combinations. Early in life he fixed his gaze upon a society where individuals enjoyed a healthy, sensitive relationship with their work, and he never relinquished the vision. Calling that relationship the instinct of workmanship and exalting it as the ethical basis for society, he inclined late in the nineteenth century toward some form of preindustrial paradise. But Veblen's own scientific talents led him to discover great potentialities in modern industrial society. Elevating the scientific method as the means to his end, he substituted the engineer —bureaucracy's perfect symbol—for the cottage spinner as tomorrow's hope. In a grand effort to preserve daily human satisfactions in an evolving, impersonal world, he dreamed of a self-operating utopia where dispassionate, expert engineers would oversee a society of individuals comprehending and loving their work. Natural law, instinct psychology, organicism, teleology, and bureaucracy competed and coalesced in his private answer to a variety of modern civilization's basic problems.

The new middle class supplied the largest body of adherents to bureaucratic thought. Leaders in a major social reorganization, these men and women required values suitable to their new sense of location. More simply, they were the ones who thought that way. From an urban vantage point, they quite literally saw that impersonal life in flux which they could understand most readily as the interaction of groups—theirs relating with others. In the city people daily felt the need for continuity and regularity. These were the natural values of the trade associations and somewhat later of the craft unions as well. Experts in administration supported by a variety of professionals sought solutions to the city's problems through proper procedures and continuous enforcement, rather than by simple, self-fulfilling rules. These same professionals naturally conceived of science as a method for their disciplines instead of a set of universal principles. Relaxed in each other's company, they helped to limit the appeal of the new values by smothering them in a private, technical language that only confused their larger audience.

The sanguine followers of the bureaucratic way constructed their world on a comfortable set of assumptions. While they shaded many of the old moral absolutes, they still thought in terms of normal and abnormal. Rationality and peace, decent living conditions and equal opportunity, they considered "natural"; passion and violence, slums and deprivation, were "unnatural." Knowledge, they were convinced, was power, specifically the power to guide men into the future. Consequently, these hopeful people also exposed themselves to the shock of bloody catastrophe. In contrast to the predetermined stages of the idealists, however, bureaucratic thought had made indeterminate process central to its approach. Presupposing the unexpected, its adherents were most resilient just where the idealists were most brittle.

An even more serious weakness than this deceptive optimism was a failure to explain precisely what they sought in these all-important social processes. It was not that the exponents of bureaucratic thought sacrificed ends to means but that they merged what customarily had been regarded as ends and means into a single, continuous stream, then failed to provide a clear rationale for the amalgam. Endless talk of order and efficiency, endless analogies between society and well-oiled machinery, never in themselves supplied an answer. Instead of careful definitions, they offered only tendencies.

Among these, two assumed the greatest importance. One explained process through human consent and human welfare: adjust interactions according to the wishes and needs of the people involved. That spirit informed significant sections of urban reform, social work, and progressive education, and even a portion of scientific management. The second construed process in terms of economy: regulate society's movements to produce maximum returns for a minimum outlay of time and effort; to get, in other words, the most for your money. Touching almost every area, this view appealed particularly to business, labor, and agricultural organizations, and to a large majority of professional administrators. Which of the two, what blend of the two, or what alternative to them would predominate not only lay in the future but was actually irrelevant to the basic weakness itself. By failing to probe the implications of their own ideas, they opened themselves to any number of thoughtless shifts in emphasis. Too often they followed the glittering phrase and the bright hope without testing its substance. In later years some of them would see Benito Mussolini, who made the trains run on time, as a somewhat peremptory democrat.

Close to the center of each theory of change lay the problem of society's cohesion. What held it together as it moved? The original classical theory answered that cohesion came as a by-product of the natural laws. Entrepreneurial genius, self-interest, and habit combined to integrate any society that was abiding by fundamental principles. Yet in the face of actual conflict, its advocates could only threaten greater wreckage as an incentive to unite. Nothing guaranteed cohesion. A society could always commit suicide, it seemed, if its members chose. The utopianism of such men as Henry Demarest Lloyd and Washington Gladden emerged in part to fill the need for a more satisfying solution. Accepting the current signs of disruption, even relishing them in a certain grim fashion, they described an enveloping moral unity to come as the very essence of their visions. In other words, they replaced threat with promise.

As emotions calmed after the mid-nineties, America no longer appeared a savage jungle where prayers went unanswered until tomorrow. Now the nation warranted hope today, and the idealists struck just the right note of considered optimism. Each of their disembodied Ideas—Richard Ely's Christian Commonwealth, Simon Patten's Creative Economy, Frederic Howe's Free City—contained a complete and healthy integration. The closer a society moved to its destiny, the greater control an Idea exercised over its affairs, and consequently the tighter its unity became. America, already well advanced, could anticipate that final stage, "a union of all the people," quite soon.

Through the use of natural laws and the concepts of idealism, all of these theories ultimately explained cohesion by way of some agency apart from men's lives. Bureaucratic thought, on the contrary, attempted to resolve the issue exclusively from within. Most simply, it predicated unity upon a perfect meshing of society's parts, a frictionless operation analogous to the factory under a pure scientific management. In a certain sense, bureaucratic thought reverted to the visions of the original classical theory, substituting an internally derived dynamic—a social process—for the externally justified balance of a John Fiske or a William Graham Sumner. Both theories, at least, sought to create unity out of diversity, instead of requiring some form of homogeneity as did an idealist like Lester Ward or a utopianist like Edward Bellamy. In combination, the destruction of those comforting outside forces and the acknowledgment of society's inevitable pluralism raised difficulties that would plague bureaucratic thought for years to come. Whenever general anxieties rose across the nation, followers of the bureaucratic way had to turn for help to one of several traditional techniques for achieving tighter cohesion.

One of these time-honored devices was exclusion: draw a line around the good society and dismiss the remainder. Just as the defenders of the community and the men of power late in the nineteenth century each had denied their enemies a place in the true America, so worried people in the twentieth also separated the legitimate from the illegitimate. The most elaborate method —a compound of biology, pseudo-science, and hyperactive imaginations—divided the people of the world by race and located each group along a value scale according to its distinctive, inherent characteristics. Those alternately called Anglo-Saxon or Teutonic or Nordic always rested at the top. Bristling with the language of the laboratory, such doctrines impressed an era so respectful of science. At the same time, they remained loose enough to cover almost any choice of outcasts: one could discard all new immigration as "refuse of the murder breed of Southern Europe," all slum dwellers as "degenerate," all Jews as congenitally treacherous, all people of yellow, brown, or black skin as innately inferior. Even in the more moderate guise of eugenics, or selective breeding, racism was used to shut out those who did not belong, not to improve those who did.

A more charitable tradition held out the possibilities of assimilation, a prospect better suited to the temper of the early twentieth century. Where the spokesmen for respectability in the late nineteenth century had usually claimed that only a worthy elite should rule, their reform-minded successors in the twentieth increasingly insisted that all should be made worthy enough to rule. Education of many kinds came to assume an exceptional importance. Although the significance of imparting morality through the schools had not been lost on such men as Gladden and Josiah Strong, public education for them was largely a holding operation until other great forces could transform society. Idealists like Ward and Giddings were the first to assign the schools a central role. Through a curriculum rich in civics and through classes for adults as well as children, immigrants as well as natives, the schools would facilitate the arrival of Social Rationality, preparing the nation for a higher civilization. Nor did instruction end in the classroom. Patten exhorted social workers to educate the poor, the social worker Peter Roberts urged trade unions to educate the immigrants, and Ward expected the State to educate everybody. Within their own framework, those of a bureaucratic persuasion carried on the passionate crusade. In fact, an uncritical faith in "education" almost matched the devotion for "science," with which it was closely identified, and extraordinary hopes for an alert and informed citizenry were invested in its promise.

Yet these traditional supports alone simply did not suffice.

Theoretical racism remained basically uncongenial to bureaucratic thought, and education in the abstract offered little comfort. Exponents of bureaucratic thought felt obligated to find a
more emotionally satisfying bond among all citizens. They required a mundane common denominator that in its own way
would draw a diverse nation together as neatly as natural law
had. Deeply impressed by America's economic productivity, a
number of them sought the answer within a context of abundance. Their fascination with the processes of an urban economy
led them naturally to the distribution of goods and from there to
the consumer. Here, announced such men as Walter Weyl and
Walter Lippmann, was a primary function for the citizens of a
bountiful society, a singularly American source of consciousness
that in turn would underwrite its common action. But they
seemed at a loss to know how they might use the discovery. It
generated little excitement and even fewer applications. Others
anticipated cohesion through a common rationality, an idea
drawn from everyday life rather than an Idea attached from
above. But the scientific method as the nation's popular philosophy merely brought them back to the same fluid, indeterminate
order with which they had started.

Out of a continuing frustration, bureaucratic theorists indulged
in an odd assortment of ruminations about the bases of a man's
life, those bedrock fundamentals which would surely explain
society's underlying unity. Some tried a tame version of the
Marxist doctrines concerning men's relationship to the means of
production. A very few welcomed some variant of Freudian
sexuality, although again they could not seem to build upon the
idea. Most often, they returned as if by habit to the land. Without
knowing precisely what they found there or why, they just talked
about it. Despite ample evidence on mechanized agriculture and
abundant harvests, they conceived the countryside in frozen
demographic terms. They joined in the laments over a declining
rural population, over abandoned farms and eroded hillsides. Less
directly, they discussed the "correct" concentration of people in
the center city and applauded plans to ring it with garden

suburbs. In effect, they retained elements from a powerful American tradition—unity through contact with the soil—because they could not do without it.

These many efforts never did resolve the problem of cohesion within a bureaucratic system. That failure in part accounted for the endurance of idealistic thought, whose simple, automatic answers remained the best available to a good number of educated citizens. Cohesion was a basic American issue. Weakness here would encourage men normally inclined toward the new ideas to fall back upon other systems or to adopt harshly coercive methods in any time of troubles, such as the one surrounding the First World War. Meeting little resistance, crisis had a way of twisting their otherwise generous, if patronizing, impulses into the gnarled forms of an enforced patriotism.

Systematic thinkers of all kinds early in the twentieth century gravitated to political theory in an effort to explain what seemed the most pressing problems of their time. Here an immediate heritage offered them practically nothing of value. The economic principles in the original classical theory had relegated government to the role of a small, wasteful necessity. Cooperative utopias such as those of Bellamy and Lloyd had moved the final step and effectively dissolved the government. Less systematically, commentators of all sorts late in the nineteenth century had approved a simple government of moral men whose good sense would keep it out of society's affairs. When the maintenance of order and balance required an occasional intervention, it should act promptly and then withdraw at once. Precise lines of authority separating the branches of government and close limitations surrounding each official task would help preserve these virtues.

A strikingly different conception of government arrived with the new century, a conception that received at least some support from almost every prominent theorist of the time. A few, such as Herbert Croly and Walter Weyl, discussed the new political theory at book length; a great many more, ranging from such enthusiastic reformers as Frederic Howe and Jane Addams to such cautious publicists as Albert Shaw and Benjamin De Witt, explored parts of it in a way that generally presupposed the whole.

A blend of many ideas, the new political theory borrowed its most revolutionary qualities from bureaucratic thought, and the heart of these was continuity. Trained, professional servants would staff a government broadly and continuously involved in society's operations. In order to meet problems as they arose, these officials should hold flexible mandates, ones that perforce would blur the conventional distinctions among executive, legislature, and judiciary. Above them stood the public man, a unique and indispensable leader. Although learned enough to comprehend the details of a modern, specialized government, he was much more than an expert among experts. His vision encompassed the entire nation, his impartiality freed him from all prejudices, and his detached wisdom enabled him to devise an equitable and progressive policy for the whole society. Corps of servants received his general directives and translated them into their particular areas. At the same time, they channelled basic information back to the public man, so that all government activity was ultimately coordinated in his mind. Because he could best determine where and how the government should expand or contract, he should have the broadest discretionary power, including the right to bend unnecessarily rigid constitutional limitations.

As the nation's leader, the public man would be an educator-extraordinary. He bore the greatest responsibility for raising mass intelligence to the level of true public opinion. That, as Franklin Giddings explained, "is rational like-mindedness. . . . Public feeling, public sentiment, the most ardent conviction of belief, may exist with scarcely an admixture of real public opinion. We can derive . . . no assurance that a stable popular government can be maintained in a nation which ceases to be hourly creative of genuine public opinion—the fruit of rational discourse." Thus the very future of democracy rested with the public man's instructional talents. In time, after a "long tutelage in public affairs," the electorate would come to participate directly in certain aspects of government through the initiative, referendum, and recall. The proper use of such mechanisms, however, depended upon the prior existence of that rational public.

The political theorist from 1880 could recognize a good deal of familiar terminology: good men in high office, minimum waste, a rational electorate, civil service, direct democracy, a harmonious, growing society. In a new setting, however, words could play strange tricks. The good men were no longer moral exemplars but leaders of broad power; minimum waste implied a smoothly functioning bureaucracy, not a handful of honest men on low salaries; a rational electorate presupposed the eventual inclusion of all citizens, instead of its restriction to one class; civil service promised increasing government service throughout the nation rather than its further withdrawal; direct democracy no longer replaced the government in Washington, but strengthened it; and the harmonious society, now usually composed of interacting groups instead of isolated individuals, depended upon the government's presence, not its absence.

The theory was immediately and persistently attacked as undemocratic, an accusation that never ceased to sting its defenders. Sensitive to the traditional suspicion of an overweening government, uneasy as they trod so close to elitist rule, they still believed they were only modernizing, not destroying democracy. In fact the theory was not as boldly authoritarian as it sometimes appeared. It assumed, first of all, a frictionless bureaucracy. The theory's advocates were convinced that the process of becoming an expert, of immersing oneself in the scientific method, eradicated petty passions and narrow ambitions, just as it removed faults in reasoning. The product was the perfect bureaucrat, whose flawlessly wired inner box guaranteed precisely accurate responses within his specialty. The latitude he enjoyed in administration existed only because no one could predict the course of a fluid society and the expert would require a freedom sufficient to follow it. At this level, the theory purported to describe government by science, not by men.

Second, the theory also presupposed an ethereal communion

between leaders and citizens. As all citizens became rational, they would naturally arrive at the same general answers. Experts, of course, would always know more in their particular fields, and the public man would always see the whole more clearly; but national rationality would assure consensus on the big issues, the matters of principle. Here the question of who led and who followed became academic. All were moving reasonably, scientifically, in the same direction, with power distributed merely to ensure a smooth, efficient operation of the whole society.

Finally, the entire realm of leadership was left exceptionally vague. All of the theory's exponents envisaged some form of instructions welling up from below and then transmuted, or translated, or transmitted by the government into public policy. Viewed in one way, that left the public man an ominous freedom of action, and his communion with the masses suggested the lockstep of totalitarianism. In another light, however, leaders served as little more than highly intelligent coordinators who responded to all manner of rational public demands, integrated them, and arranged for their fulfillment. In this sense, the public man was chief of a huge bureau of service, bound at one end by the citizen's initiative and at the other by the discipline of science. The theory itself never indicated which way the balance might tip.

In fact, fuzziness in crucial matters constituted its gravest weakness. How could the electorate recognize a public man? Did the government require only one such man or a sizable cadre? However one might interpret the theory, these questions were fundamental. Not only was government inoperative without its public men, but with false leaders the whole system turned into a nightmare. Nevertheless, its spokesmen waited until the public man was in office before acknowledging him. In the end, the public man remained a mystical, self-evident truth, and countless Americans simply made it an article of faith that at the right time he would materialize and lead.

Idealism supplied most of the new theory's superstructure—the philosopher-kings, the rational public, the social consensus. Bureaucratic thought filled the interior—the beautifully functioning administration, the perfect administrative types, the interacting groups, the society in indeterminate process. Many men never accepted any of the theory. Others borrowed only a piece here and there. No candidate ever won high office on such a platform. Yet this revolutionary approach to government, incomplete as it was, eventually dominated the politics of the early twentieth century.

7

Progressivism Arrives

ATTRIBUTING omnipotence to abstractions—the Trust and Wall Street, the Political Machine and the System of Influence— had become a national habit by the end of the nineteenth century. This was the American way of expressing the contrast between a familiar environment and the strange world beyond. In the town, or even in restricted areas of the city, power was personal. Almost any interested citizen could separate the leader from the follower and the partisan from the apathetic. If he cared, he could also discover the men who combined to make the important decisions; and among these, who controlled wealth or votes, who held the strategic posts, and who simply had a reputation for offering wise counsel. With a little more effort, he could probably uncover the men who financed campaigns and something of the privileges they reaped. Never simple, often fluctuating, it was still a manageable pattern, an eminently human network of relations.

As long as Americans were content to operate within that familiar setting, the outside world posed no serious problems. They translated its events into the language of local power, then dismissed them. When they moved into a broader arena, however, they soon found that they could neither see, know, nor even know about the people upon whom they had to depend. The legal framework changed; new groups, some abiding by quite different values, complicated the pattern; and relationships often followed an alien logic. The system was so impersonal, so vast, seemingly without beginning or end.

Some sallied forth and returned, licking their wounds, to stay. But the urge to fight again and again infected ever increasing numbers, particularly those from the new middle class. They demanded the right to pursue their ambitions outward rather than simply to be left alone at home, and that in turn required far-reaching social changes. To improve public health, for example, doctors might insist upon the renovation of an entire city. Some social workers quite literally called for a new American society. Expansionists in business, labor, agriculture, and the professions, in other words, formulated their interests in terms of continuous policies that necessitated regularity and predictability from unseen thousands.

These men and women stood in the forefront of the reforms that had spread across the land by the beginning of the twentieth century. In contrast to the grim defenses of the community only a decade before, these movements were founded in stability. If frustration also drove the new reformers, it was a frustration born of confidence, an impatience with the inertia that slowed their irresistible march to victory. Most of them lived and worked in the midst of modern society and accepting its major thrust drew both their inspiration and their programs from its peculiar traits. Where their predecessors would have destroyed many of urban-industrial America's outstanding characteristics, the new reformers wanted to adapt an existing order to their own ends. They prized their organizations not merely as reflections of an ideal but as sources of everyday strength, and generally they also accepted the organizations that were multiplying about them. Theirs was an unusually open, expansive scheme of reform which took them farther and farther into modern society's hitherto unexamined corners. The challengers of the late nineteenth century had, in almost all instances, sought a single objective—the autonomous community—through sweeping, redundant programs. Their successors sought a great variety of objectives through a technique of reform which they came to believe could resolve each of these problems, and tomorrow's as well. The heart of progressivism was the ambition of the new middle class to fulfill its destiny through bureaucratic means.

The two initial centers of progressive reform were the large cities of the East and Midwest and the predominantly agrarian states of the Midwest and portions of the South. By priority, complexity, and sophistication, the urban wing led the rural. It was in the major cities that a fair number of citizens first gained a sufficient grip upon their lives to look anew at the society around them. Making sense out of this impersonal world had been a slow, painful process that the depression of the nineties had seriously retarded. Those who did find their way emerged with a consuming sense of accomplishment, a conviction that now no challenge could overwhelm them. Later changes would largely appear as more of the same—additional electric trolleys and broader expanses of commuter housing, more modern factories and stronger trade unions, bigger skyscrapers and denser tenement districts. An elusive yet fundamental maturity appeared in the great cities around 1900, with an aggressive, optimistic, new middle class the prime beneficiary.

Urban progressivism originated in these calculated second thoughts. No divine logic designated this place and this time for full-scale reform. If anyone had cared to examine them, county governments were at least as corrupt and incompetent, but their half-hearted renovation awaited the twenties. Rural poverty and disease were just as obvious and as appalling in their setting as slum squalor was in its, but aside from some educational philanthropy and Dr. Charles Stiles' attack upon hookworm few paid them much attention. Moreover, as city officials gained some experience in dealing with metropolitan problems late in the nineteenth century, urban government had gradually grown more efficient and more responsive. At that same steady, unspectacular rate both the government and the privately owned utilities had been expanding, improving, and lowering the costs of their essential services. A change in the quality of perceptions, not in the quantity of unique evils, produced a broad reappraisal of the cities around 1900.

In the larger cities, the hectic period of growth—what Theodore Dreiser called "the furnace stage of [their] existence" when "everything was in the making"—had largely passed, and the heroes of yesterday had become the villains of a more settled era. Once city dwellers had noticed only the presence or absence of a basic service. Now they took its existence for granted and scrutinized the details, grumbling over inconveniences and omissions and shoddy work. Contracts excused or ignored in the panting demand for sewers and fresh water now seemed vicious, and franchise privileges granted out of a confused need for something at once were regarded as nothing less than theft. Some of the critics were the very ones who had promoted the city's helter-skelter growth only a few years before. Many more, however, were rising young men and women who had had no part in the decisions, who had never shared the moon-struck atmosphere surrounding them—and could not comprehend it. They arrived fresh, intolerant, and eager to take hold.

At the center of their discontent lay a fairly simple condition. A patchwork government could no longer manage the range of urban problems with the expertise and economy that articulate citizens now believed they must have. In one of the grand ironies of the era, the reformers described their opposition as a devilishly effective pact between bosses and businessmen which financed the machines and sold public favors on request. Partly in self-delusion and partly in self-defense, they declared that they would destroy that System and, by implication, substitute a natural, individualistic democracy. Of course the urban progressives were the systematizers and their opponents the slovenly, albeit sometimes democratic, governors. The typical business ally of the boss, moreover, was a rather marginal operator anathema to the chamber of commerce. The few important businessmen who did purchase franchises invariably complained of political larceny. Hidden behind the stereotypes, well-to-do merchants, manufacturers, and bankers who sought more dependable and rewarding relations with government were moving in the vanguard of urban reform.

Impatiently dismissing all half-measures, the reformers reached out for the power to reorder the government themselves, and though they fell short, they did accomplish a good deal. In a series of highly publicized struggles involving almost every major city, they extended the scope of utility regulation and sharply limited the privileges and duration of the franchises. Tax assessment, decades out of date and badly skewed in favor of large corporations, was modernized. Completing an older movement to introduce the secret ballot, urban progressives also shortened the ballot, and that, in conjunction with the expansion of government services, increased the number of appointive posts. Reformers were remarkably successful in reserving these positions for specialists, either by broadening the civil service or by private understandings with the city's leading officials. The experts in turn devised rudimentary government budgets, introduced central, audited purchasing, and partially rationalized the structure of offices. Bureaus of research provided endless data on all of these matters as well as the skill for drafting some of the more complex ordinances.

While some reformers were streamlining the government, others entered the slums. Settlement houses multiplied in the new century. Campaigns for public health, originating in the eighties as drives against filth and then broadening into attacks upon particular diseases, developed around 1900 into integrated, citywide programs. Just as naturally, slum life involved the progressives in housing and factory conditions, and that in turn led to new regulations covering both areas. These reformers asked and to a surprising degree received one another's assistance. When a child labor committee brought its bill before the New York legislature in 1903, for instance, an extraordinary collection of settlement workers, union officials, young lawyers, public administrators, and other professionals eagerly gathered to lobby for the measure. With some exceptions, the humanitarian progressives came to form a loose confederation, increasingly aware of the ways their special interests fitted into a common cause.

If humanitarian progressivism had a central theme, it was the child. He united the campaigns for health, education, and a richer city environment, and he dominated much of the interest in labor legislation. Female wage earners—mothers in absentia—received far closer attention than male, movements for industrial safety and workmen's compensation invariably raised the specter of the unprotected young, and child labor laws drew the progressives' unanimous support. The most popular versions of legal and penal reform also emphasized the needs of youth. Something more than sympathy for the helpless, or even the powerful influence of women in this portion of progressivism, explained that intense preoccupation. The child was the carrier of tomorrow's hope whose innocence and freedom made him singularly receptive to education in rational, humane behavior. Protect him, nurture him, and in his manhood he would create that bright new world of the progressives' vision. Here was a dream utterly alien to the late nineteenth century. Instead of molding youth in a slightly improved pattern of their fathers, like cyclically reproducing like, the new reformers thought in terms of fluid progress, a process of growth that demanded constant vigilance.

Whatever the reformer's specialty, his program relied ultimately upon administration. "For two generations," Frederic Howe wrote in 1905, "we have wrought out the most admirable laws and then left the government to run itself. This has been our greatest fault." Now laws established an outline for management, a flexible authority to meet and follow the major issues of urban living. In fact, the fewer laws the better if those few properly empowered the experts, for administration was expected to replace the tedious, haphazard process of legislative compromise. In the regulation of factory conditions, for example, urban progressives spent far less time listing novel rules than perfecting inspection according to the basic ones. Of course discretionary phrasing had long been a common part of legislation. But where the leeway in the New York Housing Act of 1867 served as a sieve through which any agile landlord might escape, the latitude in the New York Health Law of 1913 enabled the state commissioner to manage such matters as quarantines by his personal standards of medical efficiency. Because the reformers viewed organization quite simply as anti-chaos, they conceived their administrative solutions in terms of broad executive mandates, with a mayor holding full general authority and subordinates enjoying virtual autonomy in their limited areas of expertise. The model government formed a simple pyramid free from the cross-checks and intersecting lines of divided responsibility.

Scientific government, the urban reformers believed, would bring opportunity, progress, order, and community. Once emancipated from fear and exploitation, all men would enjoy a fair chance for success. The coarseness, the jagged violence, of city life that so deeply disturbed them would dissolve into a new urban unity, the progressive version of the old community ideal. At first, the urban progressives had expected to transplant village intimacy into the city, either directly through the kind of neighborhood cohesion settlement workers were cultivating or through the "organic city" of brotherhood and compassion, their mystic compromise between the town's face-to-face society and the metropolitan crowds. Early in the twentieth century this goal rapidly lost ground to a very different one predicated upon the assumption that every man, properly educated, would desire a functional, efficient society. The new bureaucratic vision accepted the impersonal flux of the city and anticipated its perfect systematization. When a band of urban progressives went in search of utopia in 1916, they travelled not to a country retreat but to an industrial subdivision of Cincinnati where they tried to build a model for the professionally serviced city. If memories of the friendly village still lingered about the corners of their thoughts, most of them were now dreaming of an urban world that they would control for the benefit of all, a paradise of new-middle-class rationality.

Although many topics of late-nineteenth-century reform reappeared after 1900, most of the old issues had changed beyond recognition. Civil service, for instance, had once been a negative, absolute goal, self-contained and self-fulfilling. Now the panacea of the patrician had given way to the administrative tool of the expert, with efficiency rather than moral purity its objective. The long-standing ambition of urban home rule underwent a comparable metamorphosis. Earlier it had anticipated no more than the removal of outside influence, a simple dream of the uncontaminated community reclaimed. Now it was a precondition for reform. It prepared the laboratory for uninterrupted experimentation. Similarly, the enemies of child labor changed an uncomplicated demand for abolition into a complex social movement. What would become of the emancipated children? The urban progressives advocated nurseries and kindergartens, better schools and tighter attendance laws, recreational facilities and social clubs. Was the child any safer outside the factory? They spread the gospel of personal hygiene and public sanitation, proper diet and prompt inoculation. And what of the child's home environment? Many of them supported adult labor laws and adult education, trade unions and family courts. Perhaps only half-aware of what they were doing, they transformed the sin of child labor into the sin of the unprotected child.

As these changes occurred early in the twentieth century, the industrial centers of the East which had set the pace in almost every area of reform now retraced their steps and modernized their pioneer accomplishments. Massachusetts, for example, which in 1900 had seemed so far advanced in the regulation of industry, was undertaking a general renovation of its reform laws only five years later under Governor Curtis Guild, Jr. Moreover, many of the experiments in the nineties, such as the first purified milk stations and the first campaigns against diphtheria and tuberculosis, had been financed by private funds, a natural extension of nineteenth-century charity reform and obviously unsuitable to the progressive goal of systematic, city-wide coverage. For that the government had to assume responsibility, which it began to do around the turn of the century. The change in orientation among settlement workers illustrated the same process. Dedicated in the nineties to personal service among the poor, they had operated from a most traditional attitude about the private nature of man's improvement. Only as they grew convinced that their ambitions involved a whole society and required a modern government of experts did they become an important part of the new urban progressivism.

Of course the older brands of reform did not suddenly disappear. Just as progressivism was emerging, in fact, a rash of old-fashioned graft prosecutions spread among many of the nation's major cities: Joseph W. Folk, for instance, attacked bosses and bribers in St. Louis, righteous citizens battled an alliance between criminals and city hall in Minneapolis, and Francis J. Heney prosecuted a corrupt triangle of politicians, labor leaders, and businessmen in San Francisco. In a widely read series for *McClure's*, the muckraker Lincoln Steffens described the uprisings as if they were startlingly new phenomena, and to many then and later these moral crusades seemed the finest flower of a new reform. Actually the labors of such men as Folk and Heney lay outside the mainstream of progressivism. With no purpose beyond disclosure and conviction and very little organized support behind them, they captured the headlines, then disappeared.

Divergent types of protest often marched side by side within the same city, especially where someone loosely identified with "reform" gained power. In 1901 a diffuse discontent over greedy traction executives and complacent city councilmen threw out the old crowd in Cleveland. The new mayor, Tom L. Johnson, had gained a fortune manipulating franchises before his conversion to Henry George's single tax, and he was able to fight the traction companies on their own terms for eight exciting years. Reformers of the old school, sweeping and moralistic, collected in and around city hall throughout his tenure. If a group of zealous and well-trained young men had not counselled Johnson, his administration would have accomplished little more than Hazen Pingree's sterile war against the utility "octopus" in Detroit a decade before. Such men as Frederic Howe, Newton D. Baker, and Edward Bemis brought a wealth of new ideas on tax assessment, the treatment of criminals, and rational executive procedures; they even contributed expert knowledge about the regulation of utilities that fell beyond the mayor's experience. Willing to listen and eager to succeed, the unpretentious Johnson allowed his lieutenants to fashion their own programs. Early in the century these amalgams of old and new were the standard content of any reform administration, whose simple, popular slogans—"a three-cent fare for Cleveland"—usually concealed the more substantial changes within.

Actually, reformers never fully controlled the government of a metropolis. The larger the city and the more heterogeneous its life, the looser its power structure. A multiplicity of functions created many independent centers; ethnic differences spawned more. No one group could possibly manage more than a fraction of its political services, and that complexity encouraged ambitious citizens to try their luck in the scramble. A New York or Chicago, impersonal and diffuse, invited competition. At the same time, the problems of consolidation were immense. The very intricacies that produced so many cracks kept the way open to one's enemies as well. In a very rough sense, the power to decide came increasingly to be parcelled along lines of functional specialization. Businessmen who restricted themselves to particular taxes and economic regulations, administrative experts who concentrated upon the government's procedure, doctors who limited themselves to public health, tended to have more and more success, while the men who attempted to combine all of these programs into general policy seldom left a mark on the big city.

In order to compete effectively, members of the new middle class organized to ensure a continuity of influence. Where respectable citizens in the eighties typically had called a conference and passed resolutions, the new breed around 1900 formed associations with long-range policies and delegated one or two officers to act for the entire body. As late as 1894 only Chicago boasted an urban reform league with a paid executive; ten years later comparable associations in every major city employed full-time directors. Although the new professional, business, and labor organizations had some grumbling members and even an occasional palace coup, these scarcely affected the trend. For instance, when the so-called socialist opposition won office in the United Mine Workers and the International Association of Machinists, its leaders, too, shelved their plans for democratic unionism in favor of a centralized command.

As reformers sought to expand their influence, they found two important avenues open before them. Newly self-conscious businessmen offered one. They alone among the prominent progressive groups had the inherent resources—the critical positions in the local economy, the money, and the prestige—to command some sort of response from the government. Weaker reformers, therefore, tried to attach their causes to these men's ambitions, relying upon their need for expert advice and their general sympathy for systematization and order. The boss provided the second avenue. "Professionally [the boss] desires to play his role [as benefactor] in the fullest sense," wrote the settlement worker Robert A. Woods, "and if public improvement or general welfare be part of the tradition he is among the first to catch and hold it." Capable of recognizing when he was beyond his depth, the boss also depended upon the special skills of the new reformers.

It was the expert who benefited most directly from the new framework of politics. The more intricate such fields as the law and the sciences became, the greater the need for men with highly developed skills. The more complex the competition for power, the more organizational leaders relied on experts to decipher and to prescribe. Above all, the more elaborate men's aspirations grew, the greater their dependence upon specialists who could transcribe principles into policy. A chamber of commerce, mobilized and formidable, desired a cleaner, safer, more beautiful, and more economically operated city. Only the professional administrator, the doctor, the social worker, the architect, the economist, could show the way. Knowing that, the chamber's president had to accept at least some of their technical schemes or abandon his goals. By placing a specialist, Lawrence Veiller, in charge of New York City's movement for better housing in 1898, its backers transformed an expensive avocation into an efficient campaign. Meanwhile, professors like Frank Goodnow, Leo Rowe, and Edmund James were telling the National Municipal League what urban reforms it really wanted. For the same reason, legislators faced with such involved problems as utility franchises and factory inspection also came to depend upon the new professionals who as a result proved to be remarkably effective lobbyists. As the definer of general impulses, the expert who timed his entry properly and presented his plans cleverly could become the indispensable man.

Supplementing these primary routes to power, some progressives also used moral suasion to excellent effect. In particular, women of good families such as Jane Addams and Florence Kelley were learning how to shame their contemporaries with surprising results. Rant though they might, men in authority simply could not seal themselves from these voices as they had a generation before from a Terence Powderly or a Henry George. Politicians who would otherwise have turned their backs gave at least token response, and the rich subsidized many a venture that on its own merits would never have appealed to them.

Such a heavy reliance upon other people's good graces meant that many urban progressives functioned under constant pressure. At any moment the very rich might close their checkbooks. The boss would never willingly relinquish any control he deemed essential to his organization's power. The reform-minded businessman, moreover, usually pictured the ideal city as an extension of his commercial values. Desiring continuous services that were also inexpensive, he resented taxes that would take away with one hand the benefits he was just then extracting with the other. His modern city was a business community; a clean, attractive appearance, an atmosphere of growth and progress, raised the general level of the economy. This excluded a great deal that other progressives were urgently seeking, and as dependents they had somehow to show their sponsors that better schools and parks in the slums would produce a more peaceful, industrious citizenry, that higher costs for welfare services would save the taxpayer "in the long run." Tortuous logic brought limited results. By 1905 urban progressives were already separating along two paths. While one group used the language of the budget, boosterism, and social control, the other talked of economic justice, human opportunities, and rehabilitated democracy. Efficiency-as-economy diverged further and further from efficiency-as-social-service.

State progressivism in the industrial East simply rephrased urban problems in the artificial terms of a larger jurisdiction. During the late nineteenth century, the rising metropolitan centers had already come to dominate these states' politics, which often comprised so many responses to the dynamics of their major cities. Progressivism deepened that tradition. In New York, for example, the great victory of the progressive Governor, Charles Evans Hughes, was the creation of a state commission to regulate urban public utilities, particularly those in New York City; and in Ohio the triumph of reform merely relieved the cities of excessive interference from the state legislature.

State governments in the East were certainly not the cordial allies of urban progressivism. By a combination of custom, majority rule, and the gerrymander, they served as rural strongholds where the enemies of the city generally held sway. Assistance came grudgingly and sparingly. When the New York legislature passed measures to regulate urban housing and public utilities, it did so primarily out of upstate Republican antagonism to Tammany Hall. The laws pried the city open to state politicians. Urban home rule succeeded in Ohio largely because a number of country legislators hoped to tip a very close electoral balance in favor of their party. More often, these state governments rejected urban reforms almost as a matter of policy.

In most of the Midwest, South, and Far West, however, state progressivism enjoyed an independent existence. Once again, a new social maturity lay immediately behind the reform movements. Out of the disruptions of the late nineteenth century, a number of men on the farms and in the towns and smaller cities had gradually built stable careers around the new modes of distribution and finance. Slowed by the uncertainties of the late eighties and nineties, they had suddenly found themselves in highly advantageous positions around 1900. They were prospering, and tomorrow's promise now seemed exceptionally bright. These merchants and commercial farmers, bankers and lawyers, promoters and editors—men whose success was rooted in their own areas even as it drew them far into a national society—constituted an indigenous socioeconomic power that their regions had not known in any strength since the full-scale arrival of the railroads. Like the urban progressives, they were taking a calculated second look at the world around them.

Generally younger men with a passion for the future, they manifested much of that same zest and self-confident drive which characterized the urban progressives. Yet by contrast they were quite narrow. Lacking a strong contingent of new professionals, they concentrated upon a relatively few matters of economic policy and political power. The nature of reform in the smaller cities of the Midwest and South provided one excellent illustration of that difference. In these centers of limited function—a commercial way-station, a home for one or two simple industries —a handful controlling its primary business usually monopolized power. Progressivism generally emanated from an influential group of citizens who were just then appreciating the advantages of modernization as an aid to their expanding interests. Implemented with little of the pulling and hauling that attended urban progressivism, their reforms moved far more smoothly to a logical conclusion. In many instances, that meant substituting either a city manager or a set of specialized commissions for the mayor and introducing city-wide, nonpartisan elections to break down all little enclaves of political power. By the First World War about six hundred of these smaller cities had adopted such a system, an utter impossibility in the metropolis, and quite often the local chamber of commerce or its equivalent openly selected the important officials.

Even in a city the size of Memphis, which passed one hundred thousand early in the century, reform followed a similar pattern. A commercial center specializing in the cotton trade, Memphis contained relatively few elements of a complex urban-industrial society. When leading citizens suddenly became dissatisfied with an alliance between city hall and the underworld, they brought in a new mayor, Edward H. Crump, who modernized taxes and rationalized government in a businesslike fashion. If Crump later asserted his independence and outlasted his sponsors, that told much more about his political acumen than it did about the lost opportunities of progressive reform. In a Memphis the sources for social-welfare reform scarcely existed.

That narrowness, which characterized the towns and farms as well as the smaller cities, also stood in marked contrast to late-nineteenth-century reform. Very few of these progressives had looked kindly upon Populism or its near relations. Struggling to secure a place for themselves during the eighties and nineties, they had either avoided such movements or opposed them as a direct threat to their ambitions. Now they replaced the older programs with far more concrete yet subtle proposals which envisaged an administered progress rather than immediate wholesale changes. It was men of this stripe, no less determined and much better organized than their predecessors, who collected about Governors Robert La Follette in Wisconsin, Albert Cummins in Iowa, John Johnson in Minnesota, and Walter Stubbs in Kansas, Braxton Bragg Comer in Alabama, Robert Glenn in North Carolina, and Hoke Smith in Georgia, and somewhat later Hiram Johnson in California, as well as the lesser figures in several other Western and Southern states.

They gathered, but they did not necessarily control. Without the focus of a big city, politics in these states tended toward a diffuse factionalism. Local leaders endlessly jostled each other for petty advantage, and only the skillful manager of loose coalitions held any chance of success. Except for Alabama's Comer, a Birmingham businessman turned politician, each of the important progressive Governors launched his state career as just such a factional chieftain, concentrating initially upon intraparty power rather than upon a specific program. Consequently, even after he had allied himself to certain new-middle-class groups, his campaigns continued to reflect a much broader segment of the state's population. In Wisconsin, for example, La Follette's early margins of victory came from newly assertive Americans a generation removed from Scandinavia who had relatively little at stake in the Governor's progressivism. Cummins of Iowa constructed his first coalition out of Republican antiprohibition sentiment, an issue that bore only tangentially on progressive reform. And Hoke Smith's dependence upon the followers of Tom Watson, now a pathological racist, meant that as Governor of Georgia he would have to mix a large measure of Jim Crow into any plans for reform.

Leadership played an exceptionally important role in the state progressivism of the West and South. The Governors not only had to maintain their coalitions, but they had to do so while directing legislative and administrative programs of unprecedented complexity. The best of them compensated in two ways. They marshalled the reformers to browbeat legislators; and they veiled much of their program with those traditional appeals to localism which still attracted a large if disorganized rural audience. The kings of state progressivism—La Follette, Cummins, and Johnson of California—mastered these managerial and rhetorical techniques with startling results. As Governors they set standards for the nation; and when they moved on in time to the Senate, they still commanded the kind of veneration at home that almost assured re-election. A fumbling leader, on the other hand, such as Stubbs of Kansas or Folk of Missouri only scattered the reformers and stunted his own career.

Not all of the localist rhetoric was a sham. Most members of the new middle class in these agricultural states also felt something of that vague threat which had obsessed the community reformers of the late nineteenth century, and a desire to break the grip of oppressive national forces continued to influence their progressivism. Particularly in the South, where the economic dominance of outsiders was too pervasive for any ambitious man to ignore, the urge for local independence remained a very powerful sentiment indeed. After 1900 the familiar cries to emulate a successful Northern capitalism included a new and stronger emphasis upon Southern control. A younger group of promoters still called for a modern South but one in which they would hold the power. Similar themes, though somewhat more subdued, appeared in the Western movements as well.

Partly from expediency and partly from conviction, therefore, the progressive platforms in the West and South included a good deal of old-fashioned reform. Leaders demanded stern antitrust laws, discriminated in favor of state enterprise in such areas as insurance, and insisted upon rigid rules to restrain the political activities of the large corporations. In several states, moreover, they introduced direct primaries and some version of the initiative, referendum, and recall with all the fanfare of a Populist camp meeting. At the same time, however, they expanded the discretionary power of the executive, copied many of the new techniques for efficient government, stressed the law's continuous implementation, rationalized tax structures, and in many of these matters drew upon the new professional's advice.

In this mingling of old and new, of suspicion and optimism, the new clearly predominated. Railroad regulation, the major issue in state progressivism, illustrated that supremacy. Earlier champions of the community had demanded an arithmetic equality in rates and a flat prohibition against anything hinting at special privilege. They had looked to the legislature for relief. The right laws, often designating exact rates, would ensure right principles. In this conception the regulatory commission had served exclusively as an arm of the legislature, to enforce its laws and to gather its data. In the twentieth century the commission became the master instead of the servant. Once empowered, it operated apart from the legislature, administering rather than enforcing. It was expected to oversee adjustments not only in rates but also in such highly technical matters as storage, transfer, and the general handling of cargo. Business-minded progressives, in other words, expected the commission to act as their agent in an endless series of maneuvers with the railroads. No precise legal wording could possibly have captured their purpose; that required an independent body responding to the flow of circumstances. In the end these commissions accomplished relatively little. Irrelevant to the natural flow of people and goods, the states simply could not manage the major problems of a national economy. Nevertheless, railroad regulation suggested how deeply a new orientation, derived from urban-industrial society and championed by a new middle class, had penetrated the minds of reformers throughout the nation.

Progressivism was the central force in a revolution that fundamentally altered the structure of politics and government early in the twentieth century. In no sense, however, did it monopolize the field. In fact the major corporations tended to move somewhat ahead of the reformers in attempts to extend the range and continuity of their power through bureaucratic means. Most large corporations had spread their nets far more rapidly during the eighties and nineties than their officers could comprehend, let alone manage. Beginning with the railroads, a few companies made an uneven start toward assimilating these gains toward the end of the century. Then around 1900 the rush to reorganize commenced, with one giant firm after another adopting some variant of administrative centralization. An age that assumed an automatic connection between accurate data and rational action naturally emphasized a few leaders linked by simple lines to the staff below. Information would flow upward through the corporate structure, decisions downward. A scheme guaranteed to produce ulcerous executives and evasive underlings, it still represented an important advance in marshalling the corporation's resources for long-range, nationwide policy.

As their interests grew more refined and their need for technical services increased, big businessmen also leaned more and more upon expert assistants. The first to profit from this trend had been a few specialists in corporate and financial law. Then around 1900 they were joined by a great variety of experts. When John D. Rockefeller wanted to do good with his millions, he turned to Frederick T. Gates, a pioneer specialist in spending other people's money, and when he wanted to rehabilitate his reputation, he hired a second pioneer, Ivy Lee, professional in public relations. The magnate no longer relied upon the family friend and the cooperative newspaper editor. In 1901 J. P. Morgan brought a partner into his firm who simply did not care much about stocks, bonds, and mortgages. George W. Perkins—organizer, mediator, publicist, and politician—added a new dimension to one of the nation's major centers of power. As one commentator remarked, Perkins served as "Secretary of State" for a company that had become involved in an increasingly complex set of public and private negotiations.

The political implications of the desire for continuity turned big businessmen into political innovators, and campaigning was one of the first areas affected. Particularly after 1896, such magnates as John McCall of New York Life Insurance, Henry H. Rogers of Standard Oil, and Edward Harriman began both to contribute more consistently and to grant funds for a party rather than a man. They were attempting to buy a good reputation, to incline all important party members in their favor instead of stringing a few as company puppets. The more extensive the magnate's political concern, the more important it was to condition countless, unknown officials in all parts of government to respond appropriately whenever his interests came under consideration. The managers of the Republican party, which was almost the exclusive beneficiary, were naturally delighted. Businessmen's detached representatives had only weakened party discipline. Discretionary funds now brought prestige and control back into the hands of such men as Mark Hanna, George Cortelyou, and Nelson Aldrich, and regular donations allowed them to plan campaigns rather than approach each election hat in hand.

The centralized associations from the new middle class had exactly the opposite effect on party discipline. When an office-seeker accepted their support, he was expected in return to abide by their platforms and their ideals. Unlike such precursors as the Grand Army of the Republic or the American Iron and Steel Association, which had become adjuncts to the Republican party, the new-middle-class groups showed far less regard for the party as such. A man became known as the candidate of the chamber of commerce or the social workers, whatever his party label, and in time a slate might appear as the candidates of Toledo's Independents or Chicago's Municipal Voters' League. Moreover, the directors of these organizations, often zestful political amateurs, usually held a tight rein on all funds. Such groups compiled impressive local gains early in the century; the most effective among them approximated small, autonomous political units with all the paraphernalia for nominating, electing, and controlling a handful of officials. Little wonder, then, that party professionals, especially Republicans, preferred corporate executives to earnest, middle-class reformers.

Lobbying underwent comparable changes around 1900. A time-honored and universally condemned device, it had never been the simple, static technique its enemies claimed. Again, the major corporations were the earliest experimenters. As long as they had viewed political problems as isolated challenges, they had awaited a crisis before throwing together a lobby. The railroad wanted a land grant or the utility a franchise, the insurance firm opposed a tax bill or the oil company a restriction on monopoly. Then, as their critics described the process, corporate agents—wealthy, smiling, and persuasive—would "descend upon the legislature." As formidable as it seemed to an onlooker, lobbying of that sort was casual, almost sloppy, predicated on the assumption that legislatures usually did not matter. Precisely that assumption had to be abandoned by the nineties, and along with it went the cavalier approach to lobbying. Perpetual ferment in dozens of states demanded the corporate leader's constant attention, so he assigned full-time agents to the important posts. He needed a continuous flow of political information, so he paid strategically placed men to supply it. He required coordination, so he often hired a manager to supervise these many local activities. Andrew Hamilton, whose expenses in the decade after 1895 exceeded a million dollars, directed a nationwide network of lobbies for New York Life Insurance with as much skill in his line as the company's president demonstrated in his. Other organizations adopted the same systematic approach on a smaller scale, employing a professional agent of their own or pooling resources in order to share one. The American Medical Association expected its county and state directors to train themselves in politics. Strictly local leagues simply designated men—or women—to follow the city council throughout its sessions.

Scores of alert, critical eyes, representing thousands of crucial dollars and votes, radically altered the operation of a legislature, and political managers discovered that they could no more dispense with the lobbyists than could the organizations who had hired them. Now it was the politician who required information. In former years, when agents had come from a corporation or a church league with their bill, lobbyists had been self-evident propositions. Everyone had known what they wanted and had either bowed or resisted. After 1900, that simple precision vanished. Varieties of competing organizations, often with diversified programs, left the legislative leader without the basis for decisions. Nor could he depend upon partisan loyalties to mellow their spirits. Only if the lobbyists translated the wishes of their clients, negotiated with other agents, and offered reasonable assurance of how their constituents would react to particular measures could the political broker calculate the risks and fashion the compromises. The reliable lobbyist had become an indispensable intermediary in representative government.

Relatively, however, legislatures were declining in importance. People who wanted a definite, self-contained political favor—a tariff or a tax exemption—had almost always sought it in the form of a law. Services of an indefinite duration covering somewhat nebulous fields—railroad regulation, for example—just as naturally led them to the administrators. Although many corporate executives had long added state and local officials to the payroll as a matter of course, no precedents really existed for the imaginative uses of administration as a means to widespread, long-range control. After 1900 the dynamics of American politics increasingly concentrated in administration, where businessmen sought freedom from antimonopoly rules, farmers the basis for modern marketing, urban reformers the techniques for economy or systematic law enforcement, professionals the right to police their fields, and countless conflicting interests the mechanisms for adjustment and compromise. To a striking degree, the major legislative battles now involved which administrative agencies would receive what mandates under whose supervision.

By far the most important part of that political revolution transformed the national government. Because most progressives chose to concentrate initially upon a government close at hand and because few of them had easy access to national power, the pressure for change mounted more slowly in Washington than it did in the city halls and state capitols. Nevertheless, a rudimentary national progressivism was already taking shape around 1900. Some reformers were turning to Washington because they needed truly national solutions to their problems. Even more looked there because the scope of their operations, though far less than nationwide, had still entangled them in too many conflicting jurisdictions. Others simply sought national weapons to use in their local wars.

One issue of rising concern was the conservation and rational management of natural resources. The most complicated political story of its time, the movement for conservation grew out of the confusion created over many decades of feverish exploitation. Railroad promoters and lumber kings, land speculators and mine owners, stockmen and farmers—a few rich men growing richer and many poor ones forever scrambling—had ripped through forests, abused precious water supplies, squandered minerals, and stripped grazing lands in a rape of Gargantuan proportions. By the end of the nineteenth century, enough bitter conflicts and blasted dreams had combined with a vague sense of diminishing bounty to generate a strong demand for order. Yet despite an assumption that somehow Washington should be tackling the big issues, neither the tradition nor the means for effective action existed. In what passed for public policy, innumerable centers of power, located mostly in the states that held the natural resources, had made the important decisions. The few Federal laws passed in the name of conservation had scarcely changed even the rules of procedure. Early in the twentieth century these feelings were beginning to acquire direction and consistent purpose.

A second issue was railroad regulation. The process of consolidating the railroads had gained such momentum during the nineties that within a few more years seven large groups dominated the nation's system. At each step the reorganizations followed Morgan's original formula: a heavy burden of common stock and, of course, generous bonuses for the financiers. Apparently no group of Americans had greater confidence in their nation's future, for only an unprecedented prosperity could have relieved that mountainous debt. As it was, the good times early in the century were not good enough. The roads still required investments they could no longer attract. Consequently they raised rates. Their customers protested; Wall Street's agents replied that they had no choice. Meanwhile, the carriers' equipment deteriorated and their services remained undependable. By 1900 a small but growing number of militants, largely new-middle-class businessmen who shipped to and from the major cities of the Midwest, had already lost faith in the value of piecemeal controls through state government and were demanding an expansion of the Interstate Commerce Commission's powers.

At the same time, certain magnates were themselves developing a new interest in the national government. The passion for stability in business had grown even more urgent during the depression of the nineties, and America's tiny elite of finance capitalists eagerly awaited an opportunity to apply its techniques of reorganization to other portions of the economy. In 1899 Standard Oil publicized the latest device for these experiments when it changed into a holding company, a more flexible, enduring form than the trust, less susceptible to prosecution, and uniquely suited to the liberal issuance of common stock. In a trend that included many smaller enterprises as well, companies of all sorts hastened to the states with the laxest incorporation laws—New Jersey, the early favorite, issued about two thousand charters each year from 1899 to 1901—and overnight the face of American business seemed transformed. Most prominent were the giant new holding companies, climaxed in 1901 by the nation's first billion-dollar concern, United States Steel. Behind these lurked the master organizers: Morgan; Kuhn, Loeb; the National City Bank of New York; Lee, Higginson of Boston; and a number of powerful financial satellites, most of which revolved about Morgan's firm.

The view was far more impressive at a distance. Each year more enterprising men competed with the original finance capitalists for access to America's investment surplus. Though Morgan's towering prestige enabled him to eliminate some of the least scrupulous independents during the panic of 1907, others always materialized, disrupting the work of the mighty. The magnates also struggled with the consequences of their own greed, as untimely and hollow promotions periodically glutted the stock exchanges. Their paper dragons, moreover, faced the challenges of an increasingly diversified urban market which was confusing executives throughout the business system. Little wonder that huge enterprises like Standard Oil and U.S. Steel not only lost ground to their competitors but often did not even contest the trend. It was enough to consolidate what they had, try to keep abreast of technological changes and new sources of raw materials, and seek some way of moderating the flux about them.

The old problems of establishing and maintaining order, then, continued without pause. If conditions never approached the chaos of the late nineteenth century, in the twentieth they produced a more conscious sense of individual helplessness. The best minds in business, it appeared, were not equal to the task. In part, the disappointments stemmed from higher expectations.

Once stability had meant no more than the grossest forms of economic discipline; now it increasingly suggested elaborate patterns that might cover everything in a field of business from wages to a division of the market. Perhaps, as a few thoughtful corporate leaders were wondering, the national government could somehow be used to achieve that order which persistently eluded them when they acted alone.

At the same time, a rising group of financiers from the major cities of the Midwest were demanding a revision of the nation's archaic banking and currency laws in an effort to free themselves from the dominance of New York. In place of the ethical economics of the gold standard, they argued a technical case, insisting upon a currency geared to commercial and industrial credits so that it would automatically expand and contract in response to changing business conditions. In a similar spirit, an assortment of moderately prosperous businessmen seeking cheap raw materials or increased foreign trade called for reforms that would adjust the nation's import duties year by year without necessitating a complete overhaul of the tariff laws.

These basic issues and many lesser ones combined to force major changes in Congressional procedure. In 1890, largely out of a desire for tighter party discipline, Speaker Thomas B. Reed had applied a sweeping set of new rules which enabled him to reward and punish through a variety of controls, especially his regulation of day-to-day proceedings in the House. But if Reed's coup had originated in partisan ambition, the rules remained only because of a bipartisan need to dispatch more business. Equally as impressive, the demands for greater efficiency in the Senate had placed almost dictatorial power in the hands of a few legislative directors, particularly Rhode Island's Senator Nelson Aldrich. The fundamental changes, however, came after 1900 with the flood of broad, new issues requiring national action. The premium on speed, efficiency, and technical competence mounted sharply. Powerful, impatient groups would no longer wait for a decade's deliberation. Far heavier responsibilities passed to the committees; the committees in turn relied increasingly upon experts. Congressmen learned that success meant specialization, and competition for that one choice committee assignment grew vicious. When rebels in the House broke Speaker Joseph Cannon's arbitrary rule in 1910, they made certain that no member could receive a place on more than one major committee and that each member who had won his vital post would retain it. During these same years the arrival of Congressmen infected by the spirit of the new middle class and relatively indifferent to partisan obligations was compounding the problems of the party managers.

Though not so readily evident at the time, leadership in Congress had fallen beyond the capacity of Congressmen, and the executive was rapidly acquiring that responsibility. Neither house was constituted to evaluate an array of complicated demands, place them in order of preference, pass on them swiftly, and then follow the process of administration. The executive, on the other hand, was uniquely situated to guide these functions. The conditions demanding much more joined with a man wanting much more when Theodore Roosevelt, scion of one of New York's great patrician families, became President on the assassination of William McKinley in September 1901.

A man of unlovely traits who relished killing human beings, nursed harsh personal prejudices, and juggled facts to enhance his fame, Roosevelt was at the same time an extraordinarily vital person whose effervescence and extrovertive political style appeared to catch the spirit of the nation—at least of that nation to which a great many citizens wanted to belong. For millions of Americans this politician, soldier, author, hunter, cowboy, and forceful preacher of the balanced banalities provided a delightful, warming show. Countless reformers, mistaking vigor for directness, adored him. Upon hearing of his death in 1919, the progressive Donald Richberg recalled, "I could only press my face into the pillow and cry like a child. There were many others who wept that day." Behind the flashing teeth and flailing arms lay a keen-edged intelligence and an insatiable ambition for power within the framework of popular acclaim. No one of his time better understood the operations of American politics, and no one more shrewdly turned his knowledge to the service of personal glory.

Roosevelt inherited an office of rising prominence. Those fears of the nineties which ultimately focused upon the horror Bryan would perpetrate if elected had already invested the Presidency with a new importance. Significantly, the contributions that had poured in upon Hanna in 1896 returned again in 1900, establishing a pattern for Republican Presidential campaigns. Once a man won the nomination he stepped apart from the rest of the candidates. A largely impersonal fund—an investment in the office—carried him the rest of the way. Of course if a presumed radical such as Robert La Follette had ever led the party, the tradition would have snapped. Yet only safe Republicans were nominated, and an ample fund always materialized. In that tacit fashion, a new definition for the Presidency had already received financial form before Roosevelt's arrival, a definition with great potential and sharp limitations.

Soon after assuming office, Roosevelt set three interrelated goals: to establish himself as the pre-eminent figure in the Republican party, to elevate the executive as the dominant force in national government, and to make that government the most important single influence in national affairs. At almost every step he encountered the peculiar power of a few corporate and financial magnates, and he quickly marked these men as his primary opponents. More often than not, it was at this point that Roosevelt's urge to power and the several national progressive movements intersected. To the degree that he found personal relevance in their proposals, he joined the cause. An imperious master as well as an invaluable ally, he then tailored each project to fit his special style, leaving a private stamp on the whole of the early national movement.

In his drive for power Roosevelt relied heavily upon the ambitions and talents of his subordinates. An avid aggrandizer, the President understood and encouraged those aggrandizing executive officials who sought to construct small empires out of the growing demand for public management. He enjoyed a particularly close relationship with the well-born and hard-driving Chief of the Division of Forestry, Gifford Pinchot, whose small corps of scientific experts was spreading the gospel of rational land use throughout the country. While Roosevelt more than doubled the acreage of the public reserve, Pinchot and his colleagues were rapidly extending a system of contracts for its regulated, private development. In a remarkably short span, the President and these specialists had built a permanent base within the executive for the supervision of natural resources. In 1903 Roosevelt also fought successfully to include a Bureau of Corporations in the new Department of Commerce and Labor, then urged its staff to expand their investigation and informal regulation of large business enterprises. Meanwhile, with far less assistance from the President, the ambitious Dr. Harvey Wiley, Chief Chemist in the Department of Agriculture, was coordinating a movement for pure food and drugs from an assortment of women, doctors, scientists, and those manufacturers and distributors who hoped a mild regulation would destroy their marginal competitors. With the Pure Food and Drug Act of 1906, the executive was headquarters for still another experiment in bureaucratic reform.

Drawing upon the slack resources of his office, Roosevelt employed an exceptional range of devices to spotlight his favorite issues and force Congressional action. Special conferences, dramatic investigations, public condemnations, and private encouragement all found a place in the master's repertory. He negotiated with the legislative chieftains through a mixture of implied threats, quiet bargains, and clever flattery. Roosevelt's extraordinary ability to leave men believing that they, and they alone, enjoyed his most intimate confidence pacified innumerable opponents and won the services of many a deluded lieutenant. Increasingly the important bills, including those to outlaw rebating by the railroads, regulate the food and drug industries, and revise the Sherman Antitrust Act, were either drafted in an executive department or cleared there before they were introduced. This kind of leadership meant, of course, that those reforms the President rejected rarely survived in Congress. Roosevelt's unwillingness to support major changes in the tariff or in the financial system guaranteed that for a time Congress would meet neither of these basic problems. Moreover, his commitment to a strong, stable Republican party—the indispensable means to his influence —led him to protect both its Congressional leaders and its far-flung network of professionals.

Throughout his tenure Roosevelt derived maximum benefit from each of the government's major achievements—"my policies," as he called them. After business shippers had struggled for years to strengthen the Interstate Commerce Commission, he entered late in the battle, helped to pass the Hepburn Act of 1906—perhaps the most significant law of his Presidency—and received much of the credit for establishing the Commission as a substantial regulatory agency. In the same fashion, he identified himself with the Pure Food and Drug Act by a last-minute assault against the meat-packing industry which mobilized support behind the bill. One shrewd, successful prosecution of a giant railroad combination gave him the reputation of "trustbuster," although he had little use for the Sherman Act's sledgehammer approach.

Roosevelt, in other words, transformed important contributions into dramatic, personal victories. Both his overwhelming election in 1904 and the widespread demands in 1907 and 1908 that he seek another term testified to the magician's skill. Self-advertisement was part of the process by which he elevated the President as party leader in an entirely new sense. As interest increasingly riveted upon what Congress did instead of what Congressmen said, it was the President who fixed the gauge for judgment. How did Congressional behavior measure against his program— against "my policies"? What support had the Republicans, or any individual Republican provided? Because the President had a party label, every four years the party had a national record.

What a profound change from the days of Benjamin Harrison! Then the only bills composed in executive offices had been minor enough to pass the most jealous and imperious Congressional scrutiny, often so inconsequential the President had not even known of them. Neither of the Presidents succeeding Grover Cleveland had built upon that man's isolated initiatives in legislative policy, any more than Cleveland himself had done. No President from Hayes through Cleveland had been more than a factional leader, nor had a Congressman's party standing suffered—even if his patronage sometimes did—simply because he voted with an anti-Presidential bloc. If McKinley surrounded himself with the aura of a general party leader, he had still led the Republicans with slogans, not programs. Like his predecessors, he had used his office to harmonize partisan differences and to ensure his re-election, not to guide Congress through the steps of legislation.

Now the subdivisions of the executive had assumed the task of studying and resolving the big problems. The President was expected to give priorities, then focus Congressional attention on an issue at a time; in other words, provide and direct a rather precise legislative program. The President initiated, and Congress, if it wished, could veto. William Howard Taft would run in 1908 on Roosevelt's record, an innovation of tremendous consequence in national elections.

At the center of this revolution lay the same flexible, adaptive approach that characterized the reforms in city and state government. Each new administrative power, from the expansion of Pinchot's conservation program to the birth of an effective Interstate Commerce Commission, was predicated upon the continuous, expert management of indeterminate processes. Officials inclined in certain directions rather than committing themselves to specific goals. "The American mind . . . loves to see clear and definite solutions . . . ," wrote the President's friend Albert Shaw. "But the Roosevelt policy . . . makes [them] largely a matter of experiment from time to time to discover the just degree and method of public control."

Nothing better illustrated the new spirit than the gradual emergence of a policy toward giant corporations. Initially Roosevelt adopted the tactics of the skirmisher. Through selective antitrust prosecutions, investigations by the Bureau of Corporations, and such unpredictable intrusions as his interference in the anthracite strike of 1902, he would teach the nation's magnates at whose sufferance they operated. In a game of wills, of feints and thrusts, he hoped to maneuver them into the proper attitude of deference. Though Roosevelt overestimated the effect of these lessons, he had nonetheless found a raw nerve. Just when corporate leaders were disturbed by an inability to consolidate their empires, they confronted an unpredictable government whose chief executive seemed capable at any time of doing his worst.

Some magnates tried rather clumsily to protect themselves through straightforward deals with the executive, the sort of self-contained, man-to-man bargains traditional to nineteenth-century politics. Others waited grimly until the storm passed. Two men in Morgan's entourage—Elbert H. Gary, the unctuous chairman of U.S. Steel, and George Perkins, Morgan's aggressive young political partner—had the imagination to experiment. In an effort to immunize U.S. Steel and International Harvester (and by implication all of Morgan's major interests), they arranged a general understanding with Roosevelt by which, as the magnates interpreted it, they would cooperate in any investigation by the Bureau of Corporations in return for a guarantee of their companies' legality through private negotiations with the executive. A gentlemen's agreement between reasonable people: it was the natural extension of Wall Street's stock in trade.

Too clever to bind himself, Roosevelt still found this kind of arrangement very congenial. Of course he must always reserve the power to determine which corporations were the good ones and which the bad. Nevertheless, the agreement with Morgan's men seemed to combine a promise of stability with an essential subordination to executive direction. That appeared to be as far as anyone could go. Other big businessmen who talked favorably of a benign national regulation retreated at the first signs of trouble—the sudden, noisy demands in 1905 for meat inspection, or New York State's investigations that same year of chicanery between insurance executives and Wall Street bankers.

Roosevelt did not remain in office long enough to institutionalize his policy. Yet the parties to the gentlemen's agreement had roughed out a pattern that would eventually cover a large portion of progressive reform. The management of indeterminate processes invited exactly this kind of loose understanding. In order to achieve the adaptable order that both public officials and private interests sought, some sense of mutual purpose, some accommodation that still allowed each side ample room to maneuver, was considered indispensable. The bureaucratic answer, in other words, made reform a function of continuing, close negotiations.

8

The Illusion of Fulfillment

THE GAME of national power was played at high stakes, as a long line of aspirants flushed with local victories would have to discover for themselves. The hundreds claiming paternity for each law constituted an almost pathetic demonstration of how many tried and how few succeeded. It was so easy, for example, to miss the implications of the new executive and invest everything in Congressmen who could no longer manage the legislative process. In Washington the assumption that the world was merely an enlargement of one's familiar environment generated the greatest confusion. Contrary to those urban reformers who considered their city a "miniature [of] all the problems of a democracy," the President was not a grandly inflated city manager, nor the transcontinental railroad an extended trolley line. Nor, for that matter, did the government function like a giant corporation, a lesson that percolated slowly to a number of magnates. These were not peculiarly dull men but understandably perplexed ones, whose comprehension lagged behind changes only then in the process of development.

The most cherished and the most elusive form of political power was the right to initiate, a privilege monopolized by a handful of strategic officeholders and the men with access to them. As long as Republicans controlled the national government, a small number of big businessmen who sustained the party enjoyed a tremendous advantage over all other private citizens. While a friend or adviser might catch the right official at the right time and pre-empt the field, over the years only that elite of magnates was practically guaranteed a hearing.

Officeholders who were constructing new empires within the executive, however, shared their initiative grudgingly. Few precedents held them within other people's limits, and any petitioner had to work through them. Most magnates understood at least some of this. Nevertheless, partial understanding and rising ambitions led to partial adjustments and rising tempers. Within the executive and through executive-legislative conflicts, the tension between resourceful officials and traditionally powerful big businessmen mounted during the progressive years.

In somewhat uneven fashion, a looser group, similarly composed of important officeholders and their choice constituents, exercised the right of amending plans in their early stages. Only Congressional chieftains were assured of at least this much power in any legislation. In general, as national policy came to cover new areas in an increasingly technical manner, the right to modify fell to those affected by a particular measure. Thus, the railroad brotherhoods were consulted on a compensation law for workers in interstate commerce and the National Farmers' Union on a bill concerning finances in agriculture. What would later sound elementary was in fact a rather clumsy innovation early in the century. The new-middle-class expert usually entered the process here. But the specialist who attempted to move beyond his sphere almost always fell from grace. Such men as Herbert Croly and Walter Lippmann, hoping that Theodore Roosevelt and Woodrow Wilson would seek "experts" in political philosophy, only suffered frustration. In the realm of broad policy, each political leader was his own expert.

Beyond these circles lay a far larger number who were forced to work within someone else's framework. Together these men filling the lesser positions in and around the national government defined the outer limits of policy. If they mastered government procedure, if they stood upon solid organized strength, and if they learned to cooperate with men like themselves, they might exercise appreciable power of a kind. Robert La Follette built a brilliant legislative career almost exclusively on just such foundations. The hatred his name engendered paid tribute as much to his capacity for disrupting elite rule as to the quality of his programs.

The difficulties of combining these many contestants into a viable process of government radically increased around 1907 and 1908 as national progressivism entered a second phase. During its early years national reform had to a surprising extent operated apart from local progressivism. If the national and local movements shared many common qualities, different people with a different focus had still commanded at the two levels; the government officials and organized businessmen who had sustained the first national campaigns rarely had strong ties with local reform. The national progressives, moreover, had generally worked with their backs to each other. What little cohesion they did achieve had come almost entirely through the central role of President Roosevelt.

As Roosevelt was completing his second term, the hosts of local reform began to arrive in Washington. Success had bred confidence among urban and state reformers, and rather than undertake more of the same, they moved outward. Progressivism contained an inherent expansive thrust, partly from its need for ever-broader legislation, partly from its all-conquering optimism, but even more from its faith in method. If the right technique guaranteed the right results, no problems, whatever the size and scope, could withstand its magic. From that vantage point, they soon found all manner of movements around them deriving from the same source, and with the help of some wishful thinking, they pictured an entire nation in the process of a grand metamorphosis. They would join these millions of Americans in a single crusade against the inefficiency and injustice of special privilege, social ignorance, and habitual indifference.

This growing sense of interrelatedness owed a good deal to the network of communications that had spread about progressivism. Enterprising journalists had quickly uncovered the early reforms and had reported their findings in rich detail. These muckraking pieces, directed to a literate middle-class audience, were especially important during the first years of discovery. Then as Americans learned the outlines of reform, a more sophisticated, interpretive literature largely took their place. Such men as Frederic Howe and Walter Rauschenbusch not only encouraged local progressives to think of themselves as part of one grand drive, but they also supplied the rationale for integration: the skeleton of stages to an inevitable triumph, fleshed out with a new national intelligence; and at its heart the wonders of rational management. The interplay between reformers and their spokesmen could scarcely have been more effective in creating a national movement.

Some of the reformers, like the enemies of child labor, now sought national solutions to problems they had once conceived locally. Others, like Lawrence Veiller, the chief of New York's housing reformers, simply wanted to give national form to a scattering of local campaigns. Self-designated friends of labor, turning from employer-liability laws to the standardized formulas of workmen's compensation, planned in combinations of national and uniform state legislation. Talk of new commissions, Federal budgets, and a rationalized executive abounded. Everyone, it seemed, had a subject worthy of national investigation— rural life and urban children, retail prices and wholesale immigration, police brutality and medical education, and on and on. Ostensibly local projects such as the survey of Pittsburgh's slums and factories were clearly addressed to the entire country, a model of truth and a vision of reconstruction for everyone to see. Always they marched in groups: the National Child Labor Committee, the National Housing Association, the American Association for Labor Legislation, the Committee of One Hundred on National Health, and dozens more, either planned, founded, or refurbished during this critical transition.

Simultaneously, the earlier national campaigns were also achieving a new maturity. By 1907 conservationists had gathered their separate proposals into an integrated program for the development of water and land resources. That winter Morgan's men tried to empower the Bureau of Corporations as the government's official regulator of business practices and attracted many new participants into the debate on trust policy. At the same time, associations representing prosperous business shippers from every important city founded the National Industrial Traffic League, significantly altering the balance of power between the railroads and their customers. Even the champions of tariff reform finally struck upon a proposal that suited the progressive temper, a nonpartisan commission of experts to keep duties constantly in line with the economy.

Although the full impact of these changes was spread over several years, a portion of it affected Congress immediately. It was pressure of this sort that led such prominent Senators as Jonathan Dolliver of Iowa and Albert Beveridge of Indiana to identify themselves publicly with reform. For years they had cooperated with the Senate leadership as a matter of course, just as Representatives like George Norris of Nebraska had automatically worked with Uncle Joe Cannon, the crusty Speaker of the House. Then almost overnight Senator Nelson Aldrich and Speaker Cannon, symbols of a reactionary regime, became public enemies of such notoriety that the Congressman who dared deal with them might well place his future in the balance. Once a William Boyd Allison had held the rank of statesman because he subordinated every other consideration to the requirements of his party in Congress. Intelligent commentators had praised him not as a man who served his state, or expedited legislation, or exemplified the eternal verities but as a dedicated professional partisan. Now progressive critics judged Allison a hack. Their heroes were such men as Dolliver and Beveridge who cried defiance of the party whips in the name of a higher loyalty to reform.

The new national urge expressed itself most freely where reform had already established a firm base—in Dolliver's Iowa, for instance, or in Norris' Nebraska. The progressive Governors, led by La Follette and Albert Cummins, were now entering the Senate, while less famous products of these same organizations swelled the ranks in both houses. Although the Eastern reformers sent far fewer representatives, they themselves came unofficially, and in one demonstration of progressivism's new integration, a number of them arranged fruitful alliances with the Western leaders. Something approximating a progressive league had emerged in Congress.

The panic of 1907 acted as a catalyst in the ferment. Most obviously, it convinced almost everyone, including the bankers, that financial reform was imperative, and Congress created a commission to recommend revisions. In general, the panic released countless little pockets of pressure, turning concerned but comfortable citizens into active reformers and opening many more to the calls for change. That winter no one knew the worst would soon pass; those months might well be prefacing a catastrophe comparable to that of the nineties, a prospect horrifying enough to make thousands demand wholesale renovations. Roosevelt's feelings of impotence and anger typified a great many responses. Petrified by the thought of finance charging amuck, the President sent his Secretary of the Treasury to Wall Street with quantities of government money praying that somehow these men could tame the panic. At the same time in his last annual message to Congress, he outlined a reform program far more extensive than any he had publicized previously. Though memories of the panic soon faded, its effects continued long after through the many campaigns it had accelerated.

As Roosevelt left office, a number of hopeful conservatives announced that sanity would now return to the government's affairs. Instead, national progressivism had grown beyond anyone's capacity to control. New men of talent, ambition, and uncertain direction had so disrupted matters that national politics suddenly lost one of its indispensable elements, a calculable probability. President William Howard Taft inherited that maelstrom.

Taft, Roosevelt's personal choice as successor, adapted his patron's magical tactics as best he could. He hefted his great bulk from platform to platform campaigning for office, and as President he delivered more addresses than he cared to remember. Negotiating regularly with the imperial Aldrich, whom he admired, and the tobacco-chewing Cannon, whom he did not, he like Roosevelt avoided open conflict with the leaders in Congress and relied upon old-line professionals to maintain the party's national organization. His task, he believed, was to consolidate the recent progressive gains into a sensible arrangement of government.

Following McKinley, Taft might have been judged a success. Succeeding Roosevelt, he was an unqualified failure. He had neither a capacity for sustained leadership nor a talent for self-advertisement, and he proved much too stolid to maneuver with the experts in a political game. After the Republicans in Congress had broken their promise to reduce the tariff and passed the Payne-Aldrich Act of 1909, just another protectionist horse trade, it was natural for the President to attempt some defense. But Roosevelt would never have selected the heartland of its Republican opposition to call it "the best tariff" in party history. Nor would he have allowed himself to appear Cannon's champion when the revolt of 1910 stripped the old tyrant of his prerogatives.

The President might also have pleaded bad luck. The first major problems he confronted were as complex and dangerous as any of the time. Only a master could have halted the disintegrative processes of tariff making; and only an expert could have plumbed the controversy that arose over the land policies of Richard Ballinger, Secretary of the Interior. The immediate issue at stake in the Ballinger affair involved the particular ways of combining public and private development of the national domain. How to join the two, or where to divide them, defied precise definition, and the answers in a bureaucratic scheme naturally devolved upon the administrators in power. Ballinger, a lawyer from the expansive Western city of Seattle, undoubtedly leaned further toward private enterprise than Gifford Pinchot and his colleagues could tolerate. Nevertheless, the conservationists who assailed Ballinger, rather than presenting a clear alternative, essentially argued that they instead of he should have been making the decisions. Skilled in the arts of moral rhetoric, they left a Congressional inquiry widely heralded as the angels of righteousness with Taft and Ballinger dramatized as public villains.

Basically what the beleaguered President did not sense were the changes occurring in the nature of progressive reform. Well-disciplined groups of citizens were suddenly insisting upon self-evident rights that a few years before had not even been mentioned. When the Taft Administration prepared legislation to increase the investigative and rate-making powers of the Interstate Commerce Commission, many reformers only complained that it went no further. The Mann-Elkins Act, an impressive advance, was already an anticlimax in 1910. The same kind of assumptions muted the praise for Taft's vigorous application of the Sherman Antitrust Act. Even more perplexing, thousands of men and women who by the old political logic had no business in national affairs flung themselves into the contests of the Taft years. By 1909 they had shifted the arguments surrounding the tariff from the standard declamations on prosperity and fair play to a detailed examination of social costs and retail prices. Conservation had now entered the realm of great democratic issues and attracted a host of amateur prophets demanding reform in the name of all the people. Louis Brandeis, a thorough urbanite specializing in business law, served as prosecuting counsel in the hearings on Ballinger's conduct. Enthusiastic audiences cheered the Republican Senators who broke ranks to oppose the tariff. Representative Norris, field commander in the drive against Cannon, emerged a national hero. As the setting changed so rapidly, a whole range of Roosevelt's tactics became the hallmarks of Taft conservatism.

Moreover, no sooner had the urban and state progressives arrived in quantity than newcomers began crowding after them. Labor unions had been slow to enter national politics primarily because they lacked adequate power. Open-shop drives early in the century had preoccupied many of them, and the depth of their local political commitments—their first lines of defense—

had often discouraged any more extensive ventures for fear they might jeopardize these basic, protective alliances. Samuel Gompers, who warned constantly of the danger politics held for the union movement, had found such necessities a blessing. Many lesser union leaders, however, were eager to expand their influence, and as they gained some local security, they grew increasingly assertive in state politics throughout the industrial East and Midwest, even into such areas as Texas and Kansas. Gompers branded the lot of them "socialists." Radical organizations did exist along the edges of the labor movement, appealing especially to embattled miners, isolated lumberjacks, and outcast migratory workers in the West, and their combination in the International Workers of the World did haunt some unionists with the specter of a nationwide league of the unwashed. But the driving young labor managers in Chicago and Cincinnati and Pittsburgh were another breed entirely. As committed as Gompers to the American Federation of Labor, they simply followed their ambitions along other paths. They desired political power both as a right and as a means of improvement within the existing system. By and large, they distrusted the fine-spoken gentleman whose false promises had lined the late nineteenth century with dead legislation on working hours, factory conditions, employer liability, and child labor. They would write their own laws now and force their execution.

These progressive unionists, rising between men of Gompers' stripe on one side and truly radical leaders on the other, would have extracted some concessions under any circumstances. Two court decisions tightening the ring of injunctions about organized labor appreciably softened Gompers' resistance. Because the rulings in the Danbury Hatters and Buck's Stove and Range Company cases concerned types of boycotting long denied in common law, they scarcely came as a surprise. Nevertheless, they underlined a harsh lesson. Despite organized labor's strength and moderation, the judiciary still refused to acknowledge rights that respectable citizens had every reason to expect. To the sensitive Gompers, who wept at the threat of a jail sentence, the charge of "law-breaker" hurt as almost no other accusation could. Only Congress, it seemed, could grant the unions their legal legitimacy. Organized labor's national influence depended upon the revival of the Democratic party, whose weakness in the industrial East and Midwest made it particularly receptive to the requests of the unions. When the Democrats won control of Congress in 1910, progressive unionists arrived with them. Meanwhile, the unionists redoubled their efforts at home: between 1911 and 1913 twenty-one states adopted workmen's compensation laws, and many also improved their regulation of working conditions.

The peculiar difficulty farmers encountered in differentiating themselves from "the people" largely accounted for their late arrival as a distinct and organized national power. Even the commercial farmers could not easily surmount that heritage, and throughout these years such associations as the Farmers' Union and the Grange continued to appear rather feeble beside the veterans of the national lobby. Most farmers, in other words, still expected Congressmen to represent their interests as a matter of course. Nevertheless, the groups that did assert themselves after 1910 enjoyed something of the same psychological advantage the unions held. The farmer vote, like the labor vote, was a formidable phantom indeed to the officeholder. So many people lying off there somewhere, casting so many ballots, could easily determine a politician's future. With no precise way to gauge their sentiments, it often seemed the better part of wisdom to rely upon whatever spokesmen were available. Because politicians predicated a farmer vote, they feared it, and that fear gave the agricultural associations a power well beyond their strength in members.

Relatively small businessmen, both in manufacturing and marketing, were simply too numerous and too dispersed to combine as quickly as their more successful contemporaries. The late nineteenth century was a graveyard to consolidations in the minor industries, and early in the twentieth century the trend moved toward more limited, informal arrangements. Later refined into open-price agreements, these experiments sought a narrow range within which manufacturers might compete. Often more a hope than a solution, they still constituted the most promising alternatives to perpetual uncertainty; and the more committed the participants became, the more concerned they grew about possible prosecution under the Sherman Act, a threat regularly raised by the competitors they were squeezing. Independent retailers, who were reaching comparable understandings, faced an additional challenge. Just as they seemed to find their bearings early in the century, the rapid growth of mail-order houses like Sears, Roebuck and chain stores like A & P spread fresh panic among thousands of them across the country. They also wanted to amend the Sherman Act so that it would destroy the giants yet preserve their own price-fixing arrangements.

A combination of economic and regional peculiarities retarded the national arrival of progressives from the South and Far West. That deep Southern dependence upon outside capital, affecting attitudes as much as balance sheets, had already delayed the emergence of a sturdy new middle class, and where these groups did appear early in the century, they had concentrated with a particular intensity upon state affairs. Traditional hostilities toward national interference permeated the atmosphere. When the National Child Labor Committee turned from state to national legislation, for example, its leading Southerner resigned in protest. Gifts from Congress were welcomed; administrative supervision was not. This barrier did not really begin to crack until after 1907. Then the breaks spread rapidly, encouraging many Southern Congressmen to take a new national look at their problems and preparing the way for Woodrow Wilson's later victories.

In some respects the Far West, where a habit of living apart had bred an instinctive suspicion of men beyond the mountains, showed an even greater insularity. Here also a type of dependence —in this case upon the life-giving railroads—delayed the development of a strong new middle class. In the end, the railroads proved as valuable in uniting reform as they had earlier in inhibiting it. Groups that might never have found each other joined to spear the octopus, and by 1911 the progressives who had conquered California were casting their eyes across the continent to Washington.

Along with these late arrivals came a number of groups operating now in, now outside national progressivism. The Socialist party, a conglomerate of discontented plainsmen, new immigrants, reasonably settled Americans of German descent, a few intellectuals, and an even smaller number of rich radicals, had been founded in 1901 by several factional leaders with a new appreciation for organization, and gradually it gathered enough strength to poll almost a million votes in 1912. It always housed a great range of militants and moderates, but as it reached its zenith, the so-called German Socialists, led by Congressman Victor Berger of Milwaukee, gained ascendancy in the national party. This segment had so diluted its Marxism that only the party label separated it from the rest of America's middle-class reformers. After the Socialists won control of Milwaukee's government in 1910, for instance, Berger had asked the usual progressive specialists to help him establish an honest, efficient municipal administration. Under his guidance the national party offered just one more variant on the dominant doctrines of managerial reform.

Elsewhere along the periphery moved a vocal group of Protestant ministers who preached the Social Gospel. Although they finally established an organization of their own, the Federal Council of Churches, they remained institutionally weak. The major Protestant denominations had limped into the new century with a strong bias against controversy. Consequently, reform-minded clergymen either functioned nondenominationally, as some did within the Divinity School at the University of Chicago, or acted as independent spokesmen for reform. At the same time, they also were worried about the Protestant retreat before materialism, and usually they responded with vague doctrines that perpetuated the late-nineteenth-century vision of a general Christian unity. Beyond a mild infusion from the new social sciences, the Social Gospel had not altered appreciably since the first days of Washington Gladden's rebellion. In a sense, reforming clergymen served as the honorary chairmen of progressivism. It was still important for most Protestants to feel the presence of a Christian justification, and progressives regularly urged the ministers to join them, not as advisers but as sponsors who could spread that distinctive aura of righteousness about the cause.

Progressivism reached floodtide around 1912. The reformers had achieved not only their greatest strength but their tightest integration as well, and a multitude of concrete programs demonstrated how successfully they had translated the general urge of only five years before. Such spokesmen as Walter Rauschenbusch and Herbert Croly, whose earlier books had helped to crystallize national progressivism, now published sequels of glowing optimism that detailed the particulars in tomorrow's new world. Like so many others, they were talking fulfillment rather than promise. As Taft left office they had not accomplished a great deal, but as one of them exulted, "public opinion . . . has been wonderfully developed of late."

To a good many men of authority progressivism seemed to promise only chaos, not because of its bureaucratic principles but because of its challenge to their leadership. The more worried big businessmen, political chieftains, and their allies became, the more widely they felt they would have to range in order to protect their basic rights. A defense of their own power, in other words, came to mean a tighter grip over all of America; bureaucratic order as they construed it was a broad, superimposed social control. Progressive reform lived largely on tomorrow's hope even at its peak of national influence. In the struggle between an aspiring new middle class and an ensconced leadership the advantage clearly lay with the latter.

Around 1908 a qualitative shift in outlook occurred among large numbers of these men of authority, a shift roughly comparable to the one during the mid-eighties. Once again irritants became anxieties, a context of threat replaced isolated reactions, and responses acquired that cumulative, self-accelerating charac-

ter which created an increasingly urgent movement to discipline
an unruly society. Yet several significant differences suggested
how much better integrated the nation had grown over two
decades. Nothing like the wholesale instability of the eighties
surrounded the break after 1907, and the movements for control
remained noticeably cooler—more calculated—for a much longer
period. The greater emphasis upon enticements and compromises
showed a much defter hand, as if Machiavelli had taken the helm
from Savonarola. Moreover, the later campaigns had from the
outset certain elements of unity, a certain sense of the national
setting, which reflected the vastly improved system of public and
private communication. Although no two or ten or hundred men
directed these drives, participants at least understood more about
the value of other people's contributions to a common cause. And
their greater efficiency testified to a far tougher social organization beneath them.

Straws in the wind appeared everywhere around 1908. Critics
who had only grumbled about national reform earlier now cried
"socialism" and "communism." Organized labor received particularly heavy abuse, with each hint of violence reported as the first
gun of civil war. Bankers who had once tolerated the muckraking journals suddenly found them poor risks, and financial
stringency played its part in their disappearance. As always, a
rising curve of antiradicalism immediately affected attitudes toward the immigrant.

Although the discussion of immigration had not significantly
declined after the mid-nineties, its tone had mellowed noticeably.
Americans of many persuasions regained their faith in the melting pot despite a flow that on the average was bringing close to a
million people each year. What the progressives added was a
recommendation for systematic guidance. A government-directed
distribution of the newcomers, blending a faith in rational management with a belief in the mystical Americanizing powers of
the soil, emerged as their most popular answer to the problems of
mass immigration, and it was usually presented with considerable
goodwill.

Very few felt impelled to dispute this case until general fears began to erode the assumptions behind a gentle assimilation. Most Americans had always viewed assimilation as the total disappearance of the immigrant's distinguishing traits, and beyond a doubt that was not occurring. The new concern took two forms. One, reviving a theme from the nineties, demanded a restriction of the flow, specifically a literacy test; and these pressures grew strong enough to pass such a bill in 1913, only to encounter Taft's veto. The second, seeking to hasten the process of assimilation, led to a variety of private Americanization programs. Most of these experiments, which began to appear in 1909, gravitated almost by nature toward coercion, replacing the earlier paternalism with harsh demands to cast off all foreign ways at once. The debate over the immigrant had entered an indeterminate state, but the stronger thrust was now coming from the doubters.

At about the same time, the owners of large factories were reconsidering the dangers from discontented workmen. New schemes for incentive and welfare which had first been introduced around 1900 enjoyed a marked rise in popularity, and in more and more elaborate forms they came to include bonuses and stock sharing, recreation and clean washrooms, company houses and eventually company unions. Still generally benign in character, these programs did represent a more systematic effort to insulate the factory from all signs of agitation. The work card, a seal of the employer's approval to carry from job to job, was used more frequently. In addition, the various organizations that brought unionists and businessmen together for conversation and adjustment were dying from disuse. In grays rather than purples, the atmosphere surrounding labor relations darkened a bit year by year.

The magnates of Wall Street now set about the task of meeting their business critics in earnest. They convinced the Midwestern city bankers to join them behind a far-reaching yet conservative plan for financial reorganization in order to forestall any more radical measures. At the same time, railroad executives launched an impressive public relations campaign which led to a tacit understanding with the major shipping associations, and by 1912 the two sides had prepared for years of peaceful negotiation under the auspices of the ICC. These overtures brought such high immediate returns because the men who received them were also in the midst of reconsidering the nation's course. When the pace of reform quickened after the panic of 1907, large numbers of new-middle-class businessmen drew back. Progressivism run riot promised exactly the kind of turmoil they had always dreaded. As if to justify these fears, the economy bumped along an uneven trail during the next few years, while dissenters everywhere became increasingly bold. Businessmen grew noticeably more hostile to other people's progressivism and more cautious in asserting their own.

Other moderates were moving in a similar direction. Such men as Albert Shaw and Elihu Root had found the transition after 1907 almost as difficult to brook as Taft himself. Like the President, they considered reform a carefully measured process that assimilated results as it advanced, a cautious reconstruction that paid as much attention to foundations as to improvements. None of these men snapped his connections with progressivism; Taft, for instance, was still seeking a truce with the Congressional insurgents after the election of 1910. The angle of their drift, however, was clear, and before many more months they had completed the journey. Many citizens were simply losing touch with a movement that had grown beyond them. Some of them had once recommended palliatives for the factory worker under the assumption—so familiar to the progressive unionists—that gratitude would calm him. Another group had thought of reform largely in verbal terms, welcoming dissent as a release for more dangerous emotions. "Settlement Safety Valves Vindicated," boasted Graham Taylor, the kindly master of Chicago Commons, whose instinct was always to mollify rather than to correct. Still others merely wanted peace in their own time. When it did not come, the publisher Hamilton Holt, a veteran of many melioristic causes, supported Taft as the true progressive in 1912.

The greatest hidden source of strength in the drive against progressivism came from the very cities that had once led the movement. Beneath the glitter of national reform, local progressivism was declining, and the basic causes lay within the dynamics of the movement itself. By the latter half of the decade, an appreciable number of local reformers had either achieved their major objectives or found satisfactory substitutes. Businessmen who had sought an amenable, efficient government, experts who had fought for an opportunity to administer, doctors and lawyers who had suddenly discovered a world ignorant of their wisdom, even humanitarians who had criticized the neglected schools and street-corner parks, all had won measures of victory, as much in certain cases as they had ever anticipated. Some had then pushed onward—often without consolidating their gains at home. For others, success dulled the reforming urge. Now the existing system, the one in which they had an important stake, was worth defending.

Moreover, a number of sins were catching up with the urban progressives. Beyond a doubt they had proved remarkably inventive educators. Tom Johnson's huge tent and resplendent charts gave Cleveland a festive course in utilities and taxation; and Dr. Samuel Crumbine's ingenious use of the slogan "Swat the Fly" demonstrated something of the close relationship between progressivism and the rising industry of advertising. As one reformer remarked about Florence Kelley, indefatigable crusader for industrial democracy, most progressives "paid to human beings the high compliment of believing that, once they knew the truth, they would want to act upon it." Yet they were an impatient, sometimes arrogant lot who abided very few human failings. The delusive assumption that all good citizens shared their goals—or would as soon as these were explained—led them to trample sensibilities without regard for the resentment that was accumulating about them. Millions did not care in the slightest about a city budget, or preferred their children at work instead of at school, or feared the black magic of modern medicine. In time they began to fight back. The distance between an educated new middle class and their "people" was increasing.

Other men stood ready to capitalize upon these weaknesses. Most progressives had acted as if the bosses would of necessity disappear in the face of modernity. Instead, with an impressive display of resilience, these professionals emerged late in the decade more powerful than ever. Accepting many of the innovations, opening the channels of government to groups they might neutralize or convert, and laboring among lower-class citizens whose immediate needs they and not the reformers would meet, bosses in city after city fashioned organizations that could thrive in the midst of a progressive society. The cities, moreover, contained their quotas of anxious, substantial citizens now bent upon quieting reform's turmoil. In the smaller cities, new controls in progressive guise spread with astonishing speed after 1907. The coercive purposes of efficient government there, and in such major cities as New York and Philadelphia, grew so obvious that a discontented band of urban progressives organized in 1914 in an effort to undo reforms they had once championed. By the First World War the urban progressives who remained were hard pressed to defend what they still held.

In state government, on the other hand, the battle against progressivism was open for all to witness. Politicians who had once tried to ward off the challengers a blow at a time now undertook systematic campaigns to retain—or recapture—their power. In New Jersey, for example, the Republican leadership rallied to halt the climb of George Record and his progressive colleagues; in New York, Republican bosses now refused any concessions to the reformers despite numerous efforts in behalf of compromise; and in Indiana, fellow Republicans successfully undermined Albert Beveridge's bid for re-election to the Senate. Similar stories were repeated everywhere, in Democratic states like Missouri as well as in the Republican ones.

The states were natural centers of opposition to progressivism. For decades they had served as the fulcrum of American policy.

The community had automatically looked there for help, and the national government had granted them assistance with only nominal supervision. Now the balance was tipping rapidly away from the states, as both the cities and the national government drew in power at their expense. Men with so much invested in the state system resisted that decline as best they could. However rational it may have been by the new bureaucratic standards for Roosevelt and Pinchot to centralize control over huge tracts of land, such a fundamental change created upheavals that would reverberate for decades to come. Around 1907 the opponents of conservation in the Western states mounted an increasingly effective counterattack. Similarly, the enemies of national incorporation, child labor laws, and women's suffrage were investing more and more of their resources in a state-by-state defense. The results of their efforts gradually weakened progressivism even in such a major center as Wisconsin.

The strain of these actions and reactions took a far greater toll within the Republican than within the Democratic party. The majority party had drawn a large portion of the active new middle class, who now operated within a framework that had been erected before their arrival. Overarching the structure stood that imposing set of relations between prominent Republicans and wealthy businessmen, a national apparatus with ramifications into the affairs of many states, which placed a ceiling on their climb. The harder the challengers drove for national power, the more these arrangements reinforced the resistance from above. Grim party chieftains in Congress no longer pretended to negotiate with the progressives, and an increasingly angry President withdrew patronage, a policy that soon broadened into a full-scale purge. For most old-line Republicans the overriding objective was to maintain control of the national party organization. Financially secure even in defeat, they could afford to allow the Democrats a victory in 1912. "When we get back in four years," one of them explained, "instead of the damned insurgents, we will have the machine."

For a time it appeared that the progressives might yet capture the party. Their enthusiasm, their popularity among articulate Americans, and their impressive leadership spread an aura of victory about the cause, and many of them came to believe that they had only to select the right general. La Follette, who coveted the position, remained the most prominent candidate through 1911, in part because very few of his co-workers cared to meet that tenacious fighter in open combat. But the bold and brittle Senator commanded respect without kindling affection, and the great majority of progressive Republicans would not take their eyes from the one person they longed to follow, Theodore Roosevelt. After an African hunting trip ("I trust some lion will do its duty," Morgan had snorted) and a triumphal tour of Europe's capitals, the former President had returned unhappy with his successor, uncertain about his own future, and obviously unreconciled to retirement. Dreaming of how he could harness the party if only he were in office, he knew that short of Taft's abdication the lone route back lay with the progressives. Readily convinced he was the indispensable man, he placed himself in charge of the reformers early in 1912 and swept through the primaries the clear choice of the Republican rank-and-file.

Roosevelt, who realized very well that the odds always favored an incumbent, could scarcely have been surprised when the convention selected Taft. At this juncture, the odds also favored Roosevelt's retirement. He could no longer win the Presidency, and he could never lead his party again if he broke with it now. Yet the Progressive party materialized precisely because Roosevelt agreed to be its candidate. Like many others, he decided that his factional battle had already carried him beyond a point where he could influence the Republicans in authority. Great things were pending in 1912, events he might at least affect. Aware of the respectable organization behind him and assured of sufficient financial support, he seized the more congenial alternative, the one that kept him at the center of the action.

Disorganization spared the Democrats most of these problems while adding others. Since the nineties the minority party had fallen into component parts that feuded rather listlessly every four years over a Presidential candidate. Where the Republican party faced—and generally failed—the test of bending its structure to accommodate striving, younger members, the Democrats were perennially trying just to maintain a structure. Many of the components had also suffered during these lean years. Democratic organizations in such diverse states as Massachusetts and Montana, for example, had been purchased by individual rich men who wanted a private political vehicle, a fate the Republicans with their many dependable donors could almost always avoid. Furthermore, the Democrats badly needed respectability. Memories from the nineties—memories that Bryan's candidacies in 1900 and 1908 helped to perpetuate—had fixed a reputation for inferior leadership in national affairs.

At the same time, these weaknesses contained the wherewithal of victory. The Democrats' looseness had invited progressive latecomers like the unionists, the commercial farmers, and the small-business groups, many of whom had found the Republican party both cool and congested. A fairly substantial number of state and local reformers, younger products of the new middle class who were bent upon fashioning a modern party, asserted themselves rather easily in national Democratic affairs. Finally, Republican rigidity had opened the way to those successes in 1910 which injected a new confidence into the Democratic party and provided the incentive to sacrifice at least some of the old ways as the price of victory in 1912.

The nomination of Woodrow Wilson that year neatly suited the party's requirements. He had been the candidate least identified with any one faction, he embodied the hopes of younger Democrats for responsible guidance, and he clearly meant to serve as a national leader. Southern-born, he had been bred in Northern, urban politics. With considerable *élan,* the Democrats closed ranks behind a magnetic candidate.

The son of a minister, Wilson pictured himself the champion of great moral causes. Unlike Roosevelt, who expected others simply to accept his judgment, Wilson anticipated men flocking of their own free will behind his banner. His keen sense for factional maneuver had sent him up the ladder of academic politics at Princeton into the Governorship of New Jersey, where he astonished friend and foe alike by his skills for command. He had learned as he rose. Once a Cleveland Democrat, he quickly absorbed the elements of progressivism when his ambitions took him actively into party politics. The scholar who had first won fame by advocating legislative government after the British model now became an exponent of executive direction through that voice of all the people, the President. In microcosm, he underwent the intellectual migration of his generation. Outside a circle of intimates, people did not warm to this lean, intense man whose gaze seemed to fasten a bit beyond them. Friends too found his anger a biting lash. Yet there was an electric quality about Wilson, as gripping in a crowd as in a private audience. Millions who had known nothing better than Roosevelt's pomposities and La Follette's statistics would thrill to his soaring rhetoric.

Despite the emotions accompanying the birth of the Progressive party, the campaign of 1912 was not a particularly lively affair, perhaps because everyone knew the Democrats would win. In comparison with the battle of 1896, the nation's last formative election, relatively little distance separated the candidates. Not only was there no comparable breakdown in communication, but in several important respects the three leaders reasoned from the same premises: they accepted the legitimacy of power residing in voluntary, cooperative groups, they assumed the responsibility of the national government for guidance, and they conceived of that guidance in bureaucratic terms. All major parties, in other words, claimed the privilege of completing the national progressive movement.

Taft and his Republican minority unquestionably stood farthest to one side. Reflecting the concerns of powerful men, they thought of reform in terms of control. Where others looked forward to a general release of national energies, the regular Republicans wanted to build channels for safe change. The

Progressives, in turn, offered the most detailed plan of a new world under careful government supervision. Remarkably free from the hacks and the hangers-on, the new party contained a high proportion of those men and women who had created the progressive movement, and the New Nationalism, as its program was called, reflected that constituency. As strikingly different as the Democratic party was from this wing of Republicanism, Wilson's New Freedom did not deviate greatly in approach from the New Nationalism. If Wilson relied more heavily upon platitudes about equality and individualism, Gifford Pinchot could declare in all honesty that "equality of opportunity" and "the individual's rights" were also fundamental to Roosevelt's doctrine. The New Nationalism saw merits in industrial concentration which the New Freedom denied. Yet as the philosophers sketched it—such men as Charles Van Hise on behalf of concentration and Louis Brandeis on behalf of decentralization—the distinction dimmed. Both men believed in an outer ring of rules and an inner core of administrative management. This formula, Van Hise concluded, would "secure efficiency . . . , freedom for fair competition, elimination of unfair practices, conservation of our natural resources, fair wages, good social conditions, and reasonable prices"; and Brandeis could not have disagreed with a word of it. Though important questions of balance and emphasis did separate them, a common orientation—one not at all alien to Taft's Republicans—meant that bureaucratic reform would dominate the discussions to come. The advocates of a sweeping, moralistic reform, scattered through both parties, could not significantly alter the outcome without strong national leadership.

A cautious man might have worried about a popular mandate no greater than 42 percent. Despite an overwhelming victory in the electoral college, Wilson had apparently slipped into the Presidency between halves of the Republican majority. Roosevelt had received 28 percent of the popular vote and Taft 24. Neither timid nor retrospective, the new President proceeded to make the best use of his opportunities. His party in Congress invited strong leadership. A heavy percentage of the Democratic majority were newcomers, men without either the urge or the experience to strike out on their own. Among the Democratic veterans in both houses the habit of commanding in opposition ran deep. They were not prepared to fight the executive for the right to manage a complex legislative program. Like Democrats across the country, they wanted very badly to belie the party's reputation for incompetence in national affairs, and with considerable relief they rallied about the standard Wilson thrust before them.

The nature of the program, on the other hand, fell largely beyond the President's control. By 1913, as the new Congress met in special session, years of struggle had already defined the issues it would debate. A full complement of private groups stood at hand to demand their due, and their firmness betokened scant leeway for the politicians, legislative or executive. The challenge before Wilson, therefore, lay in balancing, in imaginative compromise, rather than in evoking or initiating. The latitude he did enjoy came from a temporary short-circuiting of political communication. After so many years of Republican rule, the familiar figures and customary routes to influence had abruptly given way to new faces and new patterns of authority, and it would take even the most skillful citizens a little time to acclimate themselves. During the interim, the President could substitute his own direction. Nevertheless, the conditions that had allowed the unique creativity of Roosevelt's Presidency had dissolved. Wilson would have to serve as regulator, as taskmaster, and above all as final arbiter, combining the many pressures to some constructive purpose. He handled each masterfully.

By the fall of 1914 Congress under Wilson's guidance had dispatched three fundamental reform issues. Succeeding where Taft and the Republicans had failed exactly four years earlier, the Democrats fulfilled an ancient party promise in the Underwood-Simmons Act by substantially lowering the tariff. To this was appended a mild, graduated income tax, now cleared of the Court's shadow by a constitutional amendment. With greater commotion, the new Congress then passed the Federal Reserve

Act, which made currency a function of commercial and industrial credit and provided a rough unity to national finance
through twelve regional reserve banks and a Federal Reserve
Board. Finally, after several months of uncertainty, the Democrats established a Federal Trade Commission to oversee corporations within the rather vague rules listed in a companion measure, the Clayton Act.

With the completion of that agenda and the outbreak of war in
Europe, Wilson allowed his grip on Congress to relax. The
reforms of the next two years came piecemeal, bearing the mark
of the jerry-builder. This was the time when the late arrivals to
national progressivism claimed their measure. Although organized labor failed to gain its major objectives, the unions won a
mixed bag of laws protecting the rights of seamen, outlawing
child labor, and imposing higher wages in the railroad industry
at the moment of a threatened strike. Commercial farmers
received a separate financial structure to handle their type of
credit, a permanent place within the Department of Agriculture
for the extension service, and a start toward the regulation of the
important produce exchanges. The appointment to the Supreme
Court in 1916 of Louis Brandeis, who was identified with the
causes of small businessmen and unionists, also belonged to this
later stage of Democratic reform.

These were also the years when traditionally powerful businessmen regained a fair portion of their lost influence. The
magnates of Wall Street, who had had little direct effect on the
laws concerning the tariff, finance, and the corporations, returned
in strength with the European war. Like Roosevelt, Wilson and
his Cabinet depended upon these wizards of popular myth to
stabilize finance in the face of a sudden disturbance, and once
welcomed back the magnates remained to modify a variety of
economic policies—railroad rates and the application of the antitrust laws among others. At the same time, protectionist organizations redoubled their efforts to alter the Underwood-Simmons
Act. The Democrats finally agreed to a commission that would
advise in a policy of tariff adjustments.

In all, the Wilsonian compromise covered an impressive range. Scarcely a significant question of the era did not fall somewhere within its scope, and no well-organized group was denied. The genius of the New Freedom lay in its capacity to respond at least partially to each of the many claimants in a way that granted none of them a clear victory over his competitors. The new professionals helped to formulate legislation ranging from the Federal Reserve and Federal Trade Commission Acts to the bills on child labor and scientific agriculture, then staffed and counselled the bureaus which were to manage these problems. New-middle-class businessmen, who asserted themselves in 1913 and 1914 while the magnates were sulking in their tents, played an especially important role in the construction of the basic laws on finance and corporation control as well as such later measures as the Tariff Commission. Legislation concerning agriculture and labor openly served the organized elites in these two areas. Yet at no time did any of these groups, or a combination of them, have the power to exclude their opponents, as the smooth return of the big businessmen late in 1914 demonstrated.

Neither Wilson, his advisers, nor the leaders in Congress could pretend that this remarkable balance followed a master plan. The original agenda had merely set priorities, and in the end had included far too little. Yet the Democrats could take pride in a most dextrous management. The new majority had proved surprisingly sensitive to organized pressures from all sources, and the President had shown an exceptional talent for administrative compromise, the essence of bureaucratic leadership. Although many of the beneficiaries would never vote for a Democrat, enough did in 1916 to re-elect Wilson by a fraction over a reunited Republican party.

The New Freedom, in combination with the reforms preceding it, cemented the basic progressive principles into the American system. With the Tariff Commission Act in 1916 every area of reform had been affected by the new values of bureaucratic management. The executive beyond a doubt was now the focus of national government. Party leader and Congressional director, he held an authority no one could challenge, and people across the land looked naturally to him for guidance. Even after 1914, as Wilson's interest often drifted from domestic affairs, almost every new reform had first to clear the White House before it could pass Congress. The mold of the modern executive was set. In times of weak Presidents, cabinet officers would have to divide the tasks, but beyond an occasional incident the initiative would never return to Congress.

From the President's office radiated departments supervising matters that ranged from the cutting of trees to the slaughtering of cattle and supplying expert services for a host of organized citizens. Where the executive did not have jurisdiction, an independent commission usually did. This progressive favorite dominated the regulation of corporations and held promise of exercising a significant influence over finance and the tariff as well. Throughout the pattern ran the central themes of modern reform: functional specialization, continuity, adjustment. And behind it rested the assumptions of a bureaucratic order: a society of ceaselessly interacting voluntary groups assisted in their course by a powerful, responsive government. The people still existed, it was assumed, giving the nation its mystic coherence, but day by day administrators would deal with them in rational subdivisions.

So a great many reform-minded citizens indulged the illusion of a progressive fulfillment. The contours of a new society spread before them, and in the pride of victory the ambiguities of their success understandably eluded them. Who was to lead and who to follow? The riddle of that gentlemen's agreement between Roosevelt and Morgan's men lay close to the heart of the whole progressive puzzle. How would power distribute among officials and citizens, regulator and regulated? Where for that matter would power reside in their society of equals—weighted according to intrinsic strength? What the reformers failed to comprehend was that they had built no more than a loose framework, one malleable enough to serve many purposes, and that only its gradual completion would give meaning to an otherwise blank outline. They had carried an approach rather than a solution to their labors, and in the end they constructed just an approach to reform, mistaking it for a finished product.

To what end—or, better, by what inclination—was it all moving? Bureaucratic management lent itself equally to social control and to social release. In fact each of the new reforms involved a blend of the two. Yet not only would different people mix these in very different ways, but the same people regularly altered the proportions as their outlook changed. Of course there were still the public men, those demigods of leadership. Here the progressives might have taken a cue from their masters; neither Wilson, Roosevelt, nor La Follette could abide either of his competitors in the role. Indicatively, the sharpest clashes of the New Freedom concerned appointments to the new commissions. Somehow the impartial experts had not automatically materialized. No one could turn back to the old certainties; for so many, a new orientation had replaced them precisely because it made better sense out of their world. The challenge lay in understanding the implications of that bureaucratic approach as it applied to a changing society. In 1916 the most arduous tasks still stretched ahead.

9

The Emergence of Foreign Policy

DURING THE LATE nineteenth and early twentieth centuries, the mind's eye of an American swept world affairs with marvellous freedom. So little obtruded upon the senses. The consciousness which centuries of abrasive contact had worked into men's psyches, the *Weltanschauungen* that bound "us" and "them," nation inextricably interlocked with nation, into bundles of hates and hopes, simply did not apply in the United States. East and west were the great buffer oceans, insulators against a jagged proximity. To the north, Canada—Britain's sparsely settled outpost, America's poor half-brother. To the south, Mexico—land of bright shawls covering lazy peons, and then jungles beyond. Or so at least it appeared from Wichita or Austin or Washington.

The very conditions inviting the imagination to soar kept its passage narrow. In a basic sense, what lay beyond the nation's boundaries did not exist. Almost nothing abroad had that immediacy, that imperative quality, which could force an American's recognition as he speculated about the world. He viewed the universe as an elementary extension of his everyday experience because that, essentially, was his only experience. As that experience changed—as the fragmented society of the nineteenth century gave way to the increasingly bureaucratic one of the twentieth—both the attitudes and the ambitions involving foreign lands altered markedly. Yet however radical these changes, the

American was still using a strict domestic standard to interpret his world. Throughout these years, in other words, he remained remarkably undisciplined by an external reality.

The late nineteenth century did contain several protections against the effects of these flights into fancy. The national government treated foreign relations much as it did the rest of its business. In almost all cases the initiative lay elsewhere—with private citizens or foreign countries—and unless some event touched the political needs of the responsible officials, they usually did not react. The chances of missing the mark were always high. Little in the wide world had relevance in that parochial context. When issues did reach the government, it offered replies one by one. Foreign relations were composed of incidents, not policies—a number of distinct events, not sequences that moved from a source toward a conclusion. The same Grover Cleveland who sorted his domestic problems into niches and dropped simple, self-contained solutions after them gave an equally tidy moral answer to each matter coming from abroad. And so it went from administration to administration.

Of course these responses were not merely private whims. The government's officials, along with a great many Americans, shared certain predilections about their world which gave their decisions a general consistency. One of these separated the world into two parts. Above lay the civilized powers, principally Europe and the United States; below fell the subjects of their imperialism in Asia, Africa, and Latin America. If some nations straddled the line—Turkey, Japan, even Russia—by and large the nature of the division drew them either up or down. Thus Russia was generally regarded as a backward great power, whereas Japan was a sport, that one fascinating exception to the colonial rule. The first was scaled down from civilization, the second measured up from barbarism. This segregation involved much more than an allocation of status. Basically it concerned intrinsic worth and inherent capacities and carried with it a clear moral differential, one that not only attributed meager sensibilities to the barbarian but also freed advanced nations to deal with him by a code they would never have dreamed of applying to each other. One would no more accord China the same rights as Britain than one would expect the same honor from a Chinaman as from an Englishman.

Give or take certain exotic peculiarities, barbarians all seemed very much alike. Civilized peoples, on the other hand, differed significantly, and a second American habit of mind managed these distinctions by assigning each European nation one or two dominant traits. Individuals often disagreed in their analyses: France might be "radical" or "gallant," Russia "treacherous" or "romantic." Yet for Presidents as much as for village editors, just such stick-figure nations, each moved by an elementary little motor, constituted an important portion of the American's world reality.

A third predisposition recast the matter of national characteristics into a comparison between the United States and the whole of Europe, and on the surface Americans everywhere arrived at a common, unequivocal conclusion. Europe was old and tired and declining, America young and vigorous and rising. In fact, Europe was not only decaying but decadent—jaded, a bit corrupt, and enslaved by centuries of prejudice. America, on the contrary, joined virtue with youth, moral vision with power, imagination with thrust. "America is slowly but surely creating the ideal of a broad and perfect equity," announced Professor Franklin Giddings, "in which liberty and equality shall for all time be reconciled and combined." "Ours is the elect nation for the age to come," cried Josiah Strong's friend, the Reverend Anson Phelps. "We are the chosen people." Yet just beneath the surface lay the uncertainties of the braggart. Europe had a cunning that innocent America could never match, or Europe had achieved levels of culture that shamed its backwoods offspring, or Europe had deadly attractions that must inevitably tangle America in its coils. Each of these secondary themes expressed the worries, the self-doubts, of an habituated dependent.

Moreover, there were the sacred principles, in particular the Monroe Doctrine and Neutrality. Serving a function analogous to Protection and Sound Money, these postulates had significance because of their emotional power rather than their contents. Neither had the precision to guide everyday affairs. Nor did the official employ them for that purpose. Instead, he used them as justification. These were the self-evident universals, the symbols of the national will to which men were supposed to respond much as they should to "democracy" or "Christianity." If the issues they sanctioned had touched vital interests throughout the nation, these doctrines, like the principles surrounding the tariff and the currency, would also have become the subject of endless debates in exegesis. But until the very end of the century they involved only marginal matters. Comfortable in their loose fit, they supplied a warming sense of righteousness to foreign affairs.

More than irrelevance kept the United States from adventures abroad late in the nineteenth century. The rare Secretary of State who devised a broad scheme immediately faced two obstacles. If he moved in private, he had no apparatus to support him. The foreign service consisted of honorary ambassadors, inexperienced ministers, and underpaid subordinates, men who came and went according to the dictates of partisanship and the availability of more attractive opportunities elsewhere. At home the Secretary had a bare handful at his disposal, scarcely enough to fill the seats at a small conference table, and it was only an exception like Alvey A. Adee, Second Assistant Secretary from 1886 to 1924, who provided continuity even in matters of procedure. The Secretary himself was almost always a stranger to his field. No experts sat close at hand to compensate for his ignorance, no network sent him a regular flow of information, no professional system stood ready to implement his wishes. Meanwhile, nothing encouraged Congress to increase the department's allotment; foreign affairs had no firm constituency. The armed services, moreover, rotted in disuse during most of these years. As officials discovered in 1881 when they contemplated intimidating Chile, that nation had a better-equipped navy than the United States. And while the Navy slowly improved, the Army remained static, a force of about 25,000 forgotten regulars until 1898. The paraphernalia for action simply did not exist.

If the Secretary moved in public, he exposed himself and his colleagues to the possibility of sharp political retribution. Foreign relations were uniquely identified with the executive, and in a manner unlike that prevailing anywhere else in government, important undertakings here placed the reputation of the Administration far more than the party at stake. The Senate, of course, held important powers over appointments and treaties, powers that might have been substantially enlarged in the late nineteenth century. Yet whatever its potential, the Senate concentrated upon partisan maneuver and the preservation of its prerogatives, leaving formulation—and public responsibility—to the executive. The Supreme Court showed even greater circumspection. In a rare display of reticence, the Court refused an effective role in the management of America's new empire after 1898. The so-called insular cases, dealing with the applicability of the Constitution to the colonies, passed the problem along to the other two branches. "Ye—es," Elihu Root was supposed to have said with regard to these muddled decisions, "as near as I can make out the Constitution follows the flag—but doesn't quite catch up with it."

Tradition and practice, therefore, left the first step to the executive. But tradition and practice also told its officers to be extremely cautious. By custom the executive did not attempt to lead the national government, and by every rule of success the politician did not hazard bold commitments. When the occasion arose, the executive could fight with unprecedented energy to protect his prestige. McKinley, in striking contrast to his deferential approach in domestic affairs, used every available weapon to force the Treaty of Paris, terminating the Spanish-American War, through the Senate. To take unnecessary risks of this sort, however, was utter foolishness. As a matter of course, the executive avoided foreign troubles.

The process by which the government opened its doors to world affairs and transformed discrete responses into policies properly belonged with the general contemporary movements to manage a disorderly environment. The same broad pattern prevailed here as well: the initial efforts to impose a crude order, the desire for regularity and predictability, the need for a government of continuous involvement, and the emphasis upon executive administration. Here also a basic qualitative shift occurred in those few critical years around 1900.

Yet a distinctive personnel operating in a unique setting gave this part of the story special significance. If a relatively few people directed domestic policy, then infinitesimally small numbers guided the changes in foreign relations. A great many Americans developed an interest in world affairs and expressed opinions about them. But only a tiny fraction combined the consistent concern with the power that would allow them to shape the nation's commitments. Although this handful dealt in matters vastly more complex than America's domestic affairs, they approached world problems with far less subtlety and far less restraint. They exemplified, in other words, that common American inclination to project familiar assumptions upon a huge and ill-perceived canvas. Neither dullards nor bunglers, they merely functioned within a singularly narrow framework of experience.

Two groups, the one profit-oriented and the other power-oriented, dominated the origins of foreign policy. The quest for profits abroad, which had continued since the seventeenth century, practically monopolized the nation's foreign affairs during the late seventies, eighties, and early nineties. Trade was the most common concern. Americans had an extraordinary variety of goods to sell coming from all manner of farms and factories and warehouses, and in ones and twos and tens they cried out for the government's assistance. Occasionally a major industry confronted the kind of challenge that required a definite response. When neo-mercantilism in Europe led to the exclusion of American pork early in the eighties, successive administrations did what they could to reopen the market until the crisis finally passed. Usually, however, the demands for government aid just dinned about the officials' ears. Too many voices made an indeterminate sort of noise which might cause men to think generally about commerce but not to work specifically for any one interest. Thus James G. Blaine, Secretary of State under both Garfield and Harrison, and Frederick T. Freylinghausen, Arthur's Secretary, pondered ways to extend the whole of the nation's trade in Latin America, and John A. Kasson, America's representative at the conference on the Congo in 1884, grandly insisted that the United States seize some port somewhere along that river as the first step in somebody's great commercial enterprise. That kind of concern lacked the precision to change customary ways.

A smaller number were concession seekers. Sometimes men of wealth, sometimes frank fortune hunters, collectively they had slight political influence. They themselves often travelled abroad in search of favors, soliciting for the right to develop mines, build small railways, and the like. In the process, they acquired close friends among America's languishing resident officials. Thousands of miles from Washington—in China or Korea or a Central American republic—these men could generate a passionate enthusiasm for the opportunities awaiting the timely intervention of the United States government; but far back home prudent politicians extinguished these flames one by one. None of the concession hunters had the power by himself to move his government, and unlike the commercial interests, their demands had no cumulative impact during the late nineteenth century. On occasion their intrigues did alter the nation's course. In 1891, for instance, the role of adventuring businessmen in Chile's civil strife had helped to precipitate an anti-American riot which for a time actually threatened war. Yet that merely demonstrated how plastic the government's responses were—no one ever thought of a policy with regard to Chile—and such freakish incidents passed as quickly as they arose.

Unquestionably the general fear after the mid-eighties that domestic opportunities were disappearing did encourage Americans to think more seriously about economic expansion abroad. Depression then gave these feelings a sudden urgency. The government showed a keener awareness of the requirements of trade, especially in Latin America, where it interfered several times during the mid-nineties to assist American commerce. More people talked yearningly about that limitless Asian market —"Four hundred million Chinese without shoes!"—and thought seriously about acquiring the Hawaiian Islands before some other power swallowed them. Yet the commercial crisis of the nineties, even more than the discussion preceding it, seemed to belong to everybody and, consequently, pointed nowhere in particular. Without someone to provide discipline and direction, these worries need not have produced anything more concrete than a headache. Certainly they demonstrated no capacity to force the birth of policy.

The men whose economic ambitions did make a critical difference bore a close resemblance to the handful directing the nation's new finance capitalism. In this case, banking establishments of lesser stature—powerful in their own right but inferior to the House of Morgan, the National City Bank, and Kuhn, Loeb—also belonged in the camp, and because no Morgan arose to take command, the group as a whole had less coordination than its smaller, tighter domestic counterpart. Particularly within this hemisphere, such names as Speyer and Co., Seligman and Co., and Brown Brothers would appear regularly as the competitors and colleagues of the greatest houses, autonomous agents in a common enterprise. All of these firms in varying degrees had access to the newly mobilized domestic surplus, and it was a number of decisions concerning its use that sent the financiers in an earnest quest for foreign profits. Trapped by the myth of waning prospects at home, they sought a far wider sphere for investment, and even after prosperity returned, they continued to find enough enticements to keep them looking abroad.

The bankers employed their funds in two ways. They invested in relatively large mining, manufacturing, and transportation projects, and they invested in governments. Often, though not always, the second came as a corollary to the first; the right administration would protect the fruits of their industrial enterprise. Both, in any case, required novel services from Washington. The needs of trade generally stopped at the port. If goods were received and paid for without unusual restrictions, commercial interests had no reason to concern themselves about conditions beyond the border. While specific discriminations did necessitate specific interventions—witness the pork crisis of the eighties —by and large a decent set of rules, once established, left matters to the businessmen's ingenuity. If some unexpected barrier did suddenly block commerce, the trader could without inordinate hardship take his goods elsewhere. The financier, on the other hand, could not pick up his railroad or mine and move on. Under duress he could only liquidate at a great loss. Consequently his investments involved him intimately and continuously in the foreign nation's internal affairs. Taxation, currency, civil strife, the rights of laborers, these and much more immediately affected his interests, and to the degree that he could not manage his own claims, he looked to the government at home for help. In fact, bankers often refused to risk much without prior guarantees of that protection. In other words, these men demanded a predictable commitment from the United States—a foreign policy, in short, to parallel their economic policy. Over the years their ambitions abroad would wax and wane in response to the business cycle and to their interpretation of domestic prospects. Nevertheless, once their roots had sunk somewhere abroad, they would require their government's uninterrupted support.

The financiers themselves could not implement a foreign policy. Nor around 1900 were they particularly well prepared to exert influence where they most needed it. Their political ties remained far stronger in legislative than executive circles. It was the extraordinary good fortune of a second, power-minded group to hold the strategic offices just at the sensitive moments of transition. Its membership included John Hay, Secretary of State under McKinley and Roosevelt; Elihu Root, his successor; Henry Cabot Lodge, member of the Senate Foreign Relations Committee; and, above all, Theodore Roosevelt. In a ring just beyond them were such men as Alfred T. Mahan, the Navy's world-famous theorist; John Bassett Moore, adviser to the State Department on international law; Whitelaw Reid, editor of the New York *Tribune;*

and Albert Shaw, editor of the *Review of Reviews*. On the periphery sat Brooks Adams, the brooding metaphysician, as well as such prominent public figures as Lyman Abbott of the *Outlook* and Franklin Giddings of Columbia University. Short of a miracle, no coterie of like-minded men could have concentrated themselves more effectively in the seats of power and publicity than this one did. Equally important, most of them regarded the others as personal friends. An easy, informal cooperation gave them an inestimable advantage in working their will.

Despite variations in temperament, these men held in common a broad range of opinions about world affairs. At the root of international affairs, they believed, lay national power, a vague concept that mixed portions of a mystic social strength with large doses of force. While the conflict with Spain preoccupied them, they exalted war as power's purest expression, "the last and most crucial test of a nation's energy," as Adams phrased it. "Nothing else in the same degree," Giddings declared, "rouses a people to positive action . . . [like] the unifying and stimulating influence of war." In a calmer setting they talked more broadly about the massed military, economic, and cultural resources of the nation, what Mahan referred to in an additive way as "national efficiency." Nations with power were obliged to use it, either because to waste it would constitute a crime against civilization or because fate decreed its use. Some, like Roosevelt and Lodge, felt a special calling to elicit America's international greatness from a tradition-bound slough; others, like Adams, bluntly offered the alternatives of world supremacy or national catastrophe; and still others, like Giddings, saw American glory rising as naturally as "the advent of spring after winter." All agreed with Shaw that the nation "must be strong for the sake of our destiny, our dignity, our influence, and our usefulness." All, moreover, accepted Mahan's dictum that "our rights should depend upon the will of no other state, but upon our own power to enforce them," for the essence of national greatness was independent authority.

America, therefore, "must accept the responsibility of a great place among the nations," ultimately, it was implied, occupying the first chair. By the same token, the United States would have to extend its sway over the world's lesser peoples. As Hay, who sprinkled his official correspondence with references to "Chinks" and Latin American "Dagoes," once remarkęd, nothing could match imperialism as "a fine expression of the American spirit." Civilization directed the control of the inferior by the superior, and to hold back out of timidity or mistaken scruples only hindered progress. The question of the morality of expansion, Mahan said, was "as little to the point as the morality of an earthquake." "Barbarism has no rights which civilization is bound to respect," Lyman Abbott proclaimed. More gracefully, Giddings explained the necessity of crushing the Filipino guerrillas in order to impose America's rule over the islands: "the legitimate and rightful appeal is always from any dissent of the governed now to that . . . consent which, we have sufficient reason to believe, will be freely given when all the facts are clearly seen, and when the reason and conscience of the governed [are] fully awakened and matured. . . ."

Although many of these men had travelled abroad—that is, to Europe—none of them depended upon a regular fund of information to sustain his visions. They were armchair theorists. Unlike the financiers, who at times gathered an impressive amount of data as the preliminary to an investment, the power-oriented allowed their imaginative faculties full scope. Sublime faith in first principles, coursing generalizations, and magnificently inclusive organic and mechanical analogies informed their thought. Nor did members with less of a philosophical bent like Root feel impelled to challenge these propositions. Understandably, then, their speculations had a tendency to spill over into the absurd. "The Germans cannot increase their velocity because they cannot extend their base, and augment their mass—we can and do," Brooks confided to his brother, Henry. "As long as we can increase our mass we can increase our velocity and so increase our advantage. . . . The pinch will come when all else has been absorbed and we must take China with its mines, or be undersold." Though that sort of thing might have been dismissed as the ravings of a bedeviled patrician, Presidents indulged in parlor games almost as weird. Roosevelt could contemplate England and Germany allied in a military attack on an American canal, or talk emptily about "taking" Canada in a phantom war against England he was playing in 1901 with Lodge. The fantasies of power, with nations as tokens on a worldwide board, led most of them to dream in that fashion about shadowy thrusts and counterthrusts.

Still, it was this inner circle that actually executed the change from itemized responses to policy. And if ever a group were inclined toward policy, these power-minded strategists qualified. No nagging surplus forced strange lands on their attention. Nor did they stretch outward because the world was impinging upon the United States. They quite simply wanted the United States to master that world. Obviously a nation did not claim its place with the leaders by waiting for others to move. The United States would have to plot its own special course, then calculate each step according to that guide. The most able among them were capable of learning as they acted. The earliest grand designs of such geopoliticians as Mahan, like the far more modest projects of a Blaine, showed the usual self-contained, self-fulfilling character-istics of late-nineteenth-century thought. The end resided in the outlines of the master plan. But as Roosevelt and Root in particular acquired a new sense of interrelationships and fluid process, they applied it to foreign relations, infusing their policies with a crucial flexibility. The general goals had not altered, but their means had come to include the fundamentals of bureau-cratic management.

As divergent as the approaches by way of profits and power had been, these two elites seemed to have arrived at a common destination. Both sought a rapid and, in effect, revolutionary extension of America's international commitments, a government continuously involved throughout the globe. Both counselled an initial movement into vacuums; first of all the United States should fill those colonial areas not already occupied by the European powers. Both stressed the importance of stability, and both construed stability in a way that would draw them deep into the internal affairs of other countries. Almost all of them were

Eastern, urban Republicans who looked favorably upon the centralization of power and its rational disposition, and as they demonstrated in certain areas of domestic policy, they had at least a partial appreciation of their interdependence.

But as their domestic dealings also illustrated, cooperation between such men always remained tentative and uneven. The financiers were equally caught in a simplistic projection—in this instance, of assuming that the basic requirements of American capitalism would obtain everywhere in the world. Yet they were not conscious philosophers, and the grand schemes of the power-dreamers—the wars, the colonies, the bluffs, the endless projects—alternately irritated and frightened them. The designers, on their part, could not down a feeling that bankers were at heart small men incapable of responding to the calls of patriotism and glory. "Mankind knows that there is something better [than paper profits]," read Mahan's challenge. "Its homage will never be commanded by peace, presented as tutelary deity of the stock-market."

Indeed, their cycles of assertion and caution did not fit very well. When opportunities for greatness appeared to one group, the other might draw back because of uncertain business conditions, a special hazard, as it turned out, in the more ambitious schemes for American expansion in East Asia. When financiers believed support imperative, a national election or some ripening plan elsewhere might be distracting their political allies. Once again, it was the conundrum of who should lead and who follow—and to what end? The great bankers expected the government to act as their agent, a servant in behalf of its citizens' prosperity. The apostles of power, on the other hand, saw investment, like trade, merely as one piece in an elaborate game. Even those such as Mahan and Adams who gave economic forces great weight still subordinated them—in effect, nationalized them —in the quest for that ultimate good, American power.

Two additional clusters of ideas glided about the formation of America's new foreign policy. One was the general property of the new middle class; at least its members most often voiced the principles. Foreign relations from this perspective assumed a particularly benign cast because these men saw their ideals gradually materializing about them. They sought smoothness in the conduct of world affairs, an absence of violence and disorder and all wasteful conflict. A largely negative goal, it tended to place a high premium on the correct rituals. The forms of democratic procedure, the official guarantees of peaceful intent, were optimistically transmuted into the substance of a healthy world. For the new middle class believed in progress, and believing in it, they found it. Slowly, inexorably, mankind was lifting itself upward: civilized nations were growing ever more enlightened, and barbarians were rising ever higher toward the standards set from above. Eventually—at some indeterminate point in the future—all nations would achieve unity in peace and brotherhood. Backward countries, of course, would require many more years of patient tutelage, but—in a way that contradicted the working assumptions of the guiding elites—they would some day graduate into full-fledged world citizens. In the meantime, advanced nations were rapidly approaching the ultimate stage. It was, in all, a misty extension of ideas that informed progressivism at home. The United States would fashion a paradise of middle-class virtues. In time the world would adopt America's democratic model. Before 1913 no one in high office inclined strongly toward these views, and before 1917 relatively few made them a fighting faith. Until then the new middle class was otherwise occupied.

The second cluster belonged primarily to the defenders of the community and, appropriate to its origins, presented an exaggerated version of American ambivalence toward a world of dangers and promises. On the one hand, it dwelt upon the evils of Europe, with particular reference to Britain. Lombard Street, after all, manipulated the international gold conspiracy, that "soulless despot of alien origin," which was blocking the introduction of a people's currency in the United States. Governor Altgeld, in fact, believed that England was dictating each step in

America's foreign relations, including what he regarded as a sham crisis over the Venezuelan boundary in 1895. Others extended the pattern of jeopardy far across the Channel. Julius Wayland, a leading spokesman for farmland socialism, pictured all of Europe's masters, from "Crazy Bill," the German Kaiser, to England's smug Prime Ministers, conniving against the United States. Henry Demarest Lloyd imagined that "on the day Manila fell [to American troops] the Philippine Catholics transferred their property to Cardinal Gibbons" of Baltimore as one move in a black plot against the natives' liberty.

At the same time, they could speak with sweeping assurance about America's ultimate triumph. Between assaults on the international goldbugs Bryan reminded his audience, "There is a hardy race of people between the Rockies and the Alleghenies who will legislate for themselves and declare the financial independence of the country." The Atlantic Coast, alas, had been captured, but the great hinterland would rescue democracy. No Americans envisioned a grander destiny for their nation. Edward Bellamy saw utopia in the year 2000 spreading irresistibly from the United States around the globe, with some lag among the "backward races, which are gradually being educated up to civilized institutions." Lloyd and Josiah Strong wrote ecstatically about the "Anglo-Saxon mission," by which they meant a purely American imperialism. None ever questioned the absolute good of a purified American democracy.

After 1896 the spokesmen for the community lost what little cohesion they had once had, and with that went the tenuous balance they had achieved. Threat clearly became the dominant motif, and their vacillations from crouching defense to grandiloquent expansiveness grew even sharper. Arguing to the very last minute against any foreign venture, they could then swing violently in its favor, only to return as abruptly when their inflated hopes were punctured. Voices in the debate over foreign policy rather than forces in its making, they still constituted an element of instability that would have its effect in the crisis of the First World War.

A variety of ethnic groups contributed a final lesser factor in the emergence of foreign policy. Although immigrants certainly carried deep prejudices with them as they crossed to America, the first generation had essentially no opportunity to apply them beyond their neighborhoods. Politically impotent and nationally inarticulate, they could only pass a legacy to their sons. The rising second and third generations did insist that politicians respond to these special claims, demands that Americans of both Irish and German descent were making in the eighties and nineties. As long as foreign relations were conducted piecemeal, they sometimes influenced a particular situation. Yet to the degree that their general drive for recognition succeeded, their cry lost its shrillness. By and large, that was precisely the stage at which their American journey crossed the beginnings of foreign policy. These groups—and now their sons, yet another generation removed from Europe—had won enough early in the twentieth century to ease the passion, even to blur the lines of hate. Newer immigrants from Southern and Eastern Europe had not gathered sufficient strength to strike out in their turn. Habitual responses and token declarations, rumblings and occasional outbursts, comprised the sum of their efforts during the formative years after 1900. Later the shock of a world war would disrupt the entire process of assimilation, not only eliciting acute Germanness and Irishness from reasonably well-established groups but also hastening the arrival of relative newcomers.

At its inception the heart of the nation's new foreign policy concerned Latin America and East Asia, largely because these were the territories available for expansion. Europe had already divided most of Africa into colonies and protectorates. A few American feelers early in the twentieth century did not expose very promising prospects. The Near East was too distant and, apparently, too sterile for the risks it would entail, and Britain's India dominated South Asia. Of the two major areas remaining, Latin America—by tradition, political condition, and proximity—presented a particularly inviting front. In a vague fashion Americans had long considered the lands to the south as their peculiar province, and the Monroe Doctrine, despite its ambiguities and sporadic application, suggested that here, alone in the world, the United States held certain general prerogatives which might well be broadened into predominant rights. Latin America's many small republics, weak yet independent, provided an ideal setting for penetration with a minimum of formal responsibilities. Here, moreover, the nation's military power could operate most effectively.

East Asia, on the contrary, seemed to lack every advantage. America's slender interests there had in most cases come as a consequence of Britain's initiative, and customarily the United States moved behind a shelter of European power. Although East Asia had not been sliced into colonies, a host of nations had been collecting privileges for many years, and a newcomer would automatically begin with serious liabilities, including the rapid rise of a formidable local power, Japan. The United States simply could not muster the force at such a distance either to frighten or to fight its competitors. Nevertheless, Americans persevered. East Asia was still technically free territory, and especially as China lumbered in the direction of a modern economy, the possibilities in that huge, densely populated land appeared unlimited, regardless of America's handicaps.

In spite of the great separation between the two regions, and in spite of the very different approaches each required, the two did become entwined in American diplomacy because both were objects of a common national assertion. The Spanish-American War, a prelude to the development of foreign policy, illustrated how such a joining might occur. The United States entered the war in the usual late-nineteenth-century manner, treating the conflict with Spain as just one more item in foreign relations. Early in 1896 a dirty struggle between Cuban rebels and a decaying Spanish imperial administration began to attract a great deal of attention. For a variety of reasons—some humanitarian, some strategic, some diversionary, some economic—a large number of Americans grew convinced that the United States should resolve the issue by ensuring Cuba's independence. Under pressure, Spain slowly conceded America's secondary demands, but it would not humiliate itself by a clean, complete abdication. McKinley, always alert to the cries around him, decided that was not enough. He gave an eager Congress its cue to declare war, and with a whoop and a holler Americans fell over each other in a brief, blundering contest with a third-rate power. Because of the political support the Navy had recently enjoyed, a relatively well-equipped American fleet demolished its creaking opposition. Because months earlier the Administration's leaders had agreed with an ambitious Assistant Secretary of the Navy, Theodore Roosevelt, that in the event of war a portion of the fleet should move against Spain's Philippine colonies, the United States found itself with a fingertip hold on these islands when the war ended.

The men in power could not part with territory just gained, so in the treaty that followed they kept the Philippines, adding Puerto Rico for good measure. In the midst of the turmoil, Congress by joint resolution had also acquired Hawaii, to the relief of the American businessmen dominating its economy. A disorganized group of anti-imperialists, stressing tradition and the burden of barbarian lands, failed to defeat the treaty while it was before the Senate, and Bryan's half-hearted atttempt to use the election of 1900 as a means of reversing that decision proved equally futile. Now the United States had an empire. For a time its proponents talked grandly about the nation's maturity, its pending services to backward humanity, and an endless commercial expansion in Asia. Crowing, however, did not construct policy. These colonies had not belonged to any previous plan, nor did they serve as the basis for a new one. In a routine fashion, the government set about administering its lands to no other end than their administration. Although the Army's incompetence in war led to a partial reorganization, McKinley anticipated returning it quickly to its usual size.

In fact, the whole dazzling venture lost its glow as promptly as it had come. Filipinos engaged Americans in a brutal jungle war of the type Cuba had recently experienced, two of the nation's naval heroes bickered like schoolboys over their share of the glory, another made a fool of himself seeking the Presidency in 1900, and learned men split hairs over how few rights the United States should grant its dependents. Theorists who had once blessed the war as sign and source of a new national cohesion fretted about the ill effects from so many inferior people under the American flag. When foreign policies did emerge, the officials formulating them discovered that distant colonies were worse than irrelevant. Their protection drained precious energies from the pursuit of long-term, wide-ranging influence in world affairs.

Leon Czolgosz's bullet had a greater effect upon the form of America's policy than the war with Spain. The assassination of McKinley, by elevating Roosevelt to high office, gave the management of foreign relations to men who did have designs and who also had the skill to implement at least a part of them. Systematically the new President sought to throw a net about the countries bordering on the Caribbean and to pry East Asia open to American influence. Identifying himself with the nation, Roosevelt showed an even greater inclination in foreign than in domestic affairs to answer questions of all magnitude precisely as his personal judgment guided him. Here, after all, he was expanding rather than originating an executive's prerogative. He demonstrated some of his usual tact with Congress, abandoning reciprocity treaties that irritated the Senate and relying upon his close friend Lodge to smooth the path for his projects. Moreover, he made the appropriate gestures toward such popular ideals as "peace" and "legality." (He must have approved the State Department's reference in 1912 to the "legally constituted good government" of Nicaragua directly after American troops had crushed its opposition.) Yet withal, he drove a private chariot abroad with a freedom he never dared to exercise in domestic affairs.

As in so many other areas, he bequeathed Taft an ongoing enterprise which his successor almost perforce had to manage. Because Taft relied heavily upon his Secretary of State, Philander Knox, who in turn leaned upon his assistants, particularly

Francis M. Huntington Wilson, American policy lost much of the integration Roosevelt's personal direction had supplied. In fact, these subordinates infused America's foreign relations with a belligerence that was alien to their chief's natural preference for measured legal procedure. Moreover, Taft, unlike Roosevelt, never did comprehend the basic distinction between commercial and financial involvement, and his confused efforts to assist all of American business abroad damaged both his own reputation and those interests he wanted to help.

Wilson, who then inherited the results of Taft's mismanagement, was the first President in charge of these young policies to incline toward the international ideals of the new middle class. Nevertheless, a combination of the policies' inertia and his own prejudices rendered these guidelines practically useless in East Asia and Latin America. He favored commercial over financial expansion; yet the former remained a fog, while the latter brought insistent, concrete matters to his doorstep. Seeking non-violent ways to further American interests, his mean opinion of men with yellow and brown skins left him without the patience to pursue them. It was all too easy for him, as it was for Bryan, his Secretary of State, to conclude in a particular crisis that whatever the future might hold for these lowly folk, at present they could only understand force. When Roosevelt undermined the foundations for these countries' independence, he merely acted upon a belief that barbarians were barbarians. When Wilson did the same, he destroyed the basis for an improvement he honestly wished to serve. As if half-aware of the contradiction, he and his subordinates made a fetish of the forms—the constitutions and elections and announcements of native thanks—that somehow never could cover the nakedness of the substance. In the end, the nation's policies in these portions of the world followed a remarkably steady course through their first two decades.

Latin America, the ripe fruit in the backyard, always occupied a preferential position in the nation's expansion, and here a foreign policy appeared most quickly, most clearly, and—according to the design of its architects—most successfully. The first in a rapid succession of steps concerned a canal across the slender midriff of Central America. As Roosevelt assumed the Presidency, the United States was in the process of extricating itself from a treaty of 1850 with Britain which in effect had promised to share control over any such waterway. A stubborn Senate forced Hay to continue negotiations until Britain abandoned every one of its claims, and the Secretary and his new chief then set about realizing the ancient dream of a link between the Atlantic and Pacific.

Many had talked in general terms about the great commercial potential of a canal. The Spanish-American War had underlined its strategic value. To Roosevelt and his colleagues, however, the most important part of the venture was the swift, unequivocal assertion of America's will, a declaration to all the world that the United States would establish its own goals in Latin America and achieve them without any nonsense. When Colombia's legislature balked at an agreement for a canal through its territory of Panama, Washington's officials were livid. Roosevelt scarcely cared what route the waterway took, but once the United States had decided upon Panama, no "contemptible little creatures" in Bogotá could be allowed to thwart it. Impatiently following the progress of Panama's revolution of 1903, the Administration lent the presence of a warship to ensure its success, hastily recognized the new state, and dictated terms for an American zone across the isthmus. Construction commenced almost immediately, and by 1914 the United States had its canal, a trophy to the nation's new hemispheric authority.

If Roosevelt's canal diplomacy constituted a declaration of intent, his corollary to the Monroe Doctrine outlined the means of accomplishing it. A year after taking office, he faced another version of the question which the Cleveland Administration had broached in 1895 and which had again arisen in the negotiations over the Cuban rebellion. What supervisory rights did the United States hold over the relations between European and Latin American countries? Cleveland had insisted that Britain settle a boundary dispute between its colony of Guiana and Venezuela; McKinley had demanded independence for a European possession; yet neither had set his action into a framework for continuing diplomacy. Soon after Roosevelt had discouraged England and Germany from employing military force to collect debts from Venezuela, he told the world what it might expect in the future from the United States.

If a nation shows that it knows how to act with reasonable efficiency and decency in social and political matters, if it keeps order and pays its obligations, it need fear no interference from the United States. Chronic wrongdoing, or an impotence which results in a general loosening of the ties of civilized society, may in America, as elsewhere, ultimately require intervention by some civilized nation, and in the Western Hemisphere the adherence of the United States to the Monroe Doctrine may force the United States, however reluctantly, in flagrant cases of such wrongdoing and impotence, to exercise an international police power.

In effect, the President had announced a new doctrine rather than a corollary to the old. The original pronouncement, by prohibiting certain types of action, had tried to fix outer limits around Europe's involvement in Latin America. While shrinking these limits so that they essentially excluded the use of European arms, Roosevelt concentrated upon the core the Monroe Doctrine had avoided. Fundamentally the United States would now sit in judgment on Latin America, not Europe, and with military power as its most obvious weapon, determine unilaterally the proper state of internal affairs for the nations of that region. Weakly disguised as the unhappy policeman tending other people's nasty business, the United States had declared Latin America its sphere of influence.

It required three administrations to develop the implications of the Roosevelt Corollary, and year by year the process interlaced the government's work more tightly with that of the expanding financial elite. American investments spread rapidly throughout Latin America in the first decade of the century, doubling the

total in Mexico, for example, and trebling it in the balance of
the Caribbean area. Even more important, the quality of investment was changing. Instead of many additional little enterprises,
the new ventures usually concerned major, long-term commitments and emanated from the same great banking houses.
Agents for these institutions, like their concession-hunting predecessors, cultivated close alliances with America's resident officials
abroad, supplementing an independent influence within these
countries and an impressive power at home. Consequently, as
leaders in Washington moved out to regulate their new domain,
they encountered an extensive network of American involvements, often well matured, which defined a boundary about the
government's operations. Although the financiers could not dictate the government's policy, no policy could ignore their interests. The bankers, furthermore, had the great advantage of
specificity. Protection of those definite interests provided a very
convenient, an almost unavoidable, point of focus for officials
who had only thought in the general terms of asserting United
States power.

The string of protectorates that the United States acquired
early in the twentieth century illustrated one phase of that
interaction. Following the conflict with Spain, the War Department had administered Cuba in preparation for its independence,
for independent it would have to be after the highly publicized
altruism of America's war. Under the government's aegis, the
Cuban economy revived quickly, in part because American funds
poured into the sugar-rich island. Here of all places the United
States would have to exercise regular surveillance, and bankers
anticipated this in calculating their investments. Predictably, the
government left Cuba only after the new republic had accepted
America's right to intervene in cases of serious civil disturbance.
In 1905 a more carefully planned concert of interests emerged in
the Dominican Republic, the first country to qualify under
Roosevelt's new formula. After a period of devastating internal
strife had bankrupted its government, Roosevelt decided to settle
its affairs by removing the prize of battle—the customs house.

This time New York bankers and Washington officials entered hand in hand, the one contracting to give the customs house an honest, impartial administration and the other guaranteeing to protect the bankers.

As Taft succeeded Roosevelt, the maneuvering of American banana companies in the bloody politics of Nicaragua was rendering that nation equally helpless. Unable to install a friendly faction from a distance, Secretary Knox resorted to arms in 1910. This did not stabilize matters, and in 1913 Wilson gladly ended the affair. By 1915, however, the Democratic President had witnessed all the turmoil in Haiti he could tolerate, and he in turn tried to enforce calm by troops and a treaty. In the context of Latin American barbarism, the populistic Bryan found the agent of the National City Bank, whose interests the intervention preserved, a most congenial colleague in the crusade for civilization. A year later renewed troubles in the Dominican Republic led to a second, more forceful intervention there, and to an even more elaborate system of financial controls underwritten by the United States. To Wilson's dismay, no native politicians would supply the facade, so the Navy Department conducted the government while the bankers supervised the economy. Thus while the initiative had shifted from time to time, the pattern of mutual interest remained approximately the same.

These eye-catching events tended to obscure a stream of far subtler relationships which did not always demonstrate such harmony. A caution against overcommitment and a concern for broader strategy diluted Washington's zeal for defending each major enterprise. High officials concluded that intervention in Honduras, Guatemala, and Venezuela would not serve their conception of the national interest, despite the importunities of embroiled American businessmen. Moreover, each administration channelled some energy into economically irrelevant forms of uplift. Wilson in particular never quite lost faith in the efficacy of a compulsory education. "I am going to teach the South American republics to elect good men!" he had remarked in 1913, and whenever he was free to do so, he instructed. (Roosevelt's analogous comment in 1905—"Some time soon I shall have to spank some little brigand of a South American republic"—suggested how Wilson had both elevated and extended the earlier meaning of a barbarian's education.) Twice during the protracted Mexican revolution which had begun in 1911, Wilson skirted the edge of a full-scale war with armed interventions that had practically no bearing upon the needs of American investors. Wilson wanted to secure what he called honor and decency, and he employed the nation's resources as much to impose these as to prepare Mexico for American enterprise.

Nevertheless, the main thrust of America's policy remained clear enough. Roosevelt, Taft, Wilson, and their primary advisers all acknowledged a close interconnection between imperial politics and imperial financing, and each administration provided whatever diplomatic support it felt it could for the bankers' ambitions, not merely because they were United States citizens but because they were citizens who trafficked in a power indispensable to United States policy. When Wilson successfully applied pressure on several Latin American countries to exclude an important British investing firm in favor of its American competitors, Walter Hines Page, the ambassador at London, commented with unintentional irony on "the application of the Monroe Doctrine to concessions that might imperil a country's autonomy." It represented an impeccably logical extension of the Roosevelt Corollary. All nations in the American sphere must depend upon Americans. As capital flowed southward, officials could talk more and more honestly about the fundamentals of control. In 1917 Secretary Lansing wrote that each Latin American country seeking aid abroad should as a matter of course offer any important opportunities first to Americans. To the degree the government could enforce that rule and the financiers could fulfill it, the United States would close the door in Latin America.

In East Asia, on the other hand, the challenge was to open the door and keep it open. Here American policy showed neither the clarity nor the consistency that it did in Latin America, largely because East Asia remained an optional area in the minds of too many important men. Unlike Latin America, where those responsible for American policy made commitments that varied only in intensity, in East Asia they attempted periodically to alter the nature of their involvement. The financial elite, after organizing as the American China Development Company and acquiring a choice railroad concession in 1898, sufficiently lost interest in their venture during the next few years to let control over the enterprise fall into Belgian hands. Their enthusiasm revived somewhat around the time of the Russo-Japanese War, only to drop abruptly with the panic of 1907. Again it rose early in Taft's Administration, held tentatively for a few years, then declined precipitously at the onset of the Chinese revolution in 1912. It did not really recover until the end of the First World War. Each of these fluctuations took its toll upon the continuity of the nation's policy.

The government's leaders on their part could not hold firmly to one conception of what the United States should accomplish in East Asia and how they might best achieve it. The lure of the China trade was forever intruding into their schemes. Commercial hopes, in fact, lay immediately behind John Hay's famous "open door" notes in 1899 and 1900. Riding the winds of oratory about a limitless Asian market, the Secretary made two clever but ineffectual efforts to shame the China powers into granting easy entry for American goods and foregoing its final dissection into colonies. Thoughts of 400 million customers also distracted Taft, leading him to work at odds with his investment-minded subordinates. When Wilson took office, the new President willingly chose commerce over investment as the economic rationale for American policy. Since China never absorbed as much as 2 percent of the nation's foreign trade, that enduring dream testified to the remarkable strength of a bonanza psychology among otherwise shrewd Americans. Yet its appeal also demonstrated the marginal position of East Asia in American calculations. Whatever his personal inclinations, Wilson as President would never have dispensed with the support of the financiers in the

Caribbean. In distant China, however, where the influence of the United States relied even more heavily upon investments, he could temporarily turn his back upon them because national power as such did not seem at stake. The loose requirements of a commercially-oriented policy would scarcely have distinguished China from the rest of the globe. Although Wilson later changed his mind, the very fact he thought in terms of options illustrated the sharp difference in prevailing attitudes toward East Asia and toward Latin America.

An East Asian policy originated in Theodore Roosevelt's unquenchable ambition to force the United States into the league of powers which determined its affairs. He knew as well as John Hay that however striking the Secretary's craftsmanship the open-door notes alone were immaterial in world politics. The United States had done nothing since to implement them, or in fact to demonstrate any type of continuing interest in the area, in part because of America's fundamental weakness there and in part because of the Administration's indifference to the principles it had just enunciated. It was left to Roosevelt, therefore, to find an avenue for steady, effective involvement and an occasion to announce the nation's arrival as a major East Asian power. With his unerring eye for dramatization, he managed the latter flawlessly. The outbreak of the Russo-Japanese War in 1904 attracted an extraordinary amount of international attention in an era of general peace. A skillful use of his highly placed European friendships combined with the desire of the combatants for a settlement enabled Roosevelt to bring representatives of the two countries to Portsmouth, New Hampshire, and while the world looked on, he acted as mediator. The United States could not make war in East Asia, so Roosevelt made peace. It was, under the circumstances, a brilliant maneuver, as perfectly suited to America's situation across the Pacific as an announcement by way of the Panama Canal was to its position in Latin America.

The far more important part, a route to continuing influence, posed very different and difficult problems, ones neither Roosevelt nor his successors fully resolved. Military means offered scant hope. Although the Navy grew in strength and Roosevelt sent a portion of it around the world to display the nation's power, every official agreed that Americans would not sustain a major war in East Asia. Finance proved almost as undependable. Despite Wall Street's renewed interest in the area around 1904, the bankers did not care enough to fight past the ring of entrenched Europeans and claim a secure position of their own. In a classic example of the conflict between power and profits, Roosevelt pleaded in vain with J. P. Morgan to hold his ground in China just when the ledger and the market counselled retreat. At a critical moment the President lost that precious resource because the man who controlled it was following the dictates of another god.

Roosevelt's only recourse, therefore, lay in borrowing from the nation's general fund of prestige. The path of entry he chose was the Anglo-Japanese Alliance of 1902. The most logical avenue in light of America's increasing ability to cooperate with Britain, it still contained innumerable hazards. Britain, which had arrived first and taken the most in China, looked to rising powers like Japan and the United States as shields against its European opponents, who in combination could strip the leader of its bounty. That cautious, defensive posture meant that it would take no risks assisting the United States, a nation on the make.

Japan on its part was as much America's competitor as its ally. Roosevelt hoped that by keeping relations as smooth as possible with this expansive nation, Japan in its turn would not oppose the assertions of the United States in the Far Pacific. The President, however, miscalculated the strength of Japan's drive, particularly in Manchuria. Moreover, this man of faint sensitivity to the subtler emotions never did comprehend the implications of race prejudice in his foreign policy. The violent antipathy to yellow skins along the West Coast only caricatured a prevailing American assumption of Oriental inferiority. Neither nation could surmount the obstacle of white chauvinism. Although Roosevelt managed one bitter incident in 1907 when he simultaneously convinced California to moderate its discrimination against Americans of Japanese descent and Japan to limit its immigration to the United States, he approached the matter as if he were settling a claim for property damages. A state's interference with the nation's foreign policy infuriated him, but the prejudices behind it did not.

Of course troubles would have beset any route the latecomer had chosen. At least as detrimental to American policy in East Asia was Roosevelt's imprecision in objectives. He talked a good deal about a balance of power there, the kind that would enhance American opportunities. In practice, however, that meant little more than checking Russia, which he both distrusted and despised. British influence and Japanese expansion on the continent never seriously disturbed him. (There were good and bad powers just as there were good and bad trusts.) Although he cared about the Philippines only as a repository of American prestige, the rigamarole of his imaginary war games caused him to worry inordinately about an attack upon the islands, and that too modified his approach. Prestige, again, impelled him to oppose a Chinese boycott of American goods during 1905 and 1906. Yet if Roosevelt could never allow such an affront to pass, he was equally incapable of tying his general policy to the petty interests of commerce. Nor did he share the belief of Brooks Adams and Franklin Giddings, among several others, that in some geopolitical sense the key to the world's future lay in the Far Pacific. East Asia concerned Roosevelt very much, but no more than Europe or Latin America. In the end, the ground never quite settled beneath his efforts. While he established a pattern of involvement, he could not grasp a goal greater than his initial purpose, a mere assertion of the nation's power.

Taft compounded the confusion. As he entered office, the railroad king Edward H. Harriman was mapping the most ambitious Asian scheme of the early twentieth century—domination of the Manchurian railways—as one link in his grand design for a global transportation system. At the same time, subordinates in the State Department transposed this venture into an ideal means by which the United States might gain a preponderant influence throughout all China. Manchuria would serve as the lever, opening Peking to America's full power. The slender chances of such an enterprise depended upon the most careful attention to changing circumstances and upon the most delicate diplomacy. Instead, the complexities of the situation eluded the President, who was thinking of Manchurian trade rather than Chinese investments, and he threw the nation's prestige in the breach just when America's financial elite, in another example of political-economic divergence, was retiring before too much uncertainty and too much foreign opposition. There he stood, overextended and alone, as the revolution commenced and Wilson succeeded him.

To the relief of the bankers, who desired only to escape the chaos, Wilson withdrew government support for all such elaborate proposals. As if reverting to the simple, trade-oriented philosophy of the open-door notes, he asked merely for decent treatment in China and a pause until the turmoil ceased. It did not, nor did Japan wish to wait. When the First World War drew the European powers back home, Japan issued an ultimatum to the government then installed in Peking that would have fixed China as its neighbor's vassal. Once the United States might have shrugged and accepted fate. But now Roosevelt's involvements, which Taft however ineptly had kept alive, automatically transformed that incident into a challenge to American prestige. Willy-nilly, the United States as a power in East Asia was trapped in the requirements of a foreign policy. Although Japan did relent ever so slightly, the United States deserved little credit for that. In time Wilson's frustration led him back to the fundamentals Roosevelt had examined earlier. By the end of his Administration, he also was encouraging the financiers to enter China and even calculating the value of a token military force as means for a sharper and more systematic influence in East Asia.

Two decades of erratic behavior in a marginal area gave American policy a very mottled appearance indeed. Yet somewhere close to the center of these happenings ran a continuity of purpose that the policymakers themselves only half-recognized.

Viewing China as a resource for the use of Western powers, the United States had participated in multinational efforts to hold its government at that critical level between competence and impotence. Its rulers should have the ability to ensure a minimum domestic stability without the capacity to resist imperial penetrations. Viewing Japan as an inferior nation—precocious but in the long run no match for Western power—the United States had hoped to use its ambitions as a counterpressure to Europe and thereby maintain an environment in East Asia favorable to American expansion. The belief that ultimately any Oriental nation would have to bend before a determined Occidental one would die hard. The total effect was less a balance of power than a point of tension. All factors, internal and external, would so interact that they created a stasis allowing Americans to move in and out at their discretion.

Set against comparable domestic developments, America's first ventures into foreign policy showed an unmistakable immaturity. Unlike the best of the new administrative arrangements at home, the system for gathering and assessing information from abroad never approached the nation's requirements. Nothing better illustrated that failing than the almost panicky demands in Washington for basic data once the First World War had begun. Despite a series of measures designed to increase the professional and organizational strength of the State Department, the American network of international communications had not acquired fiber or depth even in areas of special concentration. Both Roosevelt and Wilson relied heavily upon unofficial sources—either a random scattering of friends or an ill-equipped set of private emissaries—in deciding important matters of policy. That amateurish approach not only accentuated the elements of chance where consistency was essential, but it also inclined leaders toward explosive action where careful steps would have served far better. A number of the armed interventions in Latin America, while appropriate to the spirit of American policy, actually represented one form of bankruptcy, a crude replacement for the kind of indirect influence officials had sought but could not achieve. Taft's bullish behavior in China reflected much the same weakness.

The apparatus remained that faulty in part because the politicians in command did not feel the need for something superior. As long as Americans constructed a world view so thoroughly out of the materials immediately about them, and did so without sensing any disadvantage, they would continue indulging their imaginations almost at will. Roosevelt and Wilson both retained a powerful faith in the intuitive management of world affairs, contrasting markedly with their discipline in the conduct of domestic matters. Consequently, Roosevelt's wide-ranging correspondence simply suited him better than the more mundane collations of a bureaucratic staff, and Wilson's willingness to let Bryan turn portions of the foreign service into a junk heap of party patronage was actually not so very strange. In fact, the choice of Bryan, whom his chief once said had "no mental rudder," was itself suggestive. Tradition had not forced Wilson's hand. No President since 1897 had used the Secretary of State's office as an honorary reward for the dean of the party. In an era of such speculative freedom in foreign affairs, Wilson believed he could afford a useless first lieutenant. Roosevelt had indicated that if he won in 1912 he would select Gifford Pinchot, a man utterly devoid of experience in the field. The two of them looked at America's domestic problems in just about the same light, and in foreign policy it was the starting point that really mattered.

10

The Beatified Brute

THE NATION'S EXPANSION into Latin America and East
Asia was in one sense merely a way of claiming a place among
the great powers. Certainly men like Theodore Roosevelt and
John Hay saw it in that light. Yet the conditions that produced
policies in the colonial lands could never be duplicated in Europe.
The United States dealt with the weaker nations more or less as
it chose: they could scarcely resist. Relations with Europe, on the
other hand, depended upon a reciprocal willingness, and before
1914 the major nations showed little desire to include the United
States in their diplomatic system. Although they readily granted
it the title of a great power, honor was not membership. The
United States would not bind itself by treaty to any European
faction; and after 1900 only that commitment could have established it in a scheme of things increasingly predicated upon just
such alliances.

As a result, the United States remained on the periphery of
great-power diplomacy. While the number of contacts with the
nations of Europe multiplied, these did not constitute systematic,
policy relations. In fact, events in both Latin America and East
Asia discouraged that continuity. The European powers retired
quite meekly before the American onslaught in the Western
Hemisphere, where they had relatively minor interests. In East
Asia, where their stake was much larger and America's strength
far slighter, they successfully excluded the United States from

their inner circle. Nor could a variety of private transatlantic connections cover the gap. The banking elite which had risen to prominence earlier as an agent of European finance now had the capacity to mark its own path. Without endangering important friendships abroad, American bankers held somewhat aloof, neither invading Europe's domain nor brooking interference in their own. Even Roosevelt's network of well-situated European correspondents could only supplement the more traditional international relations. On those occasions when an Old World leader wished to invoke the New, a quiet exchange of letters with the American President greatly facilitated the process. In such a personal fashion Roosevelt became the mediator between Russia and Japan in 1905, and played a significant part in the settlement of a dangerous imbroglio over Morocco at the Algeciras Conference of 1906. Nevertheless, these incidents in no way qualified the United States as a partner in European affairs.

Britain represented the great exception. But then Britain was the exception in so many ways. For more than a century Americans had habitually measured themselves by a British gauge. Their freedom and their democracy, their heritage and their culture, all acquired meaning through a comparison, explicit or implicit, with the British model. No matter how much writers or philosophers or reformers might borrow from the Continent, in the last analysis they almost invariably tested their accomplishments against those on the Isles. America's ambivalence toward Europe seemed at times to narrow into this peculiar need to find merit by way of Britain. The odds always favored London as the center of any popularly suspected international conspiracy. The British example usually served as the whip in any self-flagellating account of the nation's failings. Few found it possible to deny that somehow the United States was caught up with Britain in a common destiny, a vague yet compelling belief that the American Negro soldier captured with grim unintentional humor when he spoke proudly about "us angry Saxons." Even the citizens accused of being "German-American" or "Irish-American" never thought to retaliate with "British-American," for fundamentally

"British-American" was the norm by which one calculated devia-
tions. "Anglophile," the closest counterpart, carried none of the
hyphen's divisive, disloyal connotations.

The group that came to power with Roosevelt exemplified this
involvement. None extolled British virtues more grandly. "Natural selection" had brought it international pre-eminence, declared
Alfred Mahan, who talked of Britain with "honor, reverence, and
affection." If America would only follow Britain's guide,
Franklin Giddings wrote, "we need have little fear that another
thousand years of mediaeval night will fall upon the Western
world." Hay exalted "the Pax Britannica over India, Egypt, and
South Africa" as an imperial ideal. Yet no Americans wagged
their heads more quickly over its weaknesses. In 1910, summing
up two decades of hypercritical scrutiny, Roosevelt pronounced
the British Empire "flabby." And prior to the First World War
no one demonstrated a stronger aversion against binding the
United States by any formal, restraining compact. Britain would
always stand as their model, the one nation with which America
enjoyed a natural—an inevitable—affinity, and the United States
could not conceivably enter upon a course that might over the
long run set the two countries at odds. At the same time,
America's very success as a great power depended upon its
superiority to Britain at Britain's own game, and that in turn
required full freedom to surpass the aging parent.

These were the men with whom Britain negotiated at a time
when its fortunes dictated a search for friends, and out of that
dialogue emerged America's sole policy with a European power.
In retrospect the process appeared to have begun in 1895, when
President Cleveland and his Secretary of State, Richard Olney,
shocked Britain with an ultimatum to settle a boundary dispute
between its colony of Guiana and Venezuela. For an absurd
moment the world's first navy and a country with not a single
first-class battleship verged on a war over the jungle land along
the Orinoco. Neither government wished to risk so much for so
little, and after an interval of grace, Britain coldly, quietly,
acceded to America's demands. Again during the Spanish-Ameri-

can War, Britain seemed to stand apart from an unsympathetic Europe, particularly when it urged the United States to retain the Philippine Islands. Yet the origins of policy lay just beyond these preliminaries.

The question at issue around 1900 was how Britain would react to America's hemispheric ambitions. By tradition, might, and material interests, Britain, not the United States, ranked as the foremost power in Latin America. It alone had the capability of challenging America's expansion to the south, and a variety of interested citizens, almost belligerently apprehensive, watched the lengthy negotiations over Britain's treaty rights in a Central American canal for a token of its intentions. The answer came with remarkable clarity in the final Hay-Pauncefote Treaty of 1901. Britain simply relinquished everything. Shortly afterward, London bowed before Roosevelt's insistence upon a peaceful adjustment of the Venezuelan debt controversy, and then prodded him to take the very step he eventually did in announcing the Roosevelt Corollary. To underline the new friendship, Britain simultaneously sided with the United States against Canada in the settlement of a disputed Alaskan boundary. In the years to come, without abandoning its interests in Latin America, Britain deferred to Washington whenever the United States cared sufficiently to press its point.

Withal, it was an extraordinary performance. Once deciding that it would not contest Latin America, Britain drew a maximum return by claiming no return at all. The rest of America's policy toward Britain flowed from that graceful retreat. When Roosevelt sought a companion in East Asian affairs, he naturally turned to Britain, which retained America's favor there despite the absence of any substantial assistance for its programs. Washington and London came as a matter of course to inform each other about issues of common concern and sometimes to discuss moves before they were taken. War between the two was now unthinkable. Nothing in all this was either strange or sinister. The only danger lay in the failure of Americans to comprehend the implications of what was happening. Until the eve of America's entry into the First World War, no prominent official seemed to realize that the nation had entered a tacit alliance with Britain.

In place of a European policy, Americans pursued peace. A word of manifold meanings, it managed to encompass most of their assumptions about modern civilization. Peace connoted order and stability, the absence of violence, the supremacy of reason and law. It suggested the disappearance of militarism and all other vestiges of a barbaric past. It implied, in other words, a world operating from the same general precepts so many Americans were trying to realize at home. Of course only the advanced nations qualified for such a bright future. Almost no American seriously thought of including backward peoples in his plans, except as an appended hope for some far distant time. Fundamentally peace concerned the United States and Europe.

Arbitration, a misty means to the hazy goal, easily ranked first among the techniques for peace. It promised to regularize international affairs, which to the bureaucratic mind was in itself a virtue. It appealed to a popular legalistic bent, whether the complex judicialism of a William Howard Taft or the common-sense, rules-of-the-game justice of a George Norris. It might cover almost every international issue, or almost none. For some arbitration meant no more than committing civilization's current status to paper. For others it meant a novel and elaborate structure of treaties, courts, and procedures that would draw civilized man to higher and higher levels. Thus it might serve as the initial step toward a new world order, or it might contain a single grudging concession from a coveted national sovereignty. Alfred Love, America's leading pacifist, and Henry Cabot Lodge, prickly defender of the nation's honor, joined in supporting arbitration—as a principle.

Early in the century, the translation of that principle rested with its most skeptical proponents. Ever fearful of limiting their nation's—and their own—freedom of action, the power-oriented group around Roosevelt preferred to bury arbitration rather than risk its misapplication. Mahan, as a delegate to the First Hague Conference in 1899, had set the standard by fighting passionately to limit the jurisdiction of that conference's agreements and of the international court it sponsored. In the years that followed, neither Roosevelt nor his Secretaries of State gave more than passing support to the cause. The only successful arbitration treaties they negotiated were, as Roosevelt noted, actually regressive; that is, they covered a range of issues narrower than tradition had come to include. Nor did the President regard the Second Hague Conference of 1907, which he helped to convene, as much beyond a gesture to the benighted.

With the Taft Administration, however, the executive attitude changed markedly. The new President, acting out of a faith in the curative powers of the law, and Secretary Philander Knox, reflecting the desire of the profit-oriented for predictably smooth relations with all great powers, proceeded to negotiate inclusive arbitration treaties with both Britain and France. But they ran afoul of a jealous Senate, where Lodge increasingly spoke with priestlike authority on matters of foreign relations, and consequently the most ambitious ventures of the era died. It was left to William Jennings Bryan as Secretary to salvage something from these hopes. His efforts took the form of bilateral "cooling-off" treaties, twenty in all, which obligated both sides in an inflammable dispute to postpone any warlike moves for one year while a commission examined the issues. "When men are mad," he explained, "they talk about what they can do. When they are calm they talk about what they ought to do." Likening international conflict to a street-corner quarrel appealed to the village mentality but clearly disappointed those who believed that peace would require a sophisticated legal framework.

Nevertheless, a great many Americans would not acknowledge even the possibility of a reverse. Sublimely confident that a better world was arriving and that the United States would lead in its creation, they continued to scheme and spin. Each year more voices heralded the coming peace, and each year their visions expanded, particularly in the direction of a dawning international federation. Invariably patterned after the United States, these predictions tracked the world's progress by close analogies to their own nation's history. The international tribunal at The Hague, for example, paralleled the loose compact among the states under the Articles of Confederation. A necessarily weak beginning, it would soon give way to a "constitutional era" with broadening cooperation, just as the needs of the states had produced a more perfect American union. All the while, a spreading democracy—essentially America's democracy—would march hand in hand with world federation, twins in the cause of international peace and justice.

For countless Americans it was a flawless dream, one that carried the legalistic logic of arbitration to a natural climax. Although relatively few devoted much time to world federation as a specific movement (that would have taken them into strange terrain, and the new unity, after all, was materializing of its own accord), practically no one denied its premises. Even the exponents of national greatness, so sensitive to any erosion of American sovereignty, could only argue that the most fervent spokesmen for federation were premature. It would eventually come, of course, just as the world would inevitably grow more democratic; but it would require a long preparatory period before mankind could achieve the ideal.

The rhetoric of peace suggested the outlines of a broad agreement: the desire for orderly international conduct; the emphasis upon law, with a strong tendency to rely upon mechanical devices; and above all the faith that an irresistible progress was carrying civilization beyond war. Like any such garment, it covered men's thoughts in quite different ways, hugging some, barely touching others, perhaps missing many who had never spoken their minds. It rested so easily across the nation's discourse in part because nothing disturbed it. These assumptions, of course, concerned only a fraction of the globe—the mature fraction. Brand Whitlock, "Lover of Humanity" who went as minister to Belgium expecting to imbibe the wisdom of a perfected civilization, could readily accept the "unspeakable barbarities of the Mexicans" because he already "knew those Greasers were a pretty bad lot." Two worlds, two cultures: it was so simple in 1913.

Loose fit, hidden flaws, and all, this was America's protection in the summer of 1914 when the storms broke in Europe. The chain reaction that in a matter of days mobilized Germany and Austria against France, Britain, and Russia—joined soon after by Japan and Italy—demolished each major premise about civilized international behavior. Americans everywhere mouthed phrases of horror and disbelief. What else could they say? Instinctively they drew inward, trying to stretch the moral distance between themselves and Europe, as if quarantine might yet save their principles. Citizens who a month before had located the United States with the Anglo-Saxon peoples or the great powers or the Western nations now talked about the Old World and the New. This was Europe's disaster, they claimed, not America's, and the United States must insulate itself from foreign sins.

Americans nevertheless recovered quite rapidly, given the weight of the blow, and in the following months demonstrated that remarkable ingenuity with which men bend events to fit their values. They demanded, first, a decent, law-abiding war. Europeans were not savages and could not act like such. Belligerents must abide by the rules of fair play, both written and unwritten, in all dealings with neutrals, civilians, and each other. With nothing beyond images of Roosevelt charging San Juan Hill and faded tales of the gallant Blue and Gray to give warfare some personal meaning, they clung to the belief that the gentleman's code still applied. Honor and heroism, for nations as well as for the individual soldier, still served as the standard in combat.

Second, Americans sought to comprehend the whole of the conflict in congenial terms. Though all Europe was now tainted by bloodshed, a careful examination, they knew, would still expose the more guilty and the more innocent, the aggressor and the aggrieved. Only a miracle could have altered the outcome of that search. Among almost all of the powerful and the articulate, at any rate, bias in favor of Britain automatically conditioned

Americans to cast Germany as the villain and the Allied Powers as heroes. It was not that Germany already suffered from such a bad reputation in the United States. Now and then, power-minded citizens had warned of a German threat, and others had frowned at Germany's apparent love of the military. Yet Americans had borrowed freely from Germany's rich cultural heritage, an increasingly respected minority of them had German ancestors, and many a reformer had praised its neat, efficient ways. In fact, if any European nation were peculiarly suited for villainy, it was Russia. Backward and autocratic, Russia had filled the role of the enemy in a number of popular speculations about the world's future struggle for freedom. It had, in addition, incurred the hostility of almost every prominent official who participated in the making of America's East Asian policy. "Utterly insincere and treacherous," Roosevelt had fumed in 1905, and lesser men had echoed the same sentiments.

Germany's primary disadvantage in 1914 was not its record in American opinion, but the absence of a record. So little existed to counteract the natural pull toward Britain. Moreover, with a keen sensitivity to the American mode of thought, Britain, which dominated the channels of transatlantic communication, played directly to that powerful urge for law and honor, plying the United States with doctored news of German illegalities and atrocities. It scarcely need have bothered. Germany had, after all, attacked first—and through neutral territory; its officials did refer to a treaty as a mere "scrap of paper"; it did initiate the use of poison gas; it did rely heavily upon the submarine, a devilish device that conjured visions of sea monsters and drowning infants. At each step, crude German boasts and clumsy explanations fed the American predisposition to condemn all this. The widespread habit of personifying nations worked these pieces into a simple picture—the armored, bloodthirsty Hun. Americans of German descent, defensive from the outset, had neither the skill nor the opportunity to soften the stereotype.

Third, the large majority of peace advocates rearranged their principles in order to justify a certain kind of warfare. France and Britain had been attacked. Naturally they had to defend themselves, to defeat any enemy who threatened not merely their security but the very cornerstone of modern society. The Allies, in other words, were the armed legions of law and order, and their efforts upheld the basic values of civilization. War, once condemned out of hand, became the rational means to a greater good, if the proper men waged it in the proper context. It was quite simple for many who had once labored for a reduction in armaments to join the call in 1915 and 1916 for America's military preparedness, though they hoped, even assumed, that the United States would never enter the conflict. In the correct hands, the weapons of war could not possibly serve the wrong ends. Significantly, the debate over preparedness, as bitter as it was, contained very little about the legitimacy of arms as such. It concentrated instead upon the desirability of a particular form of readiness at a specific time. Most opponents of preparedness in 1916 could support America's war effort a few months later without contradiction. After all, the countless proponents of peace included only a handful of pacifists. As the editor Hamilton Holt explained, he had enlisted in the cause because it "was not a mere revolt at the horrors of war . . . but a pro-law movement." By that light, the migration from peace to preparedness to war was not a very difficult one.

The leaders in the Wilson Administration shared this general orientation. The President and his successive Secretaries, Bryan and Robert Lansing, all thought within the framework of an orderly war, calling for humane conduct and tinkering with mechanisms that might ensure the civilized standards. Wilson, Lansing, and Edward M. House, intriguer extraordinary and the President's intimate, viewed the conflict from Britain's perspective, despite Wilson's attempts to break from the pattern. Each considered Germany not just the guilty party but the enemy. Even Bryan, whose ingrained suspicions of Europe kept him more detached from the Allied cause—or at least more fearful of America's entry into the war—indicated his clear preference for Britain on several important occasions. None of these men doubted the righteousness of a good army, however much Bryan and, to a lesser degree, Wilson recoiled at the prospect of a full military commitment. They represented, in other words, their nation's dominant predilections, a matter of considerable importance in a trying time. By the same token, they were no better equipped to deal with world problems than the ordinary, capable American politician. In spite of Lansing's general familiarity with diplomatic procedures, they brought neither diplomatic experience nor even a student's expertise to international affairs. The ignorance they would not acknowledge as weakness compounded their inevitable confusion before a turbulent world. Nor with an unrestrained British partisan in London and an inept amateur in Berlin could the nation's foreign service compensate for their deficiencies.

Assuming that the Allies would quickly defeat the Central Powers, the Wilson Administration sought in 1914 to give the United States maximum leeway with minimum involvement during the brief war. The natural means were those rules governing belligerent and neutral rights which passed under the name of international law. Ambiguous in some instances and contested in others, this body of precedents and principles still had a certain rough consistency that made them serviceable enough for a short conflict. Temporary injustices would have to be overlooked and differences postponed for later adjustment; these rules offered the best hope of maintaining civilized standards. Moreover, they expressed the strong desire to draw a clear, impassable line between America and the war. European nations were fighting, the United States was not. "Belligerent" and "neutral" would state that blessed moral distinction, that fundamental separation of two hemispheres.

But the war dragged on, acquiring a life of its own, with no end in sight. The approach that had been automatic in 1914 now promised to become an indefinite commitment unless the Wilson Administration rethought its case at once. Large sections of the economy were thriving under the stimulus of orders from the

Allies, and every month more businessmen were reorganizing to serve that profitable commerce. Democratic leaders responded by moving with the current. "Lawful and welcome," Wilson's Secretary of the Treasury, William G. McAdoo, called the war trade in August 1915. When Britain moved to mollify America's cotton industry, suffering from the absence of its usual continental market, McAdoo and important members of the Federal Reserve system quietly assisted the Allies in underwriting the entire crop at an attractive price. When immediate sources of commercial credit ran dry, the Administration withdrew its earlier disapproval of the flotation of Allied loans in the United States, and the Federal Reserve Board altered its policy to facilitate sales to American bankers. (The original distaste for loans was a striking illustration of the popular distinction between bad finance and good commerce. Anticipating a brief war, Bryan and Wilson had both turned against the one and welcomed the other. Eventually, of course, the exigencies of that good commerce forced them to embrace bad finance as well.)

In the same fashion, the Administration clung to the old rules of international behavior, despite their obsolescence. The neat row of ships that had once constituted a blockade now scattered in fear of the submarine's torpedo. The submarine, in turn, that dared abide by the traditional procedures of hailing a commercial vessel and allowing noncombatants a safe departure was simply committing suicide before the merchantman's light cannon. Modern land transportation had demolished a whole logical scheme involving the immediate and ultimate destination of goods, and the mobilization of entire nations had destroyed the elaborate lists of absolute contraband, conditional contraband, and free products. While the belligerents continued to talk the language of international law as best they could, they adjusted policy to suit the new war. In November 1914, Britain declared all of the North Sea a "war zone"—that is, open territory for its navy—and checkered it with mines. The following February, Germany encircled the British Isles in another war zone, fair grounds for its submarine, and the next month Britain proclaimed a "blockade" of Germany that covered all waters and practically all goods.

The Wilson Administration complained at every step. Even if the United States could not undo any of this—mine fields once laid would remain—the government would legitimize none of it. "The rights of neutrals," the Administration announced with far more passion than accuracy, ". . . are based upon principle, not upon expediency, and the principles are immutable. It is the duty and obligation of belligerents to find a way to adapt the new circumstances to them." No matter how much the warring powers might manipulate the setting, the United States would hold both sides responsible for every violation of the old truths. At the same time, however, almost every prominent American saw the submarine as the critical challenge to the nation's neutrality. Into this evil serpent were invested all their abhorrence of barbarism, hostility toward Germany, and compulsion about legality. Although the Administration bent policy to accommodate Britain's needs, approving that preposterous hoax, the "defensive" armament of merchantmen, and tacitly accepting much of the blockade, Wilson immediately took high ground in response to the submarine and held it tenaciously. Throughout the lengthy exchange that began in May 1915 with the sinking of the *Lusitania,* a ship that had combined the functions of liner and war transport, he maintained that if the submarine could not act according to the traditional code of decency, it could not operate at all. Actually the issue was never moot. At the outset, the United States had claimed that the very use of the submarine meant "an inevitable violation of many sacred principles of justice and humanity," and in the spring of 1916 when Germany capitulated for a time, Wilson was still denouncing it in the name of all mankind.

By one reasonable standard, the United States had adopted a sensible policy. The tacit ally of Britain for many years, it had good reason to fear Germany's success. In mid-1915 Lansing confided in a private memorandum, "Germany must not be permitted to win this war. . . . This ultimate necessity must be constantly in our minds. . . . American public opinion must be prepared for the time, which may come, when we will have to cast aside our neutrality and become one of the champions of democracy." Almost from the beginning, he and House, who strongly urged his appointment as Secretary when Bryan resigned in the summer of 1915, premised America's policy on exactly that basis: the United States must act to ensure an Allied victory— short of war if possible, as a belligerent if necessary. An appreciable number of influential men in and out of the Administration agreed.

Wilson, who once remarked that Britain was waging "our" war, seemed at times to agree. Certainly none of these men felt a deeper reverence for Britain or wished more fervently for its success. Yet in his own eyes he was a public man—of the exalted sort progressives described—and he resisted his impulses with a vehemence born of painful inner turmoil. "We must be impartial in thought as well as in action," he had told the nation as the war began. He not merely followed that will-o'-the-wisp, as only a Presbyterian could pursue his duty, but he convinced himself that in his official capacity he had achieved it. "Neutrality" was his sacred public trust, his religion. Yet what could it possibly mean? The day when belligerents fought in a separate arena had long since disappeared. From the outset the United States was incorporated into the war as a major arsenal in the Allied system. When Germany, which received no assistance from America, attempted to check this flow, the Wilson Administration set conditions that would render it impossible. In other words, the United States was making an indispensable contribution to the Allied cause and insisting upon the right to do so.

In this context the pretense of neutrality was absurd, and the debate over a neutral's legal privileges either an arid exercise in logic or simply a maneuver for advantage. To the degree that anyone desired a functional neutrality, he would have to redefine America's goal, then undertake the delicate task of altering convention to fit a modern war. Bryan, for all of his incompetence in the particulars of diplomacy, expressed this basic issue better than any of his colleagues. Even Lansing, who was a man of self-conscious integrity, acknowledged the problem. But those who believed that the United States should participate just as it was fell back upon a deceptively simple answer. It would be unfair to change the rules in the middle of the game. Argument by false analogy (war was not football nor was international law its official guidebook) served a convenient and very understandable function. Policy, prosperity, and purpose all meshed, and the fiction of neutrality covered the whole of it with the sort of legal justification so many Americans appreciated.

Of course this kind of neutrality also satisfied something deep within Wilson, as it did for millions of Americans. The greatest danger lay not in its contents but in the President's inability to evaluate them. He lived the delusion that he—and the government of the United States—was officially and effectively impartial. Then he built upon that base. A true neutral, the United States should use its power in behalf of peace. It alone could replace the keystone in Western civilization. What might have been a distinct basis for American policy became instead a natural extension of the current one.

Soon after the war began, Wilson sent House abroad to explore the possibilities of a settlement. Then late in 1915, again acting through House, he made his first important effort to end the conflict. Waiting for Britain's cue, the United States would demand that the Central Powers negotiate under the threat of America's probable entry if they refused. A striking illustration of Wilsonian impartiality in action, it did not even appeal to Britain, the prospective partner. His second effort came directly after the campaign of 1916, which to the President's distress had become a Democratic hymn to nonbelligerence. Committed more firmly than ever to an imposed peace and temporarily irritated at Britain's treatment of American commerce, Wilson now planned to call both sides to the conference table. Just at that moment, however, Germany pretended an interest in negotiations. If the President would no longer mediate from London, he still could not appear to agree with Berlin. The grand project dwindled to a request for war aims.

America's capacity to mediate rested upon the same skewed base as its neutrality. A lightly veiled sympathy, an implicit mutual appreciation, gave negotiations with Britain a fluidity and flexibility that carried the two governments over all but the roughest periods. Even then the interchange suggested the wounded feelings of friends far more than the angry clash of opponents. With Germany, however, the Wilson Administration conducted a cold, brittle dialogue, one that barely rose to the level of communication. Harsh lectures, truculent replies, then silence: each knew the other for an enemy. Each understood, moreover, that the United States could never enter the war against Britain, although it might well join against Germany. Nor short of an extremity would the Wilson Administration ever employ its powerful economic leverage in order to bend the Allies to America's will. In response to Wilson's pleas, the one side could calculate the price of refusal by increments of assistance, the other by increments of damage. A partisan and impotent mediator never threatened the determination of either alliance to fight on.

Wilson interpreted the failure of mediation otherwise. Only an insane perversity on all sides could explain the rejection of his cries for peace. When Germany gambled for a swift victory in January 1917 by unleashing its submarines against all commerce to the Allies, Wilson was gripped in anguish. Would the United States—the one remaining rational power—now be driven into that pit of passions? Hoping desperately for a reprieve, he delayed a commitment through February, then into March. Yet the myth of neutrality provided an inexorable justification for war. By 1916, it read, the United States had forced an impartial set of rules upon the combatants. Germany had smashed them. A guilty Germany, not an innocent United States, had chosen war. Nevertheless, the President would dedicate his nation to the same unsullied impartiality in war as in peace. He would hold America above the pit, asking for no reward other than a free, decent world. In a stirring presentation of these aims, he called his countrymen to arms. The Public Man would guide a Public Nation through a war to democratize the world, and Americans everywhere cheered. War, now sanctified, had become the necessary prelude to mankind's salvation.

The nation threw itself into the conflict and with surprising efficiency made its resources available to the Allies. Its navy helped break the grip of the submarine on transatlantic commerce, its raw materials—food and petroleum in particular— fueled the Allies' sputtering war machine, and by the summer of 1918, its troops, arriving far earlier than most had anticipated, gave essential momentum to the counterattack that unnerved Germany's weary leaders. At the same time, the Administration almost ostentatiously held the United States aloof. America was an "associate," not an ally of the Entente Powers, and the government kept its troops as tightly segregated under American command as a coordinated military effort would allow. As if blindness were virtue, Wilson refused to recognize the various treaties by which his co-belligerents had already divided the spoils of victory. The United States would not contaminate its crusade with Old World corruptions.

Despite the preoccupations of war, Wilson continued to pursue a peace that would justify America's sacrifice, and by the strictest progressive standards, his leadership exemplified the ideals of the public man. In January 1918, a time of uncertainty and low morale, he sketched the broad outlines of the better world to come, thrilling millions here and abroad. Later that year, when others had lost themselves in hatred of the enemy, Wilson grasped the first opportunity to negotiate an armistice with the Central Powers and skillfully led them into an agreement of his own choosing. By using the "fourteen points" of his January speech as the basis for a cease-fire, he had combined a release from death with the promise of a life freed from tyranny, national rivalries, and militarism. Victor and vanquished alike had reason to rejoice.

These same progressive principles made Wilson's next decision

—to lead America's peace delegation to Paris himself—a difficult one. On the one hand, bickering and bargaining across a conference table seemed to jeopardize the very essence of the public man, his impartiality. Once raising the banner of justice for all, Wilson had in effect declared everyone with special national claims, partners as well as enemies, his opponents, and the distance between Washington and Paris would graphically express that detachment. On the other hand, only the public man could retain that comprehension of the whole which gave meaning to specific decisions. This belief in the end proved the more compelling. By the same reasoning, he could scarcely have selected such Republicans as Lodge and Elihu Root to accompany him, however expedient their choice. To the President, as to Roosevelt and La Follette and the rest of the progressive leaders, men who disagreed with him were hopelessly narrow and partisan. There could be only one vision—Wilson's. Like a figure out of progressive theory, the President embarked with a handful of associates and a large retinue of expert assistants, the specialists whose particular, scientific knowledge would fill out his dream of world peace. "Tell me what's right," he promised them in midpassage, "and I'll fight for it."

Wilson demanded, and received, a League of Nations as the first issue before the Paris conference. Here was the heart of the entire program, the quintessence of the progressive vision. Just as the autonomous commission lay at the center of America's domestic reform, so an international agency would supply coherence for the new world. Just as a Federal Trade Commission or an Interstate Commerce Commission was expected to manage, respond, adjust, according to the flow of events, so the League would provide a bureaucratic solution to international flux. Just as progressives at home resisted a constraining list of rules, so Wilson at Paris sought a broad mandate for his organization. Time and again he emphasized how all else in the treaty hinged upon the League, how this vital agency would breathe life into the mere words of the document. It was simply the promise of the modern American system offered to the whole world. Understandably an overwhelming majority of the new middle class greeted the League with unrestrained enthusiasm, and even the members of that class who dissented, who desired a different solution in international than in national affairs, could only attack it around the edges. Wilson's assumptions were no more than their own projected onto a universal stage.

A solution admirably suited to the modern American temper, the League by the same token was projection run riot. For almost all Americans, the war had been a domestic phenomenon—buying Liberty Bonds and passing men in uniform, feeling new restraints and hearing new hopes, and always hating the Boche. As long as they could graft these novelties to a familiar framework, they had felt no need to find a new perspective. Ideas about world affairs still floated in essentially the same rarified atmosphere of two decades earlier. They continued to ignore the great gaps separating European and American and colonial objectives; the radically different orientations abroad toward peace and honor, security and revenge; the utter absence of a preliminary structure upon which world reform might be built. It was enough to talk about an emerging international consensus on peace that the League would both express and facilitate.

As its opponents demonstrated, the League contained a good many ambiguities. Somehow it never occurred to them that these represented just one more version of the confusions inherent in the whole scheme of progressive reform. The most important criticism warned of the League's uncertain purpose. Was it meant to achieve a precise, predictable stability, or would it welcome and work with an open universe? In other words, did this particular bureaucratic mechanism lean toward control or emancipation? Both its origins and the events surrounding its birth argued the former. The primary source of the idea lay in that prewar equation between peace and law, a law that clearly connoted a determinate, dependable world order. War merely accentuated that concern. Lyman Abbott's phrase, "a universe given over to lawlessness," epitomized the instinctive abhorrence in 1914 among educated Americans, and the incessantly repeated condemnation of Germany as "lawless" expressed much of the justification for entering the war in 1917. During these same years the most articulate proponent of a permanent international agency was the League to Enforce Peace, an indicative name, which set an elaborate legal structure at the core of its program.

The widespread uneasiness over Europe's upheaval at the end of the war also suggested a stabilizing League. Here the crucial event was the Bolshevik coup of November 1917. By the usual Western standards, its first principles embraced chaos. Worse than that, the success of Bolshevism touched raw doubts everywhere about the establishment's capacity to control unrest at home. Prominent Americans joined Europe's leaders in praying for its demise. If fewer Americans recommended armed intervention as a way to realize those prayers, the explanation lay in their reasoning more than their tolerance. Because Russia was only semicivilized, the common argument ran, only a strong man could rule such a sprawling state; because Bolshevism was "anarchy," it could not possibly produce that man; therefore, Bolshevism, carrying the seeds of its own destruction, would inevitably give way to a sane, conservative command. Characteristically, the United States received no official intelligence worthy of the name. Its ambassador, David R. Francis, a wealthy hack dating from Cleveland's time, remained hopelessly befuddled throughout these momentous months. Some Americans disagreed with the standard argument, relying upon a potpourri of rumors that the Bolsheviks were experimenting with a new democracy. Yet even the dissenters worried about the wholesale disorganization, particularly in Central and Eastern Europe, which accompanied the armistice.

Wilson did not deny any of the premises arguing for stability. He had predicated America's neutrality upon law and order, and he had led the nation into war to regain them. When he envisioned a world "made safe for democracy," the first two words carried the greatest thrust. With a fair opportunity, democracy would evolve of its own accord. The task of the United States was to make the world safe for that emergence. The most significant member of the League to Enforce Peace was the President himself. Like the rest of America's spokesmen, Wilson drew boundaries around permissible discord which effectively excluded violence. While he could honestly wish the masses of Russia well, he along with a host of his fellow countrymen assumed that everyone naturally aspired to a respectable middle-class life after the American pattern. Only bad leaders (Bolsheviks) or evil and abnormal circumstances (revolution) could twist those hopes into some form of radical socialism. To remove the leaders and correct the circumstances would serve the deepest desires of an otherwise trapped people. Initially concerned about the military implications of Bolshevism—the new Russian government promptly sued for peace with Germany—Wilson drifted rather easily into a support of the counterrevolutionaries whom Britain and France were sponsoring. By the end of the war not only were American troops entangled in Russia but officials in Washington were already fixing the policy of nonrecognition, of ostracism, that would continue for the next fifteen years.

Yet if Wilson believed in an imposed stability, he also shared the new-middle-class dream of releasing energies. Everything he said with regard to the League reflected that ambivalence. Certainly the new organization would oppose the bloody adjustment of boundaries, and the United States would assume a moral obligation to participate in such collective security. At the same time, Wilson's faith in the League's capacity to resolve all the errors and unfinished business in the treaty clearly presupposed that it would respond intelligently to a fluctuating world. In short, the President expected his League both to hold and to free. His inconsistencies were nothing more than the evasions of so many Americans—friends and enemies of the League alike— about the purpose of their own domestic accomplishments.

This lack of clarity pervaded the balance of Wilson's work at Paris. Once he had built the Covenant of the League into the treaty, the President then faced that mountain of particulars which the other nations had regarded all along as paramount. He earnestly desired a just settlement for each issue, and true to his calling as the world's public man, he mastered an incredible quantity of data in an effort to reach honorable solutions, one by one. It was a superhuman task. Facing an array of hard, committed bargainers, he could not possibly have his way in every case. At several points, for example, national ambitions combined with geography and demography to defeat the self-determination of culturally similar peoples, his cardinal rule in drawing boundaries. Still, if Wilson had conceived of the treaty as the single determinant of justice, he almost certainly would have compromised less. As it was, the League offered an escape from the most intense pressures of negotiation. Reluctant to alienate those nations whose cooperation would be the very fabric of the new organization, he preferred to believe, from time to time, that he could accept a dubious answer now and postpone the final one for the League.

Two other confusions materially affected Wilson's course. One involved a conflict in the meaning of impartiality. Wilson arrived at Paris confident that as the one disinterested participant he alone could ensure a purely rational, humane settlement for all parties. In fact, an Olympian fairness toward the Central Powers ranked high among his objectives. Yet his own syllogism justifying America's entry had already singled out Germany as the absolutely guilty nation. On the one hand, he would stand above the war; on the other, he had just been in it. Throughout the sessions, Wilson tried to reconcile these contesting pulls without much success. He could scarcely oppose the treaty's "guilt" clause, placing full blame for the conflict on Germany. He had often said as much himself. After a rather feeble effort to limit the reparations Germany would be required to pay, he accepted a formula that allowed the Allies to extract all they could for any war costs they wished to include. Although the President scotched the most elaborate plans for dismembering Germany, he agreed to the detachment of its important Rhineland province for the economic benefit of France, in violation of the principles he purported to serve. Wilson could never find solid ground between his ideals of equity and a victor's peace.

The last difficulty stemmed from America's traditional separation of the world into two spheres, civilized and barbaric. Wilson's wartime generalities about self-determination and the evils of colonialism had led some to believe that the New World would no longer contain this division. Vaguely aware of the expectations he had helped to arouse, the President was still not the man to implement them. Never questioning the supremacy of "the great white nations," as he called them, he relegated the weaker countries to petitioners at the peace conference, placed the future of the League primarily in the hands of the major Allied Powers, debated colonial issues within the framework of imperialism, and opposed a clause honoring the principle of racial equality. These decisions expressed his everyday convictions far more than the compromises of a conference. Nevertheless, Wilson did wish to propagate a benign paternalism. He hoped that a system of League mandates for the German colonies would replace harsh selfishness with the wise guidance of these backward peoples, and that in a land such as China the great powers would voluntarily relinquish their most degrading political privileges. A bare step away from his European colleagues, he neither presented an effective case nor used his resources intelligently to win it. Realizing he had not accomplished enough but uncertain about what he should have done, he deeply resented the charges of inhumanity levelled against his work.

Wilson returned home to a hypersensitive nation. Climaxing a process underway since 1915, a majority of citizens had become involved—continuously involved—in foreign relations. Unaccustomed to a field that suddenly seemed to dominate their future and unable to affect the basic commitments, they had mulled about the fringes of policy, restless and tense. Now at last the treaty,* the fruit of all this involvement, would give them something to grasp, an issue of fundamental importance to settle. As if the bars had raised before a mob, Americans rushed to meet the

---

* Actually the Allies settled matters by separate treaties with each of the Central Powers. The major document was the Treaty of Versailles with Germany.

document, perhaps the most widely discussed packet of paper in the nation's history. The roar was numbing. Pieces of the treaty, or the whole of it, appeared to touch everybody, and in a manner that could only bewilder the responsible officials, citizens grouped and regrouped, demanding a say in the final decision.

Some specialized. The Great War, holding Europe's future in balance, had roused dormant loyalties to the old country and had driven newcomers to speak for themselves well before anyone might have anticipated. Even when ethnic feelings alone did not move them, the fate of their birthplace, or their ancestors', gave many Americans a convenient means of judging an otherwise chaotic world of affairs. German evil and United States sovereignty also served as popular devices to clear away that confusing mass of details. But a version of Wilsonian hope, of war as the crucible for a lasting peace, of the League as mankind's grand promise, seemed to outdraw all others. Long ago Edward Bellamy and Josiah Strong had announced America's international mission to the countryside; now the cataclysmic moment had arrived. The sense of a world progressing stage by stage to perfection, though shaken in 1914, had acquired new life through the sublimation of war into a utopian agent; the treaty would express the next—perhaps the last—giant step forward. And to many members of the new middle class the League promised universal application of their progressive principles.

In spite of these efforts to understand, a combination of ignorance, uncertainty, and inordinate expectations still left most Americans highly vulnerable to the appeals of a persuasive recruiter; and Wilson, by his office and his impressive political record, seemed pre-eminently qualified for the role. Two developments nullified his advantage. Beneath a facade of victories, the organization of the Democratic party had improved only slightly during the previous decade. After capitalizing upon the Republican divisions around 1912, Democrats had been unable either to integrate their party or to secure its finances. Even the election of 1916 had depended upon transitory factors: an immediate return on New Freedom legislation, an impression of friendliness to

progressive latecomers, and an image of peace. Without an
enduring base such as the Republicans enjoyed, the Democrats
could hold their majority only by an uninterrupted flow of
benefits distributed with the utmost skill. War disrupted that
makeshift pattern of success, and a rapid deterioration followed.
The loss of both houses of Congress in 1918 presaged an approaching disaster.

Inspired leadership might have checked the decline, but
Wilson, the one man situated to provide it, would not meet the
challenge. Despite his talents in factional maneuver, he had never
liked such work in the way a Roosevelt did. Confronted with the
responsibilities of war and peace, he willingly relinquished the
task of party management in order to concentrate upon what he
regarded as the essentials. His inept call in 1918 for a Democratic
Congress to underwrite his peace mission indicated how far he
had already retreated from domestic realities. By 1919 he lived
largely in a private land of world schemes. Since the nineteenth
century everyday politics had anchored those officials who might
otherwise have soared into foreign affairs. Now Wilson had lost
his moorings. Inclined to messianic impulses and recently beset
by illness, he slipped across the fine line dividing grand plans
from fantasy. There he would make his stand—isolated, rigid—
while his political power crumbled beneath him.

The initiative passed to a number of prominent Republicans,
most of whom still responded to the logic of power or of profits.
Both lines of reasoning led them to reject Wilson's League.
Without friends in the executive, Roosevelt's once-formidable
coterie had rapidly lost influence, and talking war in the name of
America's honor and greatness when most citizens wanted peace
had only aggravated their problem. Roosevelt himself, obsessed
by the war and by what he regarded as Wilson's cowardice, had
stunned the Progressive convention of 1916 by suggesting the
incurably conservative Lodge as a Presidential candidate. He then
returned to the Republican party with belligerent speeches which
some thought had defeated its candidate, Charles Evans Hughes.
Suddenly war came, and everyone spoke that language. Too

isolated for leadership before 1917, Roosevelt and his comrades were too overwhelmed by agreement after that.

The battle over the treaty offered them one final chance of glory. For the first time, however, they differed among themselves on a crucial matter of foreign policy. Though all of them began with the assumption that Wilson's League dangerously inhibited the nation's freedom of action, some, like Root, would have amended it in order to combine sovereignty with a limited international cooperation, while others, like Roosevelt and Lodge, would have destroyed it. Quarreling, aging, and leaderless with Roosevelt's death in 1919, they ceased to act as a group.

Circumstances, on the other hand, had blessed the profit-oriented. Although they had exercised scant influence over Wilson's course, they approved almost all of it. They had thrived during the neutrality years, and they had appreciated the need for war in 1917. Regularly adding new members, the internationally minded magnates of finance emerged in 1919 powerful, ambitious, and optimistic. A world for expansion spread before them. The last thing they desired was to be tied to a crippled Europe, where potential competitors would do everything possible to undermine America's natural economic advantages. Joined by a growing number of corporate executives who also saw unprecedented opportunities for expansion, they worked through legislators, editors, and private associations to defeat the League of Nations. As a result of these efforts, the opponents of the treaty enjoyed much better organization than its advocates.

Nevertheless, confusion continued to dominate the debate. Neither side had made significant inroads into that mass of citizens who had so recently thrown themselves into the discussion of foreign policy, and no one could fathom their wishes. At first veteran politicians moved cautiously. Then in time, as nothing concrete materialized from the public discussion, many of them found it emancipating. A plethora of imprecise talk gave the politician almost as much freedom as silence did; in either case, he could easily claim that his views represented true public opinion. Leading Republicans in the Senate, almost all of whom disliked the treaty on both partisan and personal grounds, attacked with increasing aggressiveness. At their head stood Lodge —icy, shrewd, and venomously hostile to the President—who as chairman of the Committee on Foreign Relations controlled tactics in the Senate. The ensuing struggle demonstrated how a few strategically placed men—a President and a handful of Senators—might hamstring the political process, twisting it to serve their private needs.

Lodge adopted a two-fold plan: delay and amendment. The first part, implemented largely through committee hearings, enabled him and his co-workers to publicize all dissatisfaction with the treaty while they allowed a portion of the postwar euphoria to dissipate. Although the League always remained central, Republicans welcomed the support of any ethnic group that felt its ancestral land had somehow suffered in the balance of the treaty. The second part of the plan used the desire among moderate critics to improve the League as an excuse to drown it in a flood of changes—some major, some minor. Here Lodge could also rely upon the wounded pride of the Senate, which Presidents had grown accustomed to slighting in foreign affairs and which Wilson in particular had insultingly ignored. This time, many Senators felt, they would have their say regardless.

Lodge's work had guaranteed that the treaty could not muster the necessary two-thirds majority without substantial change. Furious at the thought of compromise, Wilson, ailing and proud, drew on his final reserves late that summer to take his case to the people. Three weeks into the tour he collapsed, silencing a desperate eloquence; four days later he suffered a stroke. Though he struggled back from the grave, he remained a sick man, more than ever insulated from a political world he did not care to see. By his command, almost all of the Senate Democrats insisted upon an unaltered treaty in November when a series of votes defeated it, with and without reservations. Wilson, the man whose domestic fame had been built upon ingenious compromise, would not give an inch; and Lodge, the man who had once

helped to construct the nation's first foreign policies, now helped
to destroy its best hope of continuous participation in world
affairs. People he despised—country folk fearful of a strange
world, professional spokesmen for Ireland and Germany and
Italy—cheered him as their champion, while friends he respected
such as Root and Taft turned sadly away.

Out of a need to feel that the war had accomplished something,
that a pure battle did produce good results, most Americans
probably wanted the treaty, with the League, to pass in some
form. Cries for another vote continued, and in March 1920 a
revised version came once again before the Senate. Twenty
Democrats, either hostile to the treaty or loyal to the President,
joined the fifteen "irreconcilable" Republicans who opposed any
League to block approval. But Wilson, nursing the faith of the
progressive, had already looked beyond to one final effort. The
election of 1920, he said, should be "a solemn referendum" on the
Treaty of Versailles, the people's voice cutting through that wall
of Senatorial prejudice. An empty dream in a futile cause, it still
made some sense in his own day. Not only did men believe that a
rational public lay behind the squabbling factions, but many also
thought that the President's re-election in 1916 had, in fact, been
just such a referendum on the issues of war and peace. Why not
now, of all times, when an unprecedented public interest made it
impossible to understand the people's will? So the Democrats,
riddled and retreating, met a prosperous and powerful Republican party in the election that swept Warren Harding into the
White House and killed the League's last, faint chance.

The story of the League was more than a grotesque mixture of
myths and passions. In the strange way a surfeit of interest can
neutralize itself, the nationwide clamor had enabled a very few
men to determine the treaty's fate, and as it happened the
protagonists in the struggle represented two alternative concep-
tions of foreign policy. Lodge, the sole member of Roosevelt's
group with great authority in 1919, spoke a pure version of the

power-oriented philosophy which more than any other had struc-
tured America's world relations over the past two decades.
Wilson challenged that system with an approach derived from a
mature progressivism. In place of a sovereign assertion, a reliance
upon independent strength, and a single-minded pursuit of goals,
the President offered international coordination, systematic controls, and bureaucratic adaptability. Yet neither the old nor the
new would win that contest. The original ideas of the power-
minded had lost their force. Now the United States enjoyed an
unquestioned greatness; it did not have to assert it. After the war,
the nation militant seemed a puerile, even a dangerous notion. At
the same time, Wilson's progressive foreign policy, sketching
castles without foundations, raised expectation it could never
fulfill. Neither was distinctively idealistic or realistic; both rested
upon ethical bases, and both attempted to impose American
patterns on an imaginary world. What was truly important, by
1920 neither suited the nation's requirements.

The vacuum did not fill immediately. Once immersed, Americans would never lose their consciousness of world affairs, and
thereafter international topics assumed a natural, prominent place
in public discussions, in sharp contrast with the prewar years. But
no new groups or new guiding themes had appeared by 1920.
People talked peace again with a new urgency and simplicity,
stripped of the most elaborate legal mechanisms. Many also lost
forever that traditional ambivalence toward Europe. The opinion
that the United States—the creditor nation, the philanthropic
nation, the superior nation—could do what it liked when it liked
had run as a cheap refrain throughout the debate over the treaty.
In a certain sense, the profit-oriented elite benefited the most
from a decision they had only secondarily affected. Yet they were
verging on another major change which would broaden their
composition, weaken their cohesion, and diminish the significance of high finance. For a time they would not be able to
command. Seen in another way, the greatest gains fell to men still
scattered and weak in Wilson's era. During the twenties a new

set of public officials would fashion an approach out of the expansionist ideal of Roosevelt's coterie, the bureaucratic inclination of the progressives, and the balance-sheet philosophy of big business and stake a fresh claim to leadership. Nineteen twenty, however, merely marked a moment in the transition.

11

Doorway to the Twenties

WAR CREATED abnormalities in abundance. Sharp inflation, a new vocabulary, and a welter of government agencies each
expressed part of a strangeness that filtered rapidly through
American society in 1917. In certain cases—the drafted civilian, a
sudden prosperity or poverty—war actually altered the substance
of men's lives. Usually it just rearranged the setting. Beneath the
trappings, most Americans followed the same old goals for the
same old reasons. The impact of the war at home, in other words,
primarily affected the modes rather than the purposes of behavior.

The most powerful influence was a generalized sense of national crisis, one which millions predicated but could not define.
It was inconceivable that a good American would hang back
while his nation's fate stood in the balance. Yet what were the
right things to do? He volunteered for all manner of services
which, he was told, bore some relationship to victory. He bought
Liberty Bonds, or he sold them. He paraded. At the behest of the
Food Administration he observed meatless Mondays and wheat-
less Wednesdays. And he listened. He listened to his own impulses. He listened to those who did know precisely how to save
America. If he liked what he heard, he acted. This was certainly
no time for dainty scruples. If he did not, he probably held his
tongue, less out of fear than out of confusion, for he had no clear

alternative. The crisis of war, by stripping away a veneer of restraints, allowed Americans to translate assumptions into actions, to express normal feeling with abnormal directness; and the beneficiaries were those few with simple, persuasive answers and the means at hand to implement them.

The war itself contributed one set of answers. Germany was the enemy; therefore anything German became fair game for men in pressing need of a patriotic cause. Communities banned German music, restaurants rechristened sauerkraut "Liberty cabbage," and random gangs harassed citizens whose names or accents suggested the evil Hun. By the same token, failure to demonstrate sufficient enthusiasm for the war served as an invitation to abuse. Vigilantes scoured the neighborhood for "draft dodgers." Buying bonds, contributing to the Red Cross, uttering ritual phrases of reverence and hate became the sacred tokens of loyalty, exacted where they were not given. Yet as logical as these barbarities were within the context of war, they were basically unnatural. Few had carried a love of the Army or a detestation of all things German into the war years, and relatively few carried them out.

The essence of America's wartime patriotism derived from the familiar rather than the fortuitous. In their most important sense, the fevers of war constituted just one chapter—an intermediate one—in the developing campaigns to discipline American society. These movements supplied the neat, prefabricated explanations of the national emergency which countless citizens found irresistible. They answered the imperative yet misty questions about America's danger, they pointed to visible, available enemies, they played upon a host of incipient anxieties, and they satisfied the urge to violence. Only this exceptional appeal can account for the eagerness with which people made the most preposterous connections between foreign and domestic dangers; between the German menace and the Non-Partisan League, for example, or Bolshevism and the American Federation of Labor. If the ongoing movements for social control defined the wartime crisis,

crisis in turn accelerated the movements. In almost every case, they acquired new breadth, a new toughness, and a force that would propel them into the twenties.

The insistence upon a tight national cohesion, one prime index to the worries that had been deepening since 1907, had already inspired drives to restrict immigration and to Americanize new-comers. Both waxed during the neutrality years when a number of substantial citizens, particularly in the East, had justified ever-harsher measures in the name of preparedness, and both became obsessions with the declaration of war. Although Congress finally passed a literacy test in 1917 over the President's veto, legislators promptly called for more systematic means of exclusion. The commitment to close America's gate as far as possible material-ized during and just after the war. Even then the bulk of the fears centered not on Germans but on the peasantry from Southern and Eastern Europe. In the same fashion, plans to homogenize those who were already here also concentrated upon the most obviously "alien." New immigrants felt the brunt of the attacks against foreign languages, unfamiliar customs, and liberal citizenship requirements. Demanding an immediate transforma-tion, the grim Americanizers fulfilled their own prophesies of doom. Not only did ethnic groups hug their familiar ways in response to these assaults, but they hastened as well to organize in their own behalf. A sharpened ethnic consciousness, so evident in the debate over the treaty, merely reinforced the conviction that because the melting pot had ceased to work the nation now stood in constant jeopardy.

Rising parallel to the anxieties about cultural disunity, anti-radicalism also interpreted the threat to America by a narrowly uniform ideal, fed upon the strains of neutrality, and thrived during the war. Antiradicalism not only defined the nature of Americanization and justified the restriction of immigration, but it also demanded orthodoxy in all public education and sponsored the ominously vague Espionage and Sedition Acts for a far broader wartime control. A large majority of vocal citizens obviously believed that the nation did face "a clear and present danger" from abroad in a sweeping, furtive sense which the author of that phrase, Justice Oliver Wendell Holmes, had never anticipated. If spurious documents implicating the German government in the Bolshevik coup had not appeared, surely someone else would have invented them. By 1919 a continuing threat of alien subversion had become the necessary myth.

At the same time, antiradicalism wore another guise. Year by year, the men who felt their authority in danger had been accumulating lists of immediate enemies, of people who by their lights were nourishing the alien menace right there within the body politic. Fighting as best they could in the prewar years, groups of these determined citizens then launched a series of brutal, thorough attacks after 1917 against the most vulnerable of the so-called radicals. Through posses, state and Federal prosecutions, and government censorship, they seriously weakened the Socialist party, broke the strength of the International Workers of the World, and stamped out a variety of weaker, fringe activities that ranged from the grumblings of tenant farmers to dissenting little magazines. None of this was done under the shadow of a guilty conscience. The leaders of these campaigns— the corporate executive and the prosperous farmer, the newspaper editor and the established politician—acted on the assumption that other Americans could only praise their virtue. Public response supported that faith. Each of these radical groups could, with some justice, be identified with the critics of the war, a disconcertingly large body; and only bad men opposed a good war. In general, the radicals enjoyed neither the indigenous power nor the allies to resist popular persecution.

Once unleashed, of course, these attacks did not stop with the most obvious victims. In the region surrounding North Dakota, substantial citizens employed roughly the same techniques against the Non-Partisan League, a neo-Populist movement led by respectable farmers and townsmen who wanted to break the big city's grip over their countryside. Although no one could check their sweep to office in North Dakota, organized intimidation in neighboring states, combined with a financial boycott, first contained the League and then hurried its downfall.

Despite the efforts of the aging Samuel Gompers to win public favor by an ostentatious patriotism, the American Federation of Labor emerged from the war shaken and unpopular. Not only had many craft unions failed to capitalize upon the singular opportunities of a wartime labor shortage, but they had also joined viciously in condemning the more radical labor leaders. Immediately after the war, employers renewed an offensive which the dearth of skilled workmen had slowed and turned these same charges of "Bolshevism" and "alien" against the conservative AFL. With their left flank exposed, the craft unions did not have the strength to retaliate. By 1920 a nationwide open-shop drive, decentralized but nonetheless systematic, had gathered support from well-to-do Americans everywhere and was pushing organized labor in retreat.

And always there was that gray amalgam of slum dwellers. Life in the tenements, predicated on poverty and chance, had little more meaning to comfortable Americans in 1919 than in 1890. Before the war the ferocious suppression of strikes in the garment, textile, and mining industries, involving many unskilled workers of new-immigrant background, had expressed that rising fear of the masses, and it was the vision of danger here that lay behind the Red Scare of 1919 and 1920. A natural extension of their earlier concern, it included wholesale arrests in the immigrant quarters, concerted strikebreaking against unskilled workers in steel and other industries, and government passivity as slum-dwelling whites beat slum-dwelling Negroes back into the ghettos they had filled during the war. When the rabble seemed quiet, the violence abated.

In a similar though milder vein, prohibition had recently gained wide popularity among America's urban-industrial leadership as a new means of mass control. Around 1908, just as the Anti-Saloon League was preparing for a broad, state-by-state drive toward national prohibition, a number of businessmen had contributed the funds essential for an effective campaign. The series of quick successes that followed coincided with an equally impressive number of wealthy converts, so that as the movement entered its final stage after 1913, it enjoyed not only ample financing but a sudden urban respectability as well. Substantial citizens now spoke about a new discipline with the disappearance of the saloon and the rampaging drunk. Significantly, prominent Southerners with one eye to the Negro and another to the poorer whites were using exactly the same arguments. As a consequence, a host of predictions about sober, peaceful workmen plying their trades and minding their own business accompanied the final adoption of the prohibition amendment in 1919.

The rather abrupt entry of the Supreme Court into the battle for the good society offered one more indication of how powerful the pressures of fear had grown. For two decades after 1896 the Court—now warning, now giving ground—had followed a cautious, moderate course. On several occasions, such as those involving labor boycotts, it had upheld precedents which some in the new middle class had hoped to overturn. Also, while ordering the dissolution of Standard Oil and the American Tobacco Company in 1911, the Justices had claimed a share in the government's new regulatory activities by announcing that their personal test of reasonable and unreasonable restraint of trade would henceforth measure the legality of the large corporations. Yet in general they had used the formidable powers acquired during the eighties and nineties sparingly. They had loosened the rules covering state railroad regulation, validated workmen's compensation, accepted certain forms of legislation governing hours of work and factory conditions, and avoided a conflict when the national government undertook to supervise manufacturing concerns.

Then in 1917 the Court began a concerted drive against dissidents with *Hitchman* v. *Mitchell,* a decision upholding "yellow dog" contracts, which prohibited workers from joining a union as a condition of employment. During the next few years the Justices struck down the first Federal statute against child labor, bound unions more tightly within the antitrust laws, defended the right of the states to suppress radicalism, and prepared for an active surveillance of government policies early in the twenties. In most instances their arguments relied upon the same rubbery principles which the judiciary had formulated in the period before 1896. A strained application of the liberty of contract underlay *Hitchman;* and a substantive due process of law, which appeared to be dying before the war, now became a major means of circumscribing the state legislatures. It was precisely for such critical times as this that the Court had preserved these powerful legal weapons.

All the while, the lists of the reforming new middle class continued to shrink. Many of them had also found American society out of kilter. Wartime rumors of division and disloyalty, hints of a festering radicalism, and labor violence cast more and more doubts on the desirability of any further reform, even on the people's ultimate wisdom, and increasing numbers slipped quietly into the camp of hard controls. (What a shock to discover that thousands of draftees had never even heard of Abraham Lincoln!) Patriotism and prohibition served as especially sensitive indicators, and both were drawing heavily from new-middle-class sources by the end of the war. "The German onset brought the realization, with an intense feeling of shame and danger, that we were a nation only in a very imperfect sense," wrote a leader in the settlement movement, who also cheered the prospects of prohibition. "[We] were stirred to a new sense of responsibility for a more coherent loyalty . . . a vital Americanism. . . ." Others had lost their way in the passage from peace to war to the frustrating struggle over the League. Brand Whitlock sank into Europe's aristocratic past, Herbert Croly into mysticism. Still others subsided in the face of reforms that were now threatening them. A good number of doctors, for example, lost their enthusiasm for any social change once they were confronted with a campaign for compulsory industrial health insurance. Above all, many of these one-time challengers had simply won too much to fight on. Recognition, place, and at least a share of power had drawn them into a system with which they identified, one they could now defend as good and just. Former progressives were gradually becoming spokesmen for the status quo.

By and large, the remaining militants were those who had habitually leaned upon more powerful friends, and the loss of their allies hobbled them. This was particularly true in areas of humanitarian reform, although it also affected the union movement in ways a Gompers could never have acknowledged. The campaign for women's rights proved a partial exception. Its advocates had laid an impressive groundwork by about 1914, and the final push for the constitutional amendment enfranchising women, victorious by 1920, depended relatively little upon outside assistance. A movement that had once been sustained by the correlative values of progressivism, by the flexibility and the expectations of a society in transition, developed an independent power which in certain instances outlived that of its sponsors. Even such a pariah as Margaret Sanger, lonely crusader for birth control, could profit from the new stature of American women, at least to the degree that the courts upheld her right to proselytize. "Once Woman was my superior," the good Bishop Henry Potter sighed; "now, alas, she is only my equal."

In a more general sense the mobilization of 1917 and 1918 illuminated the degree to which an emerging bureaucratic system had actually ordered American society. When the Wilson Administration set about coordinating the nation for a modern war, a task that a great many here and abroad considered far too complex for the time allowed, the pieces for a pattern seemed to appear by magic. Businessmen who were suddenly faced with the necessity of negotiating by way of economically functional groups formed a nationwide network of trade associations. Almost as quickly, an agricultural elite organized by locality and by crop. The majority of industrial crafts were already unionized. No administration could have commanded these results. Although the needs of war did act catalytically upon the process of organization, the essential fact was that association represented a natural response. Two decades of organizational experimentation, of a deepening commitment to some form of cooperation, lay behind the record of the war years.

If the spirit and extent of middle-class organization placed it in the forefront, the trend transcended any one segment of society. Corporations that had once relied upon even greater chaos among their competitors were now planning managerial reforms that would spread from the board of directors to the repair shop. During the war, in what several veteran labor leaders mistook for a sudden change of heart, big businessmen often acknowledged the need for some union among their workers. The desire for predictability that would make Frederick Taylor a folk hero among corporate executives was also encouraging them to draw the arbitrary powers of the foreman into the hands of a specialist in personnel; and experiments in welfare capitalism, looking toward a more refined control over the labor force, multiplied each year.

There were countless applications of this general bureaucratic formula. The national Republican party, which had once derived its support from a handful of very wealthy donors, was now preparing to tap the resources of thousands of well-to-do community leaders, once more altering its structure of power as it secured its financial base. Law offices that had once depended upon the magnetism of one or two prominent names were transforming themselves into sets of highly specialized subdivisions, each with its own hierarchical staff. "Law factories" they were called. Such universities as Chicago and Columbia which had once sought fame by pursuing a single educational ideal were now increasingly eclectic centers directed by professional administrators.

Governments at every level were moving in a similar direction. Particularly in Washington and in the major cities, executive direction was an accomplished fact by the war years. Although many of the bureaus and departments of the progressive era had yet to define their functions precisely, they were at least entrenched. Nineteen sixteen marked "the completion of the federal scientific establishment," covering industry, agriculture, and an assortment of public services, and much the same was true of the basic regulatory mechanisms in both Federal and state governments. Unlike the officials during the late nineteenth century who had struck and retreated, their modern counterparts assumed continuity in their work. Agencies accumulated their files and procedures and precedents. At the time of the Red Scare, for example, the government could already draw upon a decade's sum of arbitrary practices to cow immigrants, and the birth of the Federal Bureau of Investigation formally heralded a new era. In the legislature specialized committees, often designed to mesh with an executive bureaucracy, had increasingly become the vital centers. In fact officials at all levels of government found it easier year by year to communicate with one another, just as they found it more and more necessary. In such areas as highway construction, already a major issue as the Model T streamed from Henry Ford's assembly line, Federal and state governments promptly laid a basis for long-range cooperation. The Supreme Court in 1920 declared the essential unity of American government with states and nation coordinated to achieve mutual goals, in striking contrast to its dictum of 1876 on distinct state and national systems. As if to remind citizens of the modern day while they hurried about their affairs, Congress imposed standard time zones across the land.

What had emerged by the war years was an important segment of the population, a crucial one in terms of both public and private leadership, acting from common assumptions and speaking a common language. A bureaucratic orientation now defined a basic part of the nation's discourse. The values of continuity and regularity, functionality and rationality, administration and management set the form of problems and outlined their alternative solutions. A few recognized the fact and accepted it. "There will be no withdrawal from these experiments," Elihu Root announced in 1916, referring specifically to the regulatory commissions. "We shall go on; we shall expand them, whether we approve theoretically or not; because such agencies furnish protection . . . [which] cannot be practically accomplished by the old and simple procedure of legislatures and courts. . . ." A few recognized it and rebelled, in some instances fleeing to what seemed freer air abroad. Infinitely more just lived with it, dilemmas and all, as the American way.

The ease of communications during the war astonished even the patriotic optimists. Information on allocations and production, draft procedures and bond sales, war propaganda and peace proposals, all depended fundamentally upon an extensive private network which crisscrossed the nation. Alert to the government's directives and eager to act in a quasi-official capacity, newspapers, chambers of commerce, schools, citizens' committees, and many more marshalled the home front. When the Administration wished to borrow a specialist's knowledge—or simply his prestige —innumerable experts appeared. Even such an apparent failure as the treatment of the influenza epidemic of 1918, which took a shocking toll, exemplified the new order. Although medical science could not meet the emergency, millions of educated Americans dutifully awaited the doctors' word, donning the same masks and cleansing the same foods in a remarkable display of coordinated faith.

Randolph Bourne's savage salute to war as the health of the state contained a wisdom even his small circle of listeners did not comprehend. As if countless Americans had anticipated their roles, the pieces fell into place with a neatness almost no one could have predicted. The extensive readjustment of the surface— the proliferation of laws and agencies and committees—created a perpetual noise of bustle and complaint; endless details meant endless quibbling. Nevertheless, the apportionment of tasks and responsibilities seemed to be following a prearranged schedule. Much of the secret behind this silent plan lay in the assumption running throughout the reforms of the twentieth century that no system could work without the voluntary cooperation of its leading participants. In particular, national progressivism had been predicated upon the existence of the modern corporation and its myriad relationships with the rest of American society. Chronologically, psychologically, this network had come first. It had set the terms of debate. Even as the reformers attacked trusts,

DOORWAY TO THE TWENTIES 297

slums, and the like, they had built upon them. In a way only a few of them fathomed, their alterations strengthened a scheme they disliked by weaving its basic elements into an ever-tighter and more sophisticated national system. A public bureaucracy sheltered as it regulated.

Progressives in office had not known what to do with their own revolutionary rhetoric. A La Follette, for example, could talk earnestly about a sweeping antimonopoly crusade yet premise his tax program on the growth of big business in Wisconsin. As Governor, he pruned but never attempted to uproot. A Wilson could describe the glories of old-time competition with complete honesty yet help to construct law after law that reflected an existing distribution of power. The nation required a modern financial system? Then the men on Wall Street, and to a lesser degree those on La Salle Street and Chestnut Street and even Main Street, would simply have to cooperate. Every important Democratic official agreed.

Somewhat more slowly, private leaders had come to believe that they also could not function without the assistance of the government, increasingly the national government. Only the government could ensure the stability and continuity essential to their welfare. Its expert services, its legal authority, and its scope had become indispensable components of any intelligent plan for order. And what they sought could no longer be accomplished by seizing and bribing. The nineteenth-century formula of direct control—taking an office for yourself or your agent, buying a favor or an official—now had very little relevance to the primary goals of society's most influential men, whether in business, agriculture, labor, or the professions. They required long-range, predictable cooperation through administrative devices that would bend with a changing world. Nor were they thinking about a mere neutralization of the government, the automatic reaction many had given to the first flurries of reform. They wanted a powerful government, but one whose authority stood at their disposal; a strong, responsive government through which they could manage their own affairs in their own way.

Preliminary indications of how this mutual dependence might

translate into public policy had already appeared before the war. The Federal Trade Commission from the outset had welcomed those business organizations which hurried quietly to it with their problems, and within two years it had become sponsor within the Administration for a permissive regulation quite similar to the one business spokesmen had originally requested. "It is hard to describe the functions of [the FTC]," Wilson remarked late in 1916; "All I can say is that it has transformed the Government of the United States from being an antagonist of business into being a friend of business." Similarly the county agents, who ostensibly represented the Department of Agriculture in the new schemes for demonstration and experimentation, almost invariably served as lieutenants to the local farm bureaus they had often organized. The Department of Interior under the Democratic Secretary, Franklin Lane, had come more and more to rely upon private interests in defining the conservation laws, especially in regard to petroleum.

Each of these instances duplicated a general pattern. Government bureaucrats looked to the private groups in their bailiwick as a natural constituency, men with whom they must develop good relations and from whom they expected regular support. These groups reciprocated, looking in turn to the bureaus for essential services and acting as their lobbies—just as long as the effective power of decision remained in private hands. In the late nineteenth century, the national government had delegated most of its domestic powers to the states, from whence it scattered to a thousand localities. In the twentieth, the national government parcelled an increasing amount of its power to private groups; and these then exercised it through the national government itself. Progressive legislation sketched the outlines for that new system.

The war tended to make such assumptions explicit, then apply them throughout the country. For the duration the War Industries Board under the skillful guidance of Bernard Baruch held the role such theorists as Herbert Croly had once envisaged for the FTC. The central agency for allocations and production, "it was really the town meeting of American industry," as one participant described it. "American industry virtually imposed on itself through the clearing-house of the War Industries Board, its own rules and then policed itself. . . ." Agricultural distribution fell to Herbert Hoover's Food Administration, equally dedicated to group action, voluntarism, and self-management. Both agencies established broad war goals and on rare occasions interfered by way of price incentives. Beyond that they tried to act only as referees and coordinators for all who would accept the ground rules. The private Petroleum Advisory Committee set and administered its own regulations through the government's Fuel Administration. Although decay in the railroad system forced a temporary nationalization, that industry continued to execute its own policies through the good offices of William McAdoo.

The same framework spread well beyond economics. The voluntary censorship instituted by the Committee on Public Information, for example, rested upon essentially the same principles, as did the Justice Department's wide delegation of authority to the 12,000 local units of the American Protective League, Babbitt vigilantism at its crudest. For all the makeshift quality of those procedures, they had grown naturally out of an emerging set of attitudes about the meaning of government, the proper organization of society, and the uses of power.

What was natural, however, was in no sense inevitable. Others foresaw a quite different role for this ripening bureaucracy. In 1916 the veteran reformer Frederic C. Howe as a Commissioner of Immigration organized the first Federal employment bureau in New York City. The guiding function of that small enterprise represented just as logical a development of progressive theory as the permissive practices of the War Industries Board, and a number of Wilson's appointees seemed to favor such an approach. When the Federal Trade Commission lost its central position to an array of wartime agencies, it also tried to assume more independent managerial powers. Serving as the Administration's investigator, it searched among the major industries for evidences of unhealthy monopoly and illegal profits, the impartial determiner of ethics and practices. Similarly, some members of the new Tariff Commission were attempting to establish themselves as an autonomous source of scientific data and criticism. Weaker groups in particular looked hopefully to this kind of government both as a means of defense and an opportunity for much more rapid advancement than they could accomplish on their own. With an eye to their short-run advantage, the craft unions argued not only that the government should retain a general control of the railroads after the war but that it should extend a comparable dominion over the coal mines and perhaps other basic industries as well. A few reformers even smiled upon the sixteen thousand units of Federal housing, built to accommodate war workers, as an omen of much more to come.

Firm bureaucratic traditions had yet to be made. Those who schemed so grandly about the future, however, tended to ignore that youth in this instance meant stiffness, a certain brittle quality that reflected uncertainty, inexperience, and limited talents. The war illustrated some of these rigidities with particular clarity. Belying America's pride in adaptability, mobilization depended heavily upon existing channels. When it required extensive innovation, it generally faltered. The attempts to create new shipbuilding and aircraft industries, for example, ranked among the most conspicuous failures of the war. The American system, in the idiom of that day, contained far too few interchangeable parts. Rather than a bureaucratic order, it was actually a number of separate bureaucracies, barely joined in some areas, openly in conflict elsewhere.

Other flaws had long been evident. Even during the heyday of finance capitalism, its masters had too often provided a stumbling leadership. Inordinately dependent upon the House of Morgan in domestic policies, they had moved into fields they barely comprehended, and the several billions in securities they floated early in the century had demonstrated poor judgment in their choice of consolidations and in their sense of the money market. Given the strategic power these magnates had held, they left the nation a meager legacy. By the First World War, the unique circumstances that had underwritten America's finance capitalism were rapidly disappearing. As the nationwide sale of war bonds indicated, the great bankers no longer enjoyed even an approximate monopoly over the growing surplus. Mobilization completed the destruction of a second prerequisite, the government's incapacity as an economic leader. And the increasing financial autonomy of the major corporations dealt the system a final blow. The disorder attending the brief history of finance capitalism suggested again how much of America's new bureaucracy had been resting upon a most dubious, blind faith.

It was, moreover, a system of restricted scope. The large majority of wage earners lived beyond its influence, untouched by its spirit and largely free from its discipline. Once more, the inhumanity of the suppressions during and after the war testified as much to the weakness of a ruling elite as to the quality of its ethics. By choice the men in authority would have controlled the masses through a quiet, continuous, and predictable management. The bloody club was as much a sign of their frustrations as their fears. A great many in the countryside had also escaped the bureaucratic web. An enduring rural localism, premised upon the infinite applicability of the old village values, had supplied the basic thrust to the prohibition movement, and its spokesmen now pictured a self-fulfilling climax to their campaign. By demolishing the heart of the Social Problem, the Eighteenth Amendment would automatically spread goodness where evil had once flourished. Men and women still accustomed to the unofficial enforcement of a community scarcely bothered with such matters as public administration. Much of this same time-honored approach also lay behind the rural–small town votes which passed the immigration restriction laws.

Tentative steps toward a new order had brought America to the edge of something as yet indefinable. In a general sense, the nation had found its direction early in the twentieth century. The society that so many in the nineties had thought would either disintegrate or polarize had emerged tough and plural; and by

1920 the realignments, the reorientations of the progressive era had been translated into a complex of arrangements nothing short of a revolution could destroy. But pointing a nation to the horizon did not mark its route. Neither the staff of the War Industries Board nor the advocates of railroad nationalization were corrupting the true progressivism, for its plastic center invited precisely that sort of contradictory experimentation. The unfamiliarity of new relationships and the ambiguity of new principles, the continuing debate over alternatives and the continuing struggle over place and power, all located the United States in midpassage.

Men in confusion clutched what they knew. Entering the war, the leaders of America's rudimentary bureaucracy were still conditioned to fight the battles of twenty years before. They were still imposing order upon the nation at the turn of the century, and the system's lack of resilience was partially a function of their lack of development. New problems generated in the course of solving old ones fell largely beyond these set visions. In principle they understood that growth was not a simple, linear matter. In practice they could no longer follow its intricacies. Yet this leadership was passing. In the year that Roosevelt died and Wilson crumpled, Republicans and Democrats alike were talking about the possible candidacy of a young man whose reputation had prospered enormously during the war. Herbert Hoover, born in 1874, represented a new generation, as did his closest competitor in fame, Bernard Baruch, only four years his elder. These men started with the scheme they saw about them. They had no vested interest in its origins. Fresh to the task, they longed for an opportunity to build, to integrate, to supervise a much improved version of what they could watch operating directly at hand. The future for a time would belong to them.

Bibliographical Essay

The purpose of this essay is to introduce a body of interpretive literature. By concentrating upon what historians have said about the past, it omits a whole range of primary and near-primary materials—manuscript collections, published letters and papers, memoirs and autobiographies, and a variety of contemporary printed matter. The organization of the essay derives from the books themselves. Its divisions reflect the manner in which historians have conceived their tasks, not how I have construed their findings for this book. I hope, however, that the essay will suggest at least the dimensions of my enormous debt to their work.

THE BROAD VIEW

Every effort to understand a piece of the American past depends upon the pattern from which it has been lifted. A few gifted historians have inquired systematically after that pattern. Daniel J. Boorstin, *The Genius of American Politics* (1953); Oscar and Mary Handlin, *The Dimensions of Liberty* (1961); Louis Hartz, *The Liberal Tradition in America* (1955); Richard Hofstadter, *The American Political Tradition and the Men Who Made It* (1948); Reinhold Niebuhr, *The Irony of American History* (1954); David M. Potter, *People of Plenty* (1954); and William Appleman Williams, *The Contours of American History* (1961), are all perceptive and stimulating volumes, each worthy of very careful attention. None, however, surpasses the much-maligned and invaluable Charles A. and Mary R. Beard, *The Rise of American Civilization* (2 vols., 1927).

SURVEYS AND SYNTHESES

Volumes IV and V of Ellis Paxson Oberholtzer, *A History of the United States since the Civil War* (5 vols., 1917-37), and James Ford Rhodes, *History of the United States from Hayes to McKinley, 1877-1896* (1917) and *The McKinley and Roosevelt Administrations, 1897-1909* (1922), are pioneer surveys of politics during a good portion of this period. Neither contains much of value for today. Matthew Josephson's two volumes, *The Politicos* (1938) and *The President Makers* (1940), on the other hand, remain the best introduction to the

sweep of their subject: they comprise a sustained exposition of democracy corrupted from 1865 to 1919 by business magnates and party
bosses. More recently Samuel P. Hays, *The Response to Industrialism,
1885–1914* (1957), and Ray Ginger, *Age of Excess: The United
States from 1877 to 1914* (1965), have marked out broader realms for
synthesis. Hays, who has influenced many of the historians following
him, explains the nation's changing social organization as a function
of its industrial development; he excels in the economics of politics.
Ginger explains the nation's unrelieved degradation as a function of
American capitalism; he offers particularly interesting comments on
literature. In a separate category, C. Vann Woodward's magnificent
synthesis, *Origins of the New South, 1877–1913* (1951), describes a
struggle between agrarian and industrial ways in a manner that
illuminates a national process.

THE MOVEMENTS

Populism and progressivism dominate the approaches to the history
of the late nineteenth and early twentieth centuries. As the reference
points by which historians have found their bearings, they tend to
determine the general direction of the interpretations which follow.
Each in turn has inspired a special literature.

John D. Hicks, *The Populist Revolt* (1931), a comprehensive
political narrative, outlines the structure for almost all studies of
Populism: the movement was a rational and forward-looking response
to economic hardships. Several state studies, of which Alex M. Arnett,
The Populist Movement in Georgia (1922), Roscoe C. Martin, *The
People's Party in Texas* (1933), and William DuBose Sheldon,
Populism in the Old Dominion (1935), are the best, supply further
details within this framework, as do the fine biographies of prominent Populist leaders: Stuart Noblin, *Leonidas LaFayette Polk*
(1949); Martin Ridge, *Ignatius Donnelly* (1962); and C. Vann
Woodward, *Tom Watson* (1938), which is particularly noteworthy
for its discussion of attitudes concerning class and race. Norman
Pollack, *The Populist Response to Industrial America* (1962), ex-
tends the argument on the modernity of the Populists by claiming
them as systematic radicals with an affinity to Marxism. Robert F.
Durden, *The Climax of Populism* (1965), emphasizes the political
rationality of its leadership. Underlining the economic causes of
agrarian reform, Roy V. Scott, *The Agrarian Movement in Illinois,
1880–1896* (1962), details the weakness of Populism in an area of
lesser distress.

The most significant dissent from this view appears in the early
chapters of Richard Hofstadter, *The Age of Reform: From Bryan
to F.D.R.* (1955), where Populism is described as a parochial,
romantic, and occasionally vicious cast of mind. Although no one
has developed his comments at book length, several brief accounts

have adopted their spirit. Walter T. K. Nugent, *The Tolerant Populists: Kansas Populism and Nativism* (1963), is a rebuttal to some of these charges, as well as to some Hofstadter does not make. Woodward, "The Populist Heritage and the Intellectual," *The American Scholar* (1959–1960, Vol. XXIX), is partly a reply to those of Hofstadter's persuasion and partly a modification of the author's earlier views. Many of these issues are discussed by Norman Pollack, Oscar Handlin, Irwin Unger, and J. Rogers Hollingsworth in a prickly set of papers collected in *Agricultural History* (1965, Vol. XXXIX).

Progressivism has produced a considerably larger body of works. Attempts to survey the movement have arisen from quite different questions and, consequently, have led to diverse results. Harold U. Faulkner, *The Quest for Social Justice, 1898–1914* (1931), is a general answer to what happened. George E. Mowry, *The Era of Theodore Roosevelt, 1900–1912* (1958), and Arthur S. Link, *Woodrow Wilson and the Progressive Era, 1910–1917* (1954), two outstanding books with excellent bibliographies, are primarily concerned with how national progressivism succeeded. Both assign major credit to politically skilled, educable Presidents. In the tradition of Matthew Josephson, Gabriel Kolko, *The Triumph of Conservatism* (1963), supplemented by his *Railroads and Regulation, 1877–1916* (1965), details how national progressivism failed. Big businessmen used politics to protect their economic kingdoms. Hofstadter devotes the body of *The Age of Reform* to answering why particular men did what they did when they did it, and concludes that an uneasy group of younger, middle-class gentlemen were seeking safe ways of expressing their hostility to a new and threatening set of industrial forces.

Other historians have asked very similar questions about smaller portions of progressivism. Russel B. Nye, *Midwestern Progressive Politics* (1959 edition), is a well-written story of victories; and Louis Filler, *Crusaders for American Liberalism* (1939), the best account of the muckrakers, is an examination of how momentary success led to ultimate defeat at the hands of Wall Street. From another vantage point, Richard M. Abrams, *Conservatism in a Progressive Era* (1964), explains how too much reform before 1900 and too little prosperity after undermined progressivism in Massachusetts. Two important articles analyze the social sources of reform. Samuel P. Hays, "The Politics of Reform in Municipal Government in the Progressive Era," *Pacific Northwest Quarterly* (1964, Vol. LV), emphasizes the importance of established elites; and J. Joseph Huthmacher, "Urban Liberalism and the Age of Reform," *Mississippi Valley Historical Review* (1962, Vol. XLIX), the significance of the slum-based political machine.

Variations on these themes abound. Some concern the ways men came together to form parts of the movement. Of these Mowry, *The*

California Progressives (1951), is a model study; and in that vein Jeremy P. Felt, *Hostages of Fortune: Child Labor Reform in New York State* (1965); Kenneth W. Hechler, *Insurgency* (1940); William D. Miller, *Memphis during the Progressive Era 1900–1917* (1957); Ransom E. Noble, Jr., *New Jersey Progressivism before Wilson* (1946); Frank M. Stewart, *A Half Century of Municipal Reform: The History of the National Municipal League* (1950); and Hoyt Landon Warner, *Progressivism in Ohio 1897–1917* (1964), are all useful. Another group of books analyzes how certain participants built limitations into the reform process. Mowry, *Theodore Roosevelt and the Progressive Movement* (1946), and Robert S. Maxwell, *La Follette and the Rise of the Progressives in Wisconsin* (1956), describe the dangers from faulty leadership, and Walton Bean, *Boss Ruef's San Francisco* (1952), the narrowing effects of businessmen.

Others evaluate degrees of influence. Irwin Yellowitz, *Labor and the Progressive Movement in New York State, 1897–1916* (1965), assigns precious little to his group, while Robert H. Wiebe, *Businessmen and Reform* (1962); James Weinstein, "Organized Business and the City Commission and Manager Movements," *Journal of Southern History* (1962, Vol. XXVIII); and Allen F. Davis' forthcoming volume on the social workers attribute a good deal to theirs. Samuel P. Hays, *Conservation and the Gospel of Efficiency* (1959), initiated an important exploration of the relationship between progressivism and a scientific-industrial mode of thought, and three fine books have continued the quest: Samuel Haber, *Efficiency and Uplift: Scientific Management in the Progressive Era 1890–1920* (1964); Roy Lubove, *The Progressives and the Slums* (1962); and the early chapters of Barry Dean Karl, *Executive Reorganization and Reform in the New Deal* (1963), a study far broader than its title suggests. Elmo R. Richardson, *The Politics of Conservation* (1962), is concerned largely with the complexities of a sectional conflict, and James H. Timberlake, *Prohibition and the Progressive Movement 1900–1920* (1963), finds some urban reformers supporting the later stages of that campaign.

Most biographies concentrate upon the prestige of their subjects Claude G. Bowers, *Beveridge and the Progressive Era* (1932), which John Braeman's study will supersede; Louis G. Geiger, *Joseph W Folk of Missouri* (1953); William H. Harbaugh, *Power and Responsibility: The Life and Times of Theodore Roosevelt* (1961), which includes a very good bibliography; Winifred G. Helmes, *John A. Johnson* (1949); Belle C. and Fola La Follette, *Robert M. La Follette* (2 vols., 1953); M. Nelson McGeary, *Gifford Pinchot: Forester-Politician* (1960); and Henry F. Pringle, *The Life and Times of William Howard Taft* (2 vols., 1939), in varying degrees applaud their subjects. Richard Lowitt, *George W. Norris: The Making of a Progres-*

sive, 1861–1912 (1963), the first of two volumes, attempts to establish the Nebraskan's good name on a firmer basis. John M. Blum,
Woodrow Wilson and the Politics of Morality (1956), and Pringle,
Theodore Roosevelt (1931), disparage. Some do more than assess
reputation. John A. Garraty, *Right-Hand Man: The Life of George
W. Perkins* (1960); Dewey W. Grantham, Jr., *Hoke Smith and the
Politics of the New South* (1958); and Alpheus T. Mason, *Brandeis*
(1946), while briefs in behalf of their subjects, also contribute valuable material on the events these men influenced; and the second
volume of Link's massive *Wilson* (5 vols. to date, 1947–65), is a
priceless fund of sources and information on the New Freedom.

Another group of studies fall just outside the boundaries of biography. Blum's brilliant essay, *The Republican Roosevelt* (1954),
examines both the rationale and techniques of power; the subtitle of
G. Wallace Chessman, *Governor Theodore Roosevelt: The Albany
Apprenticeship, 1898–1900* (1965), explains its purpose; and Alexander L. and Juliette L. George, *Woodrow Wilson and Colonel
House* (1956), subjects the President to a critical personality analysis.
Walter Johnson, *William Allen White's America* (1947), re-creates
an atmosphere. Daniel Levine, *Varieties of Reform Thought* (1964),
employs biographical sketches to suggest diversity; and Braeman,
"Seven Progressives," *Business History Review* (1961, Vol. XXXV),
divides his men into progressive and regressive camps according to
their attitudes toward world affairs.

POLITICS

The studies in politics are overwhelming in quantity and, on the
whole, thin in quality. Generally they develop within a tight framework of factionalism and, once again, concentrate heavily upon
reputations.

One group of these deals with the structure of government and the
process of administration. The basic work on the national govern-
ment is Leonard D. White, *The Republican Era, 1869–1901* (1958).
Earl S. Pomeroy, *The Territories and the United States 1861–1890*
(1949), examines one segment of that story with skill, and Howard
R. Lamar, *Dakota Territory 1861–1889* (1956), complements it with
an excellent account of the consequences in one area. Leslie E. Decker,
*Railroads, Lands, and Politics: The Taxation of the Railroad Land
Grants, 1864–1897* (1964), is a study in administrative irrationality.
David J. Rothman's astute analysis (which unfortunately appeared
too late to improve my volume), *Politics and Power: The United
States Senate 1869–1901* (1966), explains the development of that
body's modern political organization. Daniel J. Elazar, *The American
Partnership* (1962), explores the problem of Federal-state relations
without sufficient attention to the passage of time. Three studies

illuminate the role of the commissions in government: Robert E. Cushman's impressive general account, *The Independent Regulatory Commissions* (1941); I. L. Sharfman's monumental *The Interstate Commerce Commission* (4 parts, 1931–37); and Thomas C. Blaisdell's useful *The Federal Trade Commission* (1932). Malcolm C. McMillan, *Constitutional Development in Alabama, 1798–1901* (1955), is a good example of what has been done to explain the changing legal structure in the states. Volume I of Ernest S. Griffith, *The Modern Development of City Government in the United Kingdom and the United States* (2 vols., 1927), provides a wealth of barely assimilated data; and George M. Reynolds, *Machine Politics in New Orleans 1897–1926* (1936), serves as an interesting case study in the uses of city government.

Examinations of the political process by way of the major parties have traditionally emphasized national elections. Eugene H. Roseboom, *A History of Presidential Elections* (1958), is a general introduction; Herbert J. Clancy, *The Presidential Election of 1880* (1958), and Stanley Jones, *The Presidential Election of 1896* (1964), are careful specific studies. Paul W. Glad, *McKinley, Bryan, and the People* (1964), is a very perceptive essay on the campaign of 1896. J. Rogers Hollingsworth's valuable *The Whirligig of Politics: The Democracy of Cleveland and Bryan* (1963), describes how weak leadership damaged that party during a critical transition. Lee Benson's analytic essay, "Research Problems in American Political Historiography," in Mirra Komarovsky, ed., *Common Fontiers of the Social Sciences* (1957), contains important suggestions on the interpretation of late-nineteenth-century electoral statistics.

Other historians have explored the political process through an analysis of participating groups. Two of the best, Albert D. Kirwan's *Revolt of the Rednecks: Mississippi Politics: 1876–1925* (1951) and Horace Samuel Merrill's *Bourbon Democracy of the Middle West, 1865–1896* (1953), cast light well beyond their special areas. Peter H. Odegard, *Pressure Politics; The Story of the Anti-Saloon League* (1928), set an early standard in its field, and Mary R. Dearing, *Veterans in Politics* (1952), is a competent successor. Marc Karson, *American Labor Unions and Politics, 1900–1918* (1958), discusses in particular the restraining hand of the Catholic Church. From another vantage point, Solon J. Buck, *The Granger Movement* (1913), which is corrected at certain points by Irwin Unger, *The Greenback Era* (1964), traces the group politics of protest. Dewey W. Grantham, Jr., *The Democratic South* (1963), describes in brief a regional pattern of political change, and Jeannette P. Nichols, "Contradictory Trends in Middle Western Democracy 1865–1900," in Nichols and James G. Randall, eds., *Democracy in the Middle West, 1840–1940* (1941), outlines a balance of forces in Midwestern politics.

Another group of studies concerns matters of public policy. Louise

E. Peffer, *The Closing of the Public Domain* (1951), and John Ise's two volumes, *The United States Forest Policy* (1920) and *The United States Oil Policy* (1926), provide basic information, as do Davis R. Dewey, *Financial History of the United States* (1956 edition); Sidney Ratner, *American Taxation* (1942); Frank W. Taussig, *The Tariff History of the United States* (1931 edition); and Paul P. Van Riper, *History of the United States Civil Service* (1958). J. Leonard Bates, *The Origins of Teapot Dome* (1963), and Paul W. Gates, *Fifty Million Acres: Conflicts over Kansas Land Policy, 1854–1890* (1954), explore aspects of resource policy with imagination. Milton Friedman and Anna Jacobson Schwartz, *A Monetary History of the United States, 1867–1960* (1963), reargues the case for inflation. Henry E. Fritz, *The Movement for Indian Assimilation, 1860–1890* (1963), and Loring B. Priest, *Uncle Sam's Stepchildren* (1942), offer separate evaluations of the government's policy toward the Indians. A. Hunter Dupree, *Science in the Federal Government* (1957), is an extremely valuable account with wide-ranging implications. Hans B. Thorelli, *Federal Antitrust Policy* (1955), conscientiously supplies the background to Roosevelt's use of the Sherman Act; and William Preston, Jr., *Aliens and Dissenters* (1963), indignantly explains the background to the witchhunts of the First World War. Carter Goodrich, *Government Promotion of American Canals and Railroads 1800–1890* (1960), includes some information on state policies, and Clifford W. Patton, *The Battle for Municipal Reform: Mobilization and Attack, 1875 to 1900* (1940), some on urban.

Another set of volumes, similar in purpose, concentrates upon more precise problems of policy. Lee Benson, *Merchants, Farmers & Railroads; Railroad Regulation and New York Politics: 1850–1887* (1955), which unravels the intricacies of political economics, is the best of these. Ari Hoogenboom, *Outlawing the Spoils* (1961), ably discusses the mixture of yearning and selfishness behind the Pendleton Act of 1883. Two careful studies in self-serving factionalism, Vincent P. DeSantis, *Republicans Face the Southern Question* (1959), and Stanley P. Hirshson, *Farewell to the Bloody Shirt: Northern Republicans & the Southern Negro, 1877–1893* (1962), overlap and reinforce each other. Two others, Roger Daniels, *The Politics of Prejudice: The Anti-Japanese Movement in California and the Struggle for Japanese Exclusion* (1962), and James F. Doster, *Railroads in Alabama Politics, 1875–1914* (1957), are good examples of the many such state studies.

Among the multitude of political biographies, four are superior: Harry Barnard, *"Eagle Forgotten": The Life of John Peter Altgeld* (1938); Ray Ginger, *The Bending Cross: A Biography of Eugene V. Debs* (1948); Allan Nevins, *Grover Cleveland* (1932); and Francis Butler Simkins, *Pitchfork Ben Tillman* (1944). A second tier contributes important information on the nature of politics:

Herbert J. Bass, *"I am a Democrat": The Political Career of David Bennett Hill* (1961); Richard N. Current, *Pine Logs and Politics: A Life of Philetus Sawyer 1816–1900* (1950); Mark D. Hirsch, *William C. Whitney* (1948); John R. Lambert, *Arthur Pue Gorman* (1953); Arthur Mann, *La Guardia: A Fighter against His Times* (1959); H. Wayne Morgan, *William McKinley and His America* (1963); Leon B. Richardson, *William B. Chandler, Republican* (1940); and Leland L. Sage, *William Boyd Allison* (1956). Alongside these rank a number of studies that provide a good sense of the general setting around their subjects: Harry Barnard, *Rutherford B. Hayes and His America* (1954); James A. Barnes, *John G. Carlisle* (1931); John M. Blum, *Joe Tumulty and the Wilson Era* (1951); Elmer Ellis, *Henry Moore Teller* (1941); Hampton M. Jarrell, *Wade Hampton and the Negro* (1949); Elting E. Morison, *Turmoil and Tradition: A Study of the Life and Times of Henry L. Stimson* (1960); Nevins, *Abram S. Hewitt with Some Account of Peter Cooper* (1935); Festus P. Summers, *William L. Wilson and Tariff Reform* (1953); Joseph F. Wall, *Henry Watterson* (1956); and Edward Younger, *John A. Kasson* (1955). Paolo E. Coletta, *William Jennings Bryan I. Political Evangelist 1860–1908* (1964); Robert C. Cotner, *James Stephen Hogg* (1959); Herbert D. Croly, *Marcus Alonzo Hanna* (1912); George F. Howe, *Chester A. Arthur* (1934); David S. Muzzey, *James G. Blaine* (1934); Ben H. Procter, *Not without Honor: The Life of John H. Reagan* (1962); Merlo J. Pusey, *Charles Evans Hughes* (2 vols., 1951); William A. Robinson, *Thomas B. Reed Parliamentarian* (1930); Harry J. Sievers, *Benjamin Harrison* (2 vols. to date, 1952–59); Nathaniel W. Stephenson, *Nelson W. Aldrich* (1930); and Everett Walters, *Joseph Benson Foraker* (1948), are all useful accounts.

Three interesting studies belong next to the biographies. Glad, *The Trumpet Soundeth: William Jennings Bryan and His Democracy 1896–1912* (1960), places Bryan in his agrarian culture, and Lawrence W. Levine, *Defender of the Faith: William Jennings Bryan: The Last Decade 1915–1925* (1965), reassesses his final, futile years. Merrill, *Bourbon Leader: Grover Cleveland and the Democratic Party* (1957), where the author applies his findings from *Bourbon Democracy* to the belligerent President, attacks Cleveland as vigorously as Nevins defends him.

ECONOMICS

Once again the reader faces a mass of volumes with a disappointing net return. As in the case of the literature on politics, an excessive involvement with justification and a parochial framework account for the most serious deficiencies.

Fred A. Shannon, *The Farmer's Last Frontier: Agriculture, 1860–*

1897 (1947); Edward C. Kirkland, *Industry Comes of Age: Business, Labor, and Public Policy, 1860–1897* (1961); and Harold U. Faulkner, *The Decline of Laissez Faire, 1897–1917* (1951), Volumes V, VI, and VII in *The Economic History of the United States,* provide an approximate survey of the field. Shannon argues the cause of the suffering farmer with vigor and statistics; Kirkland defends the course of industrial development in the guise of a participant; and Faulkner covers basic material. Although each contains a full bibliography, only Kirkland's is sufficiently current. Rendigs Fels, *American Business Cycle 1865–1897* (1959), while limited in scope, offers a valuable overview; and Alfred D. Chandler, Jr., "Entrepreneurial Opportunity in Nineteenth-Century America," *Explorations in Entrepreneurial History* (1963, Vol. I), is a most important effort to comprehend the general nature of economic growth during these years.

The assumption that big businessmen were not only masters of their own domains but practically sovereign over all else they surveyed has dominated the discussion of corporate development. That, in turn, is an index to the influence of two interpretive surveys— Matthew Josephson's highly critical *The Robber Barons* (1934) and Thomas C. Cochran's and William Miller's more moderate *The Age of Enterprise* (1942). Much of the literature, in other words, concerns the good or evil consequences of omnicompetence.

With regard to the railroads, Julius Grodinsky, *Transcontinental Railway Strategy, 1869–1893* (1962), is illuminating on tactics more than strategy; George R. Taylor and Irene D. Neu, *The American Railroad Network 1861–1890* (1956), discusses problems of integration; and Cochran, *Railroad Leaders, 1845–1890* (1953), contains important documents expressing the mentality of the executives. Kirkland, *Men, Cities, and Transportation: 1820–1900* (2 vols., 1948), is a fine example of the more limited, detailed studies listed in Kirkland, *Industry Comes of Age.* The basic reference work on manufacturing is Victor Clark, *History of Manufactures in the United States, 1860–1893* (1929). Harold F. Williamson and Associates, *The American Petroleum Industry* (2 vols., 1959–63), makes a complex story comprehensible, and Ralph W. and Muriel E. Hidy, *Pioneering in Big Business, 1882–1911: History of Standard Oil (New Jersey)* (1955), tells one portion of it with skill and sympathy. Cochran, *The Pabst Brewing Company* (1948), is a model for company histories. Harold C. Passer, *The Electrical Manufacturers 1875–1900* (1953), provides a good introduction to industrial confusion; and the early pages of Chandler, *Strategy and Structure* (1962), a very valuable integration of industrial purpose and organization, analyze one of its consequences. Fritz Redlich, *The Molding of American Banking: Men and Ideas: Part II: 1840–1910* (1951), is indispensable as a guide to general policy and practice. The best accounts of a growing financial power over the railroads are E. G. Campbell, *The*

Reorganization of the American Railroad System, 1893-1900 (1938), and John F. Stover, *The Railroads of the South 1865-1900* (1955). Arthur S. Dewing, *Corporate Promotions and Reorganizations* (1914), methodically treats the financial struggles within lesser industries. Morton Keller, *The Life Insurance Enterprise, 1885-1910* (1963), is an interesting analysis of internally generated restraints within that industry.

Along less trodden paths, Boris Emmet and John E. Jeuck, *Catalogues and Counters: A History of Sears, Roebuck and Company* (1950), and Ralph M. Hower, *History of Macy's of New York 1858-1919* (1943), discuss parts of a revolution in distribution, while Lewis Atherton, *Main Street on the Middle Border* (1954), and Thomas D. Clark, *Pills, Petticoats and Plows: The Southern Country Store* (1944), ably describe its effects in the small towns. Clarence E. Bonnett, *History of Employers' Associations in the United States* (1956), is a dictionary of one type of organizational activity; and Marguerite Green, *The National Civic Federation and the American Labor Movement, 1900-1925* (1956), is an account of quite another variety.

Most biographies of the magnates are exercises in hero worship. The best of their kind are Allan Nevins, *Study in Power: John D. Rockefeller, Industrialist and Philanthropist* (2 vols., 1953), and the much more impressionistic Frederick Lewis Allen, *The Great Pierpont Morgan* (1940). Forrest McDonald, *Insull* (1962), contains useful information on the obstructive influences of high finance, and Nevins and Frank E. Hill, *Ford: The Times, the Man, the Company* (1954), on the scramble of the infant auto industry. Cyrus Adler, *Jacob H. Schiff* (2 vols., 1928); George Kennan, *E. H. Harriman* (2 vols., 1922); Burton J. Hendrick, *The Life of Andrew Carnegie* (2 vols., 1932); and Joseph G. Pyle, *The Life of James J. Hill* (2 vols., 1916-17), have limited value, as does Lewis Corey, *The House of Morgan* (1930), which, though not a biography, is an excellent example of villain worship. Grodinsky, *Jay Gould* (1957), and Josephson, *Edison* (1959), include interesting analyses. Edward C. Kirkland's felicitous *Charles Francis Adams, Jr., 1835-1915* (1965), is somewhat more detached than the rest.

The most useful surveys of labor history are the last three volumes of John R. Commons and Associates, *History of Labour in the United States* (4 vols., 1918-35); and Philip S. Foner, *History of the Labor Movement in the United States* (4 vols. to date, 1947-65), which places a wealth of data in a Marxist mold. Albert Rees, *Real Wages in Manufacturing, 1890-1914* (1961), is the most reliable study on this subject. Lloyd Ulman, *The Rise of the National Trade Union* (1955), is a very important though laborious interpretive account. The best introduction to the Knights of Labor is Norman J. Ware, *The Labor Movement in the United States, 1860-1895*

(1929). Gerald N. Grob, *Workers and Utopia* (1961), imaginatively explores the conflict between the Knights and the trade unions, and Philip Taft, *The A. F. of L. in the Time of Gompers* (1957), offers an admiring history of the young Federation. Vernon H. Jensen, *Heritage of Conflict* (1950), and Paul F. Brissenden, *The I. W. W.* (1919), provide a general coverage of radical unionism; while David Brody, *The Butcher Workmen* (1964) and Mark Perlman, *The Machinists* (1961), systematically examine conservative counterparts. Milton J. Nadworny, *Scientific Management and the Unions 1900–1932* (1955), traces a significant issue. Among the several studies of particular strikes, Robert J. Cornell, *The Anthracite Coal Strike of 1902* (1957), and Donald L. McMurry, *The Great Burlington Strike of 1888* (1956), are especially careful accounts. Two valuable efforts to recast labor's story are Brody, *Steelworkers in America* (1960), and Herbert G. Gutman, "The Worker's Search for Power: Labor in the Gilded Age," in H. Wayne Morgan, ed., *The Gilded Age: A Reappraisal* (1963). Brody places the workers within a sophisticated industrial framework, and Gutman suggests the importance of variable social settings. The best of the biographies are Elsie Glück, *John Mitchell, Miner* (1929), and Bernard Mandel, *Samuel Gompers* (1963).

Murray R. Benedict, *Farm Policies of the United States, 1790–1950* (1953), gives a brief introduction. The classic examination of general environmental influences is Walter P. Webb, *The Great Plains* (1931); and the most lucid presentation of a precise environmental determinism is Benton H. Wilcox, "An Historical Definition of Northwestern Radicalism," *Mississippi Valley Historical Review* (1939, Vol. XXVI), whose formula for agrarian discontent has been borrowed by scores of scholars. Allan G. Bogue, *Money at Interest* (1955), an imaginative case study, discovers less cause for discontent in one area than has been traditionally assumed. Theodore Saloutos, *Farmer Movements in the South, 1865–1933* (1960), and Saloutos and John D. Hicks, *Agricultural Discontent in the Middle West, 1900–1939* (1951), are comprehensive organizational studies. The best works on the emergence of a "new" farmer are Joseph C. Bailey, *Seaman A. Knapp* (1945); Gladys L. Baker, *The County Agent* (1939); and Grant McConnell, *The Decline of Agrarian Democracy* (1953). Atherton, *The Cattle Kings* (1961), and Reynold M. Wik, *Steam Power on the American Farm* (1953), are good books on specialized topics.

THEORIES AND IDEAS

Intellectual history offers fewer volumes of much richer quality. By far the most influential of these is Morton G. White, *Social Thought in America: The Revolt against Formalism* (1949), a powerful analysis whose subtitle suggests its approach to the origins of modern relativism. He has wrought so well that historians have generally left him the field uncontested. The one systematically developed alternative to White is David W. Noble, *The Paradox of Progressive Thought* (1958), also a very impressive, though unnecessarily difficult book which treats reform thought as inherently contradictory utopianism. Scholars have praised Noble's study, then ignored it—to their detriment. Other attempts to master the major trends of intellectual development are Daniel Aaron, *Men of Good Hope* (1951), another underrated work whose thesis on the broad, humane vision of the nineteenth-century reformers is very informative; Henry Steele Commager, *The American Mind: An Interpretation of American Thought and Character since the 1880's* (1950), a series of essays; Sidney Fine, *Laissez Faire and the General-Welfare State* (1956), a compendium of late-nineteenth-century thought written with an eye to the New Deal; Eric F. Goldman, *Rendezvous with Destiny* (1952), which applies White's insight in a wider setting; and Henry F. May, *The End of American Innocence: A Study of the First Years of Our Own Times: 1912–1917* (1959), which locates the origins of modern doubt among a handful of intellectuals.

Several studies of lesser scope also make important contributions. Charles Forcey, *The Crossroads of Liberalism: Croly, Weyl, Lippmann, and the Progressive Era 1900–1925* (1961), is valuable both as an examination of ideas and as a commentary on the urge to power. John Chamberlain, *Farewell to Reform* (1932), dissects literature and values by standards similar to those of Matthew Josephson, while Robert W. Schneider, *Five Novelists of the Progressive Era* (1965), analyzes four progressive novelists and a predecessor from Noble's general perspective. Frederic C. Jaher, *Doubters and Dissenters: Cataclysmic Thought in America, 1885–1918* (1964), treats a significant topic intelligently. Mark H. Haller, *Eugenics* (1963), offers a clear survey, as do Thomas F. Gossett, *Race: The History of an Idea in America* (1963), and I. A. Newby, *Jim Crow's Defense* (1965). Richard Hofstadter, *Social Darwinism in American Thought, 1860–1905* (1944), is a careful, incisive commentary. Arthur Mann, *Yankee Reformers in the Urban Age* (1954), ably discusses a quest among troubled consciences. Robert G. McCloskey, *American Conservatism in the Age of Enterprise* (1951), the intriguing account of a cumulative ideology, has, like White's study, ended discussion where it should be encouraged. Jurgen Herbst, *The German Historical School in American Scholarship* (1965), is a useful study. Stow Persons, ed., *Evolutionary Thought in America* (1950), includes a number of good, brief essays; and Edward Moore, *American Pragmatism* (1961), introduces a fundamental subject.

Two very different attempts to comprehend radicalism provide valuable insights. Chester McArthur Destler, *American Radicalism 1865–1901* (1946), discovers a fruitful dialogue between agrarian and urban dissenters. Christopher Lasch's provocative essay, *The New Radicalism in America [1889-1963]* (1965), examines his subject as a social and emotional disorder. Harry Elmer Barnes, ed., *An Introduction to the History of Sociology* (1948), and Joseph Dorfman, *The Economic Mind in American Civilization: III: 1865-1918* (1949), are useful reference works in basic areas. The excellent bibliography in Robert E. Spiller and Associates, *Literary History of the United States* (1963 edition), and in Oliver W. Larkin, *Art and Life in America* (1960 edition), cover these areas. Two surveys, Merle E. Curti, *The Growth of American Thought* (1964 edition), and Persons, *American Minds* (1958), supplement the particular studies, the former with a wealth of information and the latter with an imaginative synthesis.

Once again, the biographies prove somewhat less rewarding. The best are Joseph Dorfman, *Thorstein Veblen and His America* (1934), a full, informed account, and Ralph Barton Perry's fine appreciation, *The Thought and Character of William James* (2 vols., 1935). David Riesman, *Thorstein Veblen: A Critical Interpretation* (1953), is less favorable and less specific than Dorfman. Milton Berman, *John Fiske* (1961), is an intelligent study. Charles Barker, *Henry George* (1955), is exhaustive. Ernest Samuels, *Henry Adams* (3 vols., 1948-64), a sensitive portrayal, is better on literature than historical philosophy, and Sidney Hook, *John Dewey: An Intellectual Portrait* (1939), far better on philosophy than its historical setting. Samuel Chugerman, *Lester F. Ward* (1939), Destler, *Henry Demarest Lloyd and the Empire of Reform* (1963), and Arthur E. Morgan, *Edward Bellamy* (1944), laud their subjects.

Society

The field of social history contains the most ambitious attempts to find new means of examining old issues. In this respect Richard Hofstadter's *Age of Reform* deserves special mention. The questions he poses and the analysis he pursues in the chapters on progressivism—imaginative social history at its finest—have enriched a decade of inquiry in almost all areas.

Leadership of this quality elevates the literature concerning immigration above the rest of social history. The dominating works are Oscar Handlin, *The Uprooted* (1952), a brilliant essay on the human meaning of migration and acculturation; and John Higham, *Strangers in the Land* (1955), an excellent analysis of the responses to immigration which illuminates broad areas of American society. Supplementing these volumes are Donald B. Cole, *Immigrant City: Lawrence, Massachusetts, 1845-1921* (1963), which includes interesting material on ethnic maturation; Charlotte Erickson, *American Industry and the European Immigrant 1860-1885* (1957), a fine study

of selected issues; Edward G. Hartman, *The Movement to Americanize the Immigrant* (1948); Donald L. Kinzer, *An Episode in Anti-
Catholicism: The American Protective Association* (1964); Moses
Rischin, *The Promised City: New York's Jews 1870–1914* (1962), a
sensitive account; and Barbara M. Solomon, *Ancestors and Immigrants* (1956), a very good examination of patrician malaise. Mal-
dwyn A. Jones, *American Immigration* (1960), is a general survey.

Two works also stand apart among the studies concerning the
Negro: Vernon L. Wharton, *The Negro in Mississippi 1865–1890*
(1947), exemplar of the traditional monograph, is filled with valuable
information; and C. Vann Woodward, *The Strange Career of Jim
Crow* (1966 edition), a very influential book, explains the arrival of
legal segregation within the context of political crisis during the late
nineteenth century. Other specialized volumes are Helen G. Ed-
monds, *The Negro and Fusion Politics in North Carolina 1894–1901*
(1951), a study in white cynicism; George B. Tindall, *South Carolina
Negroes 1877–1900* (1952), a very good analysis along the lines of
Wharton; and Charles E. Wynes, *Race Relations in Virginia 1870–
1902* (1961), a substantiation of Woodward's thesis. Rayford W.
Logan, *The Negro in American Life and Thought: The Nadir
1877–1901* (1954), offers a good deal of information. August Meier,
Negro Thought in America (1963), is particularly informative on
Booker T. Washington. Gilbert Osofsky, *Harlem* (1966), the study
of a community's formation, suggests the promise of a new generation's approach to the Negro in American society. Seth M. Scheiner,
Negro Mecca (1965), also deals with New York. John Hope Franklin, *From Slavery to Freedom* (1956 edition), is a superior survey.

Histories of urbanization effectively date from Arthur M. Schle-
singer, *The Rise of the City, 1878–1898* (1933). The quantity of
books and the paucity of progress is reported in the full bibliography
of Blake McKelvey, *The Urbanization of America [1860–1915]*
(1963), an informed summary and a mine of data. Constance
McLaughlin Green, *The Rise of Urban America* (1965), presents a
broader, thinner survey. An important recent contribution is Sam B.
Warner, Jr., *Streetcar Suburbs: The Process of Growth in Boston,
1870–1900* (1962), the meticulous account of disjointed development.

The four standard works on socialism are Howard H. Quint, *The
Forging of American Socialism* (1953), an able examination of men
and ideas; Ira Kipnis, *The American Socialist Movement 1897–1912*
(1952), a study in factionalism; David A. Shannon, *The Socialist
Party of America* (1955), a careful combination of analysis and
narrative; and Daniel Bell, "Background and Development of
Marxian Socialism in the United States," in Volume I of Donald
Drew Egbert and Stow Persons, eds., *Socialism and American Life*
(2 vols., 1952), a shimmering, sneering essay with important insights.
Henry David, *The History of the Haymarket Affair* (1936), in-

cludes a full account of radical socialism in the eighties; and James Dombrowski, *The Early Days of Christian Socialism in America* (1936), is the survey of a moderate wing.

The basic works on Protestant social policies are Aaron I. Abell, *The Urban Impact on American Protestantism 1865-1900* (1943); Charles H. Hopkins, *The Rise of the Social Gospel in American Protestantism, 1860-1915* (1940); and Henry F. May, *Protestant Churches and Industrial America* (1949). Volume II of Anson Phelps Stokes, *Church and State in the United States* (3 vols., 1950), blankets his subject. Bernard A. Weisberger's lively and shrewd account of revivalism, *They Gathered at the River* (1958), touches upon a number of important trends, as does William G. McLoughlin, Jr., *Modern Revivalism* (1959). On Catholicism, Robert D. Cross, *The Emergence of Liberal Catholicism in America* (1958), is a fine sympathetic study of intrachurch conflict, a subject Thomas T. McAvoy, *The Great Crisis in American Catholic History 1895-1900* (1957), treats in greater detail. Abell, *American Catholicism and Social Action* (1960), is useful. Nathan Glazer, *American Judaism* (1957), and Handlin, *Adventure in Freedom: Three Hundred Years of Jewish Life in America* (1954), provide complementary introductions to their subject. Nelson R. Burr, *A Critical Bibliography of Religion in America,* Volumes III and IV of James Ward Smith and A. Leland Jamison, eds., *Religion in American Life* (4 vols., 1961), is excellent and annotated.

Public education has received relatively little attention from historians. Theodore R. Sizer, *Secondary Schools at the Turn of the Century* (1964), and Handlin's very brief *John Dewey's Challenge to Education* (1959) are the best introductions to the late nineteenth century. The first portion of Lawrence A. Cremin, *The Transformation of the School: Progressivism in American Education, 1876-1957* (1961), is a discriminating analysis. Rush Welter, *Popular Education and Democratic Thought in America* (1962), is a wide-ranging examination of a very important subject. Academicians obviously favor the university, and their efforts are reported in the bibliography of Frederick Rudolph, *The American College and University, A History* (1962), a smooth, informed summary. Laurence Veysey, *The Emergence of the American University* (1965), offers an intelligent framework for understanding the main lines of that development, and George E. Peterson, *The New England College in the Age of the University* (1964), complements Veysey with a perceptive analysis of compromise. Hofstadter and Walter P. Metzger, *The Development of Academic Freedom in the United States* (1955), is an interesting essay. Merle Curti, *The Social Ideas of American Educators* (1935), remains a useful survey.

The one profession about which we have adequate information is medicine. Richard H. Shryock, *The Development of Modern Medi-*

cine (1936), surveys the subject. Donald Fleming, *William H. Welch and the Rise of Modern Medicine* (1954), a very perceptive study; James G. Burrow, *AMA: Voice of American Medicine* (1963); and Thomas N. Bonner, *The Kansas Doctor* (1959), add richness. George Rosen, *A History of Public Health* (1958), covers an important adjunct thoroughly, and two good volumes—James H. Cassedy, *Charles V. Chapin and the Public Health Movement* (1962), and C.-E. A. Winslow, *The Life of Hermann M. Biggs* (1929)—supply depth here. A scattering of books treat other professions. Raymond E. Callahan, *Education and the Cult of Efficiency* (1962), is an acid, enlightening commentary on the administrative mind, and Roy Lubove, *The Professional Altruist: The Emergence of Social Work as a Career 1880–1930* (1965), an interesting examination of professionalization as a process. Willard S. Elsbree, *The American Teacher* (1939); Roscoe Pound, *The Lawyer from Antiquity to Modern Times* (1953); Alfred Z. Reed, *Training for the Public Profession of the Law* (1921); and Arthur C. Weatherhead, *The History of Collegiate Education in Architecture* (1941), are of some use.

Thomas Beer, *The Mauve Decade* (1926), and Mark Sullivan, *Our Times: The United States 1900–1925* (6 vols., 1926–35), good examples of impressionistic social history, help to introduce the ways of Americans during these years. Robert H. Bremner, *American Philanthropy* (1960), is a survey of how some used their money. Ernest H. Cherrington, *The Evolution of Prohibition in the United States* (1920), avidly chronicles that movement; Eleanor Flexner, *Century of Struggle: The Woman's Rights Movement in the United States* (1959), and Andrew Sinclair, *The Better Half: The Emancipation of the American Woman* (1965), trace parts of another. Aileen S. Kraditor, *The Ideas of the Woman Suffrage Movement, 1890–1920* (1965), analyzes the suffragettes by their attitudes toward a range of social issues. Wallace E. Davies, *Patriotism on Parade: The Story of Veterans' and Hereditary Organizations in America 1783–1900* (1955), details the diverse results of an important impulse, and James Harvey Young, *The Toadstool Millionaires: A Social History of Patent Medicines in America before Federal Regulation* (1961), tells a grim tale of success in a popular industry.

Two volumes by Frank L. Mott, *American Journalism* (1941) and *A History of American Magazines, 1885–1905* (1947), cover those fields. Two more—E. Digby Baltzell, *Philadelphia Gentlemen* (1958), and Dixon Wecter, *The Saga of American Society* (1937)—skillfully discuss complementary portions of upper-class life. Geoffrey Blodgett, *The Gentle Reformers: Massachusetts Democrats in the Cleveland Era* (1966), analyzes an interesting combination of conservatives. Bremner, *From the Depths: The Discovery of Poverty in the United States* (1956), is an outstanding work that opens the way to more studies yet undone. Edward C. Kirkland, *Dream and*

Thought in the Business Community, 1860–1900 (1956), explores a resisting subject with ingenuity, and Irvin G. Wyllie's graceful essay, *The Self-Made Man in America* (1954), tours a basic myth. Paul H. Buck, *The Road to Reunion, 1865–1900* (1937), provides useful information about the desire for unity. Robert V. Bruce, *1877: Year of Violence* (1959), offers a slice of life emphasizing the railroad strike. Donald L. McMurry, *Coxey's Army* (1929), is a narrative of frustration.

The most profitable among the biographies are Ira V. Brown, *Lyman Abbott* (1953); Richard Drinnon, *Rebel in Paradise* (1961), a sympathetic account of the anarchist Emma Goldman; Mary Earhart, *Frances Willard* (1944); Josephine Goldmark, *Impatient Crusader: Florence Kelley's Life Story* (1953); Morton Keller, *In Defense of Yesterday: James M. Beck and the Politics of Conservatism, 1861–1936* (1958); Peter Lyon, *Success Story: The Life and Times of S. S. McClure* (1963); Samuel R. Spencer, Jr., *Booker T. Washington and the Negro's Place in American Life* (1955); and Louise C. Wade, *Graham Taylor* (1964). James Leiby, *Carroll Wright and Labor Reform* (1960), and Edwin R. Lewinson, *John Purroy Mitchel* (1965), are illuminating accounts of cautious reform.

THE CONSTITUTION AND THE COURTS

The combined works in constitutional history give almost no sense of the development of the law from the late nineteenth into the twentieth century. The most suggestive volumes are James Willard Hurst, *The Growth of American Law: The Law Makers* (1950) and *Law and the Conditions of Freedom in the Nineteenth-Century United States* (1956), which though illuminating are quite selective. In the end, the only substantial body of books deals with the expanding jurisdiction of the Supreme Court during the eighties and nineties, and the best of these is Arnold M. Paul, *Conservative Crisis and the Rule of Law: Attitudes of Bar and Bench, 1887–1895* (1960), an astute analysis of evolving policy. Charles G. Haines, *The American Doctrine of Judicial Supremacy* (1932 edition), places these innovations in a wider span of time with less success; and Benjamin R. Twiss, *Lawyers and the Constitution* (1942), and Clyde E. Jacobs, *Law Writers and the Courts* (1954), supplement Haines' view of an irresistible movement toward a business-oriented, judicial conservatism. Along quite different lines, John P. Roche, *The Quest for the Dream: The Development of Civil Rights and Human Relations in Modern America* (1963), offers some material on the prewar years.

Next in quality to Paul's book are two biographies, Charles Fairman, *Mr. Justice Miller and the Supreme Court 1862–1890* (1939), and C. Peter Magrath, *Morrison R. Waite* (1963), both alert to the subtleties and uncertainties of the Court's course. The careful study by Mark DeWolfe Howe, *Justice Oliver Wendell Holmes* (2 vols. to date, 1957–63), carries this enigmatic giant to 1882. Carl B. Swisher, *Stephen J. Field* (1930), has led many an historian to inflate his subject's significance; and Willard L. King, *Melville Weston Fuller* (1950), has convinced almost no one of that man's importance. Swisher, *American Constitutional Development* (1954 edition), is a sound reference.

FOREIGN RELATIONS

No field offers such a spread of viewpoints and such radical differences over the fundamentals of interpretation. What is the proper scope of the subject? In what context should it be examined? Where and how are decisions made? Groups of historians find it difficult to agree even upon the preliminaries to an examination of these questions. It is as if the conflicts that once enlivened political and economic history have now migrated to the study of foreign relations, marking a shift from the domestic preoccupations of the 1930's to the international concerns of the fifties and sixties.

Three extremely important interpretive works suggest alternatives to the customary emphasis upon diplomatic correspondence. The initial chapters in George F. Kennan, *American Diplomacy, 1900–1950* (1951), ask the reader to view American relations as a function of parochial leadership. Robert E. Osgood's taxonomic *Ideals and Self-Interest in America's Foreign Relations* (1953) describes the dominant intellectual sets among America's policymakers and some of their consequences. William Appleman Williams, *The Tragedy of American Diplomacy* (1959), supplemented by the material in his fine volume of readings, *The Shaping of American Diplomacy* (1956), finds a single, powerful theme—economic expansion—underlying the whole of the nation's policy.

Area studies elaborate upon these as well as several other themes. On Latin American relations, Dexter Perkins, *A History of the Monroe Doctrine* (1955), is traditional diplomatic history at its best. Wilfrid H. Callcott, *The Caribbean Policy of the United States, 1890–1920* (1942), and Dana G. Munro, *Intervention and Dollar Diplomacy in the Caribbean 1900–1921* (1964), cover their subject with thorough conservatism. J. Fred Rippy, *The Caribbean Danger Zone* (1940), and Howard F. Cline, *The United States and Mexico* (1953), together give a harsh appraisal, emphasizing greed and obtuseness respectively. David M. Pletcher, *The Awkward Years: American Foreign Relations under Garfield and Arthur* (1962), is largely a study of thwarted commercial schemes in Latin America. The best survey of East Asian affairs is still A. Whitney Griswold, *The Far Eastern Policy of the United States* (1938), which concentrates upon the maneuvers of executive officials. Three very able volumes—Charles S. Campbell, Jr., *Special Business Interests and the Open Door* (1951); Fred H. Harrington, *God Mammon and the Japanese: Dr. Horace N. Allen and Korean-American Relations, 1884–1905* (1944); and Charles Vevier, *The United States and China 1906–1913* (1955)—locate the sources of policy in varieties of economic pressure. William L. Neumann, "Determinism, Destiny, and Myth in the American Image of China," in George L. Anderson, ed., *Issues and Conflicts* (1959), is a good, brief examination of the illusion of the China market, and Tien-yi Li, *Woodrow Wilson's China Policy 1913–1917* (1952), a survey of attitudes and events. Neumann, *America Encounters Japan* (1963), is a thoughtful introduction. Sylvester K. Stevens, *American Expansion in Hawaii, 1842–1898* (1945), provides adequate coverage.

Campbell, *Anglo-American Understanding, 1898–1903* (1957), supplements Lionel Gelber, *The Rise of Anglo-American Friendship* (1938), in detailing the course of rapprochement. Less obvious but important subjects are discussed in W. Stull Holt, *Treaties Defeated by the Senate* (1933), a full account; Merle Curti, *Peace or War: The American Struggle 1636–1936* (1936), largely a chronology; and Graham H. Stuart, *The Department of State* (1949), a competent organizational history. Richard W. Leopold, "The Emergence of America as a World Power: Some Second Thoughts," in John Braeman and Associates, eds., *Change and Continuity in Twentieth-Century America* (1964), explores some implications of the government's organization in a valuable essay. Calvin DeArmond Davis, *The United States and the First Hague Peace Conference* (1962); Dwight C. Miner, *The Fight for the Panama Route* (1940); Frederick B. Pike, *Chile and the United States, 1880–1962* (1963); and Robert E. Quirk, *An Affair of Honor: Woodrow Wilson and the Occupation of Veracruz* (1962), are useful studies in depth.

A good deal of the literature on foreign affairs focuses upon three events: the Spanish-American War, America's entry into the First World War, and the Treaty of Versailles. Julius W. Pratt, *Expansionists of 1898* (1936), explains the war and the peace with Spain as responses to a variegated urge for national greatness; and Walter LaFeber, *The New Empire: An Interpretation of American Expansion 1860–1898* (1963), counters with a provocative argument based on a rising panic over foreign markets. Walter Millis, *The Martial Spirit* (1931), condemns the war by setting it in an atmosphere of national hysteria; and Ernest R. May, *Imperial Democracy* (1961), justifies the war by setting it in a framework that combines American public opinion and flawed European diplomacy. Richard Hofstadter, "Manifest Destiny and the Philippines," in Daniel Aaron, ed., *America in Crisis* (1952), represents still another approach, concentrating on the nervous reactions of the nation to the crises of the nineties.

To a remarkable extent, the discussion of United States policy between 1914 and 1917 has remained within the boundaries fixed by the participants. Historians are still documenting the debate between Woodrow Wilson and Robert La Follette. Charles Seymour in *American Diplomacy during the World War* (1934) and *American Neutrality, 1914–1917* (1935) presents the Administration's case; and May, *The World War and American Isolation, 1914–1917* (1959), buttresses it by emphasizing how many critical decisions depended upon German politics. Edwin Borchard and William P. Lage, *Neutrality for the United States* (1940 edition); Charles G. Fenwick, *American Neutrality: Trial and Failure* (1940); and Alice M. Morrissey, *The American Defense of Neutral Rights, 1914–1917* (1939), on the other hand, discuss America's failings within a context of international law. A great many more studies are appraised in Leopold, "The Problem of American Intervention, 1917: An Historical Retrospect," *World Politics* (1950, Vol. II), and Daniel M. Smith, "National Interest and American Intervention, 1917: An Historiographical Appraisal," *Journal of American History* (1965, Vol. LII).

In a comparable way, the writings on Versailles have been dominated by the war that followed a generation later. In the light of history, Paul Birdsall claims in *Versailles Twenty Years After* (1941), the treaty was a reasonable settlement. In the light of history, Thomas A. Bailey claims in *Woodrow Wilson and the Lost Peace* (1944) and *Woodrow Wilson and the Great Betrayal* (1945), Wilson blundered in negotiation and then helped to destroy mankind's best hope for a lasting peace. Richard N. Current, "The United States and 'Collective Security': Notes on the History of an Idea," in Alexander DeConde, ed., *Isolation and Security* (1957), represents one of the best recent attempts to recapture the confusion surrounding the issue of the League.

Biographies have extended these discussions. Volumes III, IV, and V of Arthur S. Link, *Wilson,* by far the most detailed treatment of neutrality, constitute the most conscientious vindication of American policy within the confines of the original debate. Link, *Wilson the Diplomatist* (1957), suggests the outline of volumes to come. Daniel M. Smith, *Robert Lansing and American Neutrality 1914–1917* (1958), assigns greater importance to the Secretary of State. John A. Garraty, *Henry Cabot Lodge* (1953), gently rebukes Lodge for his part in the defeat of the League.

Another group of biographies contain useful information on the expansionists: Arthur F. Beringause, *Brooks Adams* (1955); Tyler Dennett, *John Hay* (1933); Philip C. Jessup, *Elihu Root* (2 vols., 1938); Leopold, *Elihu Root and the Conservative Tradition* (1954); W. D. Puleston, *Mahan* (1939); Paul A. Varg, *Open Door Diplomat: The Life of W. W. Rockhill* (1952); and particularly Howard K. Beale, *Theodore Roosevelt and the Rise of America to World Power*

(1956), which is a detailed, ambivalent defense of Roosevelt's greatness. Warren F. Kuehl, *Hamilton Holt* (1960); Allan Nevins, *Henry White* (1930); and Charles C. Tansill, *The Foreign Policy of Thomas F. Bayard* (1940), an encyclopedia, include material both on attitudes and on government actions.

On all of these subjects and many more, Leopold, *The Growth of American Foreign Policy* (1962), the best survey for these years, provides an excellent bibliography.

THE ERA OF THE WORLD WAR

Historians have devoted surprisingly little energy to the period of the war itself. Few events of such apparent significance have received such scant attention. Frederic L. Paxson, *American Democracy and the World War* (3 vols., 1936–48), is a methodical coverage of events. Preston Slosson, *The Great Crusade and After 1914–1928* (1935), provides an interesting but unintegrated commentary on the home front. Grosvenor B. Clarkson, *Industrial America in the World War: The Strategy behind the Line, 1917–1918* (1923), and William C. Mullendore, *History of the United States Food Administration, 1917–1919* (1941), offer reasonably accurate chronicles of the two basic wartime agencies. David F. Trask, *The United States in the Supreme War Council* (1961), details negotiations with the Allies. Lawrence E. Gelfand, *The Inquiry: American Preparations for Peace, 1917–1919* (1963), a very good study, examines the role of the expert in peacemaking.

Robert L. Morlan, *Political Prairie Fire: The Nonpartisan League, 1915–1922* (1955), and James H. Shideler, *Farm Crisis, 1919–1923* (1957), cover aspects of agricultural history; and Carroll E. French, *The Shop Committee in the United States* (1923), and Alexander M. Bing, *War-Time Strikes and their Adjustment* (1921), introduce important topics of labor history. The seamier side of domestic affairs is discussed in Stanley Coben, *A. Mitchell Palmer* (1963); Donald Johnson, *The Challenge to American Freedoms* (1963); Robert K. Murray, *Red Scare* (1955); and H. C. Peterson and Gilbert C. Fite, *Opponents of War, 1917–1918* (1957). Michael Wreszin, *Oswald Garrison Villard* (1965), is particularly rewarding on the war years. Robert L. Friedheim, *The Seattle General Strike* (1964), analyzes the distortions surrounding that event. William E. Leuchtenburg, *The Perils of Prosperity: 1914–32* (1958), contains interesting suggestions on the disillusionment of certain intellectuals.

The best volumes deal with matters relating to the Russian Revolution. William Appleman Williams, *American-Russian Relations 1781–1947* (1952), is a harsh indictment of American policy, while George F. Kennan's monumental studies, *Russia Leaves the War* (1956) and *The Decision to Intervene* (1958), analyze both the inadequacy of America's diplomatic apparatus and the reasonable nature of its mistakes. Christopher Lasch, *The American Liberals and the Russian Revolution* (1962), as much diplomatic as intellectual history, includes many insights into men's frailties. Wesley M. Bagby, *The Road to Normalcy: The Presidential Campaign and Election of 1920* (1962), ushers us into the twenties.

Index